Highways to Heaven

Highways to Heaven

The AUTO Biography of America

CHRISTOPHER FINCH

HarperCollinsPublishers

Title page photograph: Alan Becker/The Image Bank

HarperCollins books may be purchased for educational, business, or sales promotional use. For information, please call or write: Special Markets Department, HarperCollins Publishers, Inc., 10 East 53rd Street, New York, NY 10022. Telephone: (212) 207-7528; Fax: (212) 207-7222.

FIRST EDITION

DESIGNED BY JOEL AVIROM

Library of Congress Cataloging-in-Publication Data
Finch, Christopher.
    Highways to heaven : the auto biography of America / Christopher Finch.—1st. ed.
        p.   cm.
    Includes bibliographical references and index.
    ISBN 0-06-016551-0 (cloth)
    1. Automobiles—Social aspects—United States—History.
I. Title.
HE5623.F56   1991
303.48'32—dc20   90-56353

92 93 94 95 96   NK/RRD   10 9 8 7 6 5 4 3 2 1

FOR LINDA,
MY
SPARK PLUG

Contents

P A R T 1

Prologue

For all that has been written and said about the automobile, it is almost impossible to grasp the magnitude and complexity of the role it has played in shaping twentieth-century America. It is not just the visual poetry of tail fins and fenders, or the esoterica of single-gate clutches and Powerglide transmissions. It is much more than the sum of the parkways, expressways, freeways, Interstates, blacktops and dirt roads that crisscross the United States. It is also Big Macs and Mack Trucks, Burma-Shave signs and shopping malls, suburbs and cineplexes, drive-ins and drive-thrus. It is Motel 66, it is cruising on Van Nuys Boulevard, it is the economy of Detroit, it is wedding chapels in Las Vegas, it is the underground garages used for a thousand TV shoot-outs, it is smog in the folds of the Rocky Mountains, it is Daytona Beach, it is the Keystone Kops, it is Cal Worthington, it is tailgate parties in the shadow of the Yale Bowl, it is Fotomat, it is a poem by e. e. cummings, it is a painting by Edward Hopper, it is ten thousand patches of oil soaking into the parking lots at

Jones Beach, it is the Golden Gate Bridge, it is John Dillinger and Al Capone, it is the Alaska pipeline, it is a guy on a used-car lot doctoring the odometer of an '83 Dodge, it is a Minnesota auto court with cabins in the shape of wigwams, it is an orgasm in the back of a Chevy, it is a serial killer burying a corpse beside the highway, then heading for the state line in search of more victims. It is the heartbeat of America.

Even from the air the impact of the automobile is inescapable. Flying into London or Paris it is possible to make out patterns of land use that have survived hundreds of years and roads that follow meandering rights-of-way that date from the Middle Ages or beyond. But if the European landscape is still discernibly a product of the feudal system, the American landscape, seen from the air, is clearly in large part a product of the automobile age. Highways run across the deserts straight as a string stretched between two pegs. In the foothills of California's mountain ranges, roads follow canyons and snake out onto ridges wherever the automobile can bring man to a homesite that can be carved or cantilevered from the slopes. Down in the flatlands new estates are laid out along intersecting loops of tarmac that seem to have been stamped onto the land like circuitry into a microchip.

After dark the contrast is even more obvious. Fly above, say, Ireland by night and the patterns of land use observable by day almost disappear. Faint necklaces of light join towns that become luminous islands in the blackness. Fly above New Jersey by night and in some ways patterns of land use become even clearer than by day. The highways are like filaments of liquid light, and malls, shopping centers and commercial strips announce their presence with multicolored neon glows, seeming to advertise their wares even to the jumbo-jets on their approach paths to Newark, La Guardia or JFK.

From the air, in fact, New Jersey possesses a logic that is not always apparent at ground level. From a plane, the way in which the shopping strips relate to urban and residential centers is readily perceived. Exit from Route 80 or the New Jersey Turnpike, however, and drive down any of those consumer-oriented roadways and it will be found that all evidence of logic disappears. There will be plenty of familiar names—Burger King, Texaco, Miller's Outpost, Kentucky Fried Chicken, Radio Shack, Safeway, The Gap, Wendy's, Pizza Hut—but they fail to define a place the way a particular constellation of stores defines Fifth Avenue in Manhattan, or Michigan Avenue in Chicago. There are no palm trees, so the driver knows he is not in Florida, but he might be almost anywhere else because those chain names are ubiquitous. They do not define places; they are simply increments in a journey between places, and those increments become numbing because endlessly repeated.

And if the automobile has made these non-places possible, it has also transformed "real" places. Old cities like New York, Detroit and Boston were first clogged by motor vehicles, then revamped in order to accommodate them, which brought in ever greater hordes to create still vaster problems. For a while, cities that came of age in the automobile era—Phoenix, Houston and especially Los Angeles—were able to accommodate the car in their expansion, but now even these multicentered complexes are clogged with traffic. Chronically health-conscious, the upwardly mobile residents of West LA eat their high-fiber breakfasts and pound the center strip of San Vicente Boulevard with their Nikes, then, with little sense of irony, shower and head for work on the 405 Freeway, an artery hopelessly clogged with the metal platelets of automotive congestion. Yet still—and especially in places like West Los Angeles—the automobile is worshiped to the point of idolatry.

At a practical level, the appeal of the automobile is easily described. Unlike the train, or the trolley car, or the bus, it goes where and when you want, stops where and when you want. Certainly this appeals to every American's sense of God-given independence, but it also appeals to his pocketbook, since it means that he has a self-chauffeured vehicle at his disposal that can take him beyond city limits to some roadside area where rentals are cheap and the retailer can therefore sell a lawn mower or a VCR for less than he would if he were leasing expensive floor space downtown. In such ways has the automobile influenced the American economy, and the ramifications are endless, affecting retailing, distribution, advertising, real estate and a thousand other areas.

Yet to discuss the impact of the automobile in such mundane terms is to miss an entire dimension, since cars have a double existence: in the everyday world and in the world of the imagination. For many Americans they are the stuff of lyric poetry and epic drama, of tragedy and comedy (or at least nostalgic humor). Nothing has played a more potent role in the waking dreams of twentieth-century Americans than the automobile, a fact that has been celebrated in novels, movies and popular songs.

It is often said that for most Americans only the purchase of a home is a more important investment than the acquisition of a car, and that goes for the emotional as well as financial investment. But for the great majority these two areas of desire—house dreams and car dreams—are virtually inseparable, because except in a few older cities, where mass transportation still functions up to point, the humblest dream house is incomplete without a car in the driveway. In any case, the very notion of a home is intimately connected with the institution of marriage, and the ritual of courting a potential life partner is dependent upon sexual display—which in twentieth-century America is frequently fetishized as automotive hardware.

For the American male (as for men elsewhere), infatuation with the automobile is loaded with sexual freight. Worship of the car begins in childhood and reaches the auto-erotic phase at the onset of puberty, when cars, like girls, are still worshiped from afar. The older adolescent readies himself for his driver's license much as he prepares himself to lose his virginity, and so it goes until he locks himself into a union that makes no provision for divorce. Recurring bouts of vapor lock are not sufficient grounds for ending the marriage, nor will an epidemic of transmission problems justify an annulment. In a world created by the automobile, the automobile rules.

It has been commonplace since the early days of motoring to discuss the automobile in terms of erotics. The sexual charge obtained from power and speed is obvious enough, but one thing that has been largely overlooked is the car's essentially hermaphroditic nature. For men, a Jaguar seen in a glossy magazine ad or television commercial is something to be desired, and if possible possessed, and hence is perceived as feminine. A Corvette in a showroom window, a Porsche parked on a neighbor's driveway, is something to be coveted and lusted after, and hence is perceived as feminine. A man approaching male menopause who purchases a beat-up fifties Studebaker and lovingly restores it to pristine condition is resurrecting a high school sweetheart, or perhaps the homecoming queen he never dared ask for a date.

And this fundamental male-female relationship works on two levels. There are those who fall in love with the package—the preppy-proud lines of a Mercedes 190, for example—and there are those who know what's going on under the hood. The former are like readers of *Playboy* eagerly devouring a feature on girls of the Ivy League. The latter are the studs who may well get a kick out of the Mercedes but know there's a lot of fun to be had out of a well-tuned Pontiac. For the man who understands the secrets of the power unit, foreplay is an essential part of automotive sensuality with improved performance the ultimate goal.

Put that man—or the most abject voyeur—behind the wheel, though, and the car's sexuality is inverted. Fetishized femininity is converted into the ultimate symbolically enhanced erection, cleaving the air in search of unspecified conquests. Looking down on the Detroit Industrial Freeway from a helicopter, the observer sees something that resembles an unending stream of spermatozoa in search of discharge.

In its masculine guise, the automobile is often perceived as pure muscle, an extension of the owner's idealized vision of his own physique. The jock's ideal, after all, is muscles as hard as steel. The production line begins with alloys and steel and miracle plastics stronger than metal, creating a musculature unmatched in the animal kingdom. Like those of a bodybuilder, a car's muscles are kept well greased. Nor is it just a matter of appearances—Mr. Universe on wheels. If the car is seen as an incarnation of the owner, then a classic V-8 engine, or a trim turbo, lends the driver muscle power that is almost terrifying in its potential. Clark Kent steps out of his office and into his Pontiac GTO and becomes Supercharged-Man.

Supercharged-Man is likely to consign his wife and children to a Volvo station wagon, and many wives gladly accept this, perceiving the Volvo's matronly appearance and reputation for safety as an extension of their nurturing role. It should not be thought, however, that women are immune to the more overtly erotic aspects of the automobile. The hermaphroditic character of the car offers them the opportunity to engage in all kinds of role reversals, a fact that is recognized in men's long-standing and continuing efforts to brand women bad drivers. In the heroic days of feminism, few things were perceived by men as being more threatening than the woman who not only drove like a parking lot attendant but also knew how to fix cars. For some men, the notion of accepting women auto mechanics was tantamount to endorsing lesbianism.

The sexual symbolism of the automobile has always been reinforced by the auto's practical role as a provider of privacy. From the first the car was a great place to make out, away from familial interference, but the equation of the automobile with personal space has more far-reaching consequences than this. In the early days, motoring was a shared activity. The automobile was an instrument of leisure and the family outing was its ultimate expression. Most early cars were open tourers, a format that did not encourage privacy. All that changed during the twenties, when the fully enclosed sedan with fixed roof and closable windows became the norm. Now the motorist could barrel down the highway in an hermetically sealed capsule, shutting out the rest of the world. Add, in due time, an air-conditioning system, a radio, a tape or disc player and a cellular phone, and you have a controlled environment providing a degree of comfort and convenience that is hard to match.

That middle-aged man alone in the Chrysler LeBaron, crawling along the Long Island Expressway in rush hour traffic, listening to traffic reports on News 88, is leaving behind a wife who's worried about aphids in the smilax and three kids with growing pains, and he's headed for an office where he will have to deal with a new supervisor, half a dozen younger rivals who want his job (naturally they drive sexier cars), and an inept temporary secretary. He may curse at the traffic but his commute time provides him with two interludes of total privacy every business day. The last thing in the world he wants is to be part of a car pool, however sensible the idea might seem on paper. The young receptionist in the Suzuki Samurai, the dentist in the 300 SEL, the saleswoman in the nail polish–red Integra, each has a different story, a different set of reasons for cherishing his or her hour of privacy.

It's a catch-22 situation. By making the world smaller, the car helped place a greater premium on privacy, but for many this is available only at the wheel of a car. The automobile has made itself indispensable, and so it is that the majority of Americans can find themselves traveling at walking pace on a ten-lane, high-speed expressway and still be incapable of imagining a world without cars.

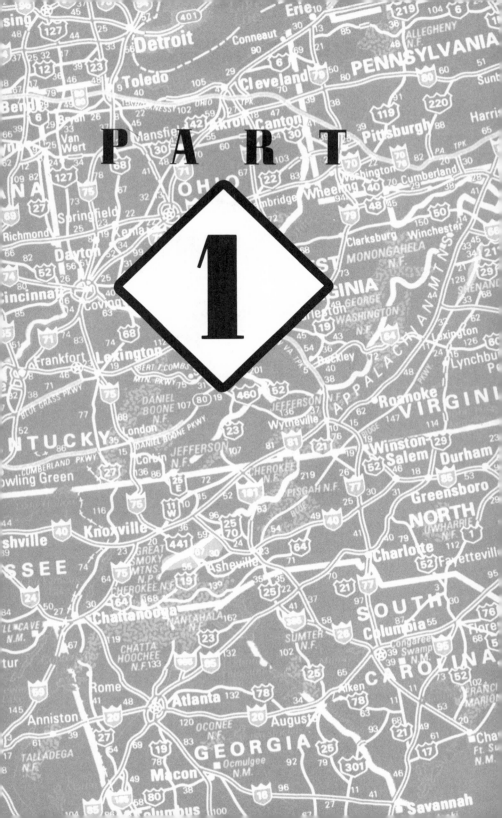

PART

1

Symbols of changing times, a dead horse and a horseless carriage.
Motor Vehicle Manufacturers Association of the United States, Inc.

Chapter 1

HIGHWAYS
TO HEAVEN

*T*here were no highways in the Garden of Eden, and in the pagan Arcadia of the Greeks, where nymphs coupled with satyrs, the only thoroughfares were those beaten through thickets by the hooves of centaurs. Some might argue that the highway came into existence as a consequence of Adam's sampling the forbidden fruit. A less puritanical viewpoint permits the highway landscape to be perceived as a twentieth-century Arcadia—the one inhabited by Vladimir Nabokov's surrogate satyr and his nymphet charge, Lolita, as they prolong their brief interlude of squabbling bliss in a succession of Sunset Motels and Skyline Courts alongside America's Interstates.

Archaeologists, anthropologists, historians, sociologists, engineers and politicians provide other perspectives, searching for concrete facts or spinning fictions that beg to be realized in concrete. Early man, the archaeologist tells us, lived not in Eden but in a dangerous world where he traveled carefully, concerned with finding the safest, most convenient route from sheltering cave to hunting ground, blazing trails with scratched signs, occasionally etching a path into the sod where several tracks converged on a ford or narrow pass. So it was for tens of thousands of years. But by the time Stonehenge was raised against the skies above Salisbury Plain, men were also creating real roads that were literally highways: well-delineated thoroughfares, such as the Icknield Way, that for reasons of safety and convenience were built on elevated ground in such areas as the chalk downs of southern England. Nor were these Bronze Age highways without their roadside attractions: gigantic horses and skeletal humans cut into chalky hillsides, bigger than any billboard and visible for miles around.

Ancient Babylonians paved the streets of their principal settlements, and the avenues and alleys of some Indus Valley cities were not only paved but furnished with covered drains. Paved highways existed in Minoan Crete, Carthage and pre-Columbian America. But the greatest road builders in history, prior to our century, were the Romans, who over a period of six centuries constructed more than 70,000 miles of paved highway, knitting together their empire with thoroughfares like the Via Appia, which ran straight as a die across the landscape, ignoring all but the most implacable geographical barriers and natural obstacles. Superbly engineered, these roads served Europe for centuries after the fall of Rome, but by the late Middle Ages had fallen into hopeless disrepair. The coming of the Renaissance did little to improve things; in *La Méditerrané* Fernand Braudel paints a dismal picture of sixteenth-century highways beset by mud, potholes, disease-bearing insects and marauding bandits. In the seventeenth century, Swiss merchants, dependent upon trade with the outside world, built and maintained good highways across the mountains to provide access to neighboring countries. Then, in the eighteenth century, the French government commenced an ambitious program of road building that reached its height during the Napoleonic era, Bonaparte recognizing the military value of highways. Soon the endless columns of the Grande Armée were marching down broad thoroughfares lined with poplars to shade men and horses from the sun. Poplars could not protect the Grande Armée from defeat at Waterloo, but by then France had the finest highway system in the world.

French road-building methods owed much to Roman models and were, in part at least, the inspiration for important advances in highway technology that took place in the British Isles in the first half of the nineteenth century, advances that would influence highway engineering in America. Thomas Telford, who built more than 900 miles of road in the Highlands of Scotland, sometimes used a pitch foundation in his attempt to improve British roads. He always insisted on good drainage combined with a cross section that featured moderate curvature, or camber, instead of the high crown that had characterized earlier roads, which often caused top-heavy vehicles to tip over. Good drainage and shallow camber were also characteristic of the roads built under the direction of John McAdam, who preferred paving roads with smallish stones instead of the large rocks that had been favored by most earlier road engineers. Often he used small limestone rocks, and when rainwater mixed with the limestone dust chipped off by horseshoes and the iron tires of coaches and wagons, it formed a kind of cement that held the rocks together so that water-bound macadam, as it was called, was to an extent a self-maintaining surface.

In cities, with their heavy traffic, cobblestones were often favored for surfacing purposes, and these found their way to many cities on the eastern seaboard of the United States, being brought back from Europe as ballast in the holds of ships that had headed out with cargoes of rum or cotton. American rural roads were another matter, however, and the sheer distances involved meant that highways in the New World were slow to be developed and improved.

It was Thomas Jefferson and his secretary of the treasury, Albert Gallatin, who first envisioned a coordinated effort to develop a U.S. highway system. Having liquidated the national debt, the Jefferson Administration turned its attention to domestic improvements. One consequence of this was Gallatin's 1808 "Report on Roads and Canals." Among other things, a ten-year program called for a turnpike running from Maine to Georgia and four great east-west turnpikes to cross the Appalachians, joining the cities of the eastern seaboard to the Midwest. Local rivalries and the War of 1812 put an end to this scheme, however. Only a few sections of the pikes were completed, and soon these were allowed to fall into disrepair.

A more lasting aspect of Jeffersonian policy was the grid system as applied to rural America. As early as William Penn's Philadelphia, American cities had adopted grid layouts (for which there were many precedents, going back to ancient Mesopotamia). However, the Land Ordinance of 1785, of which Jefferson was a principal author, institutionalized the grid and provided the basis for the Land Act of 1796, which determined that government land in the territories would be sold in rectangular packages. The grid dictated both the layout of frontier cities and the pattern of agricultural development west of the Appalachians. Inevitably, roads would have to conform to the grid; instead of reinforcing the importance of a single urban center (as in the case of Rome or Paris, cities from which roads radiated like roots from a tree), they would tend to be instrumental in decentralizing power. The fact that so many of our states have separate and distinct political and financial capitals is in part a reflection of this, as is the growth, in the twentieth century, of "centerless" cities such as Los Angeles. The system has both advantages and disadvantages, some of which did not become apparent until the automobile age put it to test.

The decentralization fostered by the grid system is just one of many American expressions of a distrust of concentrated power. When all roads lead to Rome, Rome is the center of all disenchantment. For the American colonies, London was the focus of discontent. Two centuries after independence, Americans feel free to divide their splenetic feelings among a number of centers—Washington, New York, Los Angeles—each earning its own species of scorn and suspicion in response to those areas of influence in which it is perceived to dominate. In contrast, the thinly populated midsection of the country, where decentralization has remained an effective principle, is perceived as America's heartland. It is fundamental to these attitudes that the United States is a nation made up of many states, each with its own powers, and this too has had its influence upon road building. One of the Jefferson Administration's successes had been the establishment of the so-called National Road, which linked the Potomac with the Ohio River. In 1822 Congress passed a bill intended to institute a system of tolls along that highway to pay for its upkeep. President Madison vetoed the bill, arguing that the federal government had no right to override the sovereignty of the states through which the road ran. This precedent was reinforced by Andrew Jackson when he vetoed another bill that would have permitted the federal government to purchase part of the stock of a turnpike company chartered by the Kentucky legislature. The message was clear. Road building was the business of local authorities, not the federal government, and this has remained the case until the present. Washington has pumped billions of dollars into highway building programs and has exerted its influence in innumerable ways, subtle and otherwise, but this has never been allowed to violate the principle that state, city and county governments actually build the roads and own and operate them.

In the automobile age this system has sometimes worked well. Throughout the nineteenth century, however, it tended to promote poorly kept-up roads, often just dirt tracks that were turned into quagmires by passing storms or reduced to choking dust by prolonged dry spells. Improved roads were few, though in some areas plank roads provided a good temporary surface; these were like boardwalks minus the rigid substructure of beams—but the planks rotted and needed frequent replacement. Sturdier, but hardly offering a comfortable ride, were the so-called corduroy roads made of halved logs laid side by side. For the most part the best nineteenth-century roads were the handful of turnpikes laid out by local governments and private companies, which employed a system of toll gates to raise revenue to pay for maintenance.

The fact is that road building and improvement were given little priority and did not attract the interest of the finest engineers. They were drawn instead to more prestigious efforts, such as building the canals that linked the natural waterways and, above all, to building the railroads that were to dominate the national imagination—as far as transportation was concerned—from the 1830s to the end of the century. In Europe, too, the growth of the railroads led to the neglect of highways and turnpikes. Not until the 1890s did public pressure on both sides of the Atlantic lead to a significant resurgence of interest in highways. That pressure was exerted in large part by the bicycle lobby, cycling having become a major middle-class fad that appealed to both sexes. Cyclists needed good roads in order to enjoy their sport, and they had the political clout to do something about it, at least on a small scale. City engineers began to experiment with various types of road improvement. The methods pioneered by Telford and McAdam were revived and experiments were made with asphalt and other bituminous substances used as binding materials to produce smooth, water-repellent surfaces. These experiments led to notable street improvements in major cities and wealthy suburbs, and some improved roads began to push out into the surrounding countryside, at least as far as popular picnic areas. The effect on roads linking towns or traversing the prairies was negligible, but this was the beginning of the modern highway. Just as many pioneer automobile builders received their start in bicycle repair shops, so the bicycle lobby paved the way, literally, for the automobile lobby. Momentum was slow to gather at first—it would take decades to reach its full force—but the earnest and genteelly garbed cyclists of Buffalo and Harrisburg, of Madison and Sacramento, had started a revolution that has not yet ended.

The safety bicycle, as it was first called, is a simple but remarkably efficient and even sophisticated piece of machinery. A great improvement on the "ordinary" (also known as the penny-farthing), it was invented in England and first manufactured in America by Colonel Albert A.

Pope, who opened his Boston shop in 1887. The safety bicycle was easy to ride, even in the long skirts of the period, and carried the rider in reasonable comfort, especially after the invention of the pneumatic tire, which was introduced in 1889. In particular, the bicycle had the virtues of being owner-propelled, inexpensive to feed and easy to stable.

The horse, it's true, was more versatile, but in the crowded cities of the late Victorian era its drawbacks were many. Horse-drawn vehicles were noisy and perfectly capable of creating their own species of traffic chaos. Horses fouled the streets, and dead horses, abandoned in the gutter, caused significant health hazards, especially in hot weather. Then there was the problem of housing the animals. It has been estimated that there were two million horses in New York City in the 1890s, and most of these, of necessity, were stabled in close proximity to human residences, an unsatisfactory situation, especially in those areas where the residences themselves were crowded upon one another. Overpopulated and underventilated tenements backed onto narrow alleys across which dray horses and peddlers' mules were stabled. Aromas that are reassuring in a barnyard became, in the dog days of a New York summer, intolerable stenches that rose on the night air to suffocate the residents who sought to escape the heat and humidity by sleeping on roofs and fire escapes. The horse was indispensable, but by becoming indispensable it had made man its slave.

But if you were rich or even moderately well heeled and could afford to stable your beasts at a remove from your residence, the horse still offered many advantages, and the carriages it pulled had, by Victorian times, attained a high degree of comfort and engineering sophistication. The word "comfort" could not accurately have been applied to wheeled vehicles before the seventeenth century. Egyptian and Roman chariots, the wagons of the Middle Ages, and even the coaches of Renaissance princes, were innocent of springs of any kind.

By the late 1660s experiments were being made with steel springs, and coaches became smooth-running enough to permit the installation of glass windows. Not until 1804, however, did the invention of the elliptical spring permit a rigid body to be connected directly to the axles, providing at last a truly comfortable and stable ride. The golden age of the horse-drawn carriage was, in fact, remarkably short. The important thing in this context is that by the late Victorian era the technology of coach building was ready to accommodate the internal combustion engine. Bodies, frames, suspension and running gear were all capable of evolution into the new forms that would be required by the automobile age.

Earlier experiments with self-propelled vehicles had suffered in part from deficiencies in this area, especially when bulky power units and heavy fuel supplies were concerned. This was undeniably the case with Nicholas Cugnot's steam-powered Fardier, which made its first laborious expedition onto Paris streets in 1770. This contraption resembled a farm cart from whose front end was suspended something that looked like a cross between a brewer's kettle and a cement mixer. This kettle was the firebox and boiler of Cugnot's engine, it provided steam to twin cylinders whose pistons drove the solitary front wheel. The Fardier achieved a top speed of 2¼ mph and on occasion succeeded in moving continuously for up to fifteen minutes.

The problem with Cugnot's steam wagon was that its bulky engine was completely out of proportion to the vehicle it propelled, solid and clumsy though the latter was. In addition, the engine was hopelessly inefficient and underpowered and required a daunting quantity of water and coal in order to operate, which only added to its weight. This did not discourage experimenters, however, and soon smaller, more efficient steam engines were married to better designed chassis, with improved results. In the early 1800's two English cousins, Richard Trevithick and Andrew Vivian, built a series of steam-powered vehicles, the first two of which met disastrous ends (one simply sank into the mud). The third, completed in 1803, met with greater success. Equipped with drive wheels ten feet in circumference, it must have been a strange-looking contraption, but it proved itself capable of covering respectable distances at speeds of up to 8 miles an hour.

Two years later a Philadelphian named Oliver Evans built the first American self-propelled vehicle, though it was not intended for highway use. The "Orukter Amphibolos" was a steam-powered, paddle-wheel dredge built on commission for the city fathers. Instead of having horses drag the twenty-ton vessel to the Schuylkill River, Evans hooked the engine up to a temporary set of wheels so that the dredge could proceed to its launching site under its own steam. Its novelty was such that it was exhibited in the center of the city before being set to work.

The British had taken the lead with steam power, though, and after 1830 a number of steam-powered coaches ran regular service on English turnpikes. Builders like W. H. James and Walter Hancock had considerable success with these, some of which seated up to fifteen people and serviced routes such as London to Stratford, a distance of over 100 miles. These vehicles were large and therefore could accommodate sizable engines, but Hancock also built for his own use a steam phaeton that may well have been the first private automobile.

The locomotive coaches, as they were known, were doomed, however. Operators of horse-drawn vehicles hated them (perhaps with good reason) and they were looked on as competitors by the men who ran the railroads. These two pressure groups combined to have the locomotive coaches condemned as dangerous. The result was the famous red flag law, which stated that a self-propelled vehicle could be operated on the public road only at a speed not to exceed four miles per hour and when preceeded by a man carrying a red flag. Not repealed till 1896, this law effectively crippled automobile development in the British Isles until near the turn of the century.

Steam-powered automobiles continued to be developed elsewhere, but by the final quarter of the nineteenth century more and more attention was being given to the possibilities of the internal combustion engine as a suitable power unit. Using coal gas as fuel, a Belgian named Etienne Lenoir had employed an internal combustion en-

In the early days of the automobile, steam power was a popular
alternative to the internal combustion engine.

gine to power a horseless carriage as early as 1863. The
Lenoir engine proved inefficient for this purpose, however,
and further development had to wait until the German
engineer Nikolaus August Otto built the first successful
four-stroke engine, with its now familiar induction-
compression-explosion-exhaust cycle, in the 1870s.

Otto himself had no particular interest in the idea of
self-propelled carriages. The initial application of his invention was for such jobs as powering farm machinery and
motor launches. As early as 1875, though, an Austria-based
German mechanic and electrical engineer named Sieg-
fried Marcus mounted an Otto-type engine on a wagonlike
wooden chassis and produced a primitive self-propelled
carriage. This vehicle had no direct progeny, however, and
it is generally conceded that the true genesis of the modern
automobile was the pioneering work of two younger Germans, Gottlieb Daimler and Karl Benz. Later these names
would be linked to create one of the most famous marques
in the history of the automobile. In the early days, however,
the two men carried out their experiments unknown to each
other, each independently creating self-propelled vehicles
that would announce the beginning of the automobile age.

Daimler was plant manager and technical director of Otto's Gasmotorenfabrik Deutz, and he worked with Otto, and sometimes on his own, to perfect the four-stroke engine using petroleum as fuel. In 1882 he left Deutz, along with his right-hand man, Wilhelm Maybach, and in 1890 founded his own business, whose principal concern was to improve the four-stroke engine. Almost simultaneously, Benz, another former Deutz employee, began independently to develop high-speed gasoline engines. By 1885 both engineers had produced reasonably reliable single-cylinder engines and both were at work on applying them to self-propelled vehicles. That year Daimler produced a wood-framed, gasoline-powered motorcycle that looked somewhat like a motorized version of a Regency hobby-horse. Meanwhile, Benz began building an extraordinarily elegant tricycle carriage with a single-cylinder, water-cooled engine mounted under the seat. Drive to the rear wheels was by means of chains and differential gears, like the transmission of a bicycle. This vehicle was first seen on the streets of Mannheim in 1886, the same year Daimler, near Stuttgart, installed a 462 cc single-cylinder engine in a conventional four-wheeled open carriage (bought from a local coach builder), the shafts of which had been chopped off and a vertical tiller installed for steering purposes. It was not nearly so handsome as the Benz tricycle—the engine poked clumsily through the floor of the rear passenger compartment—and is best thought of as the prototypical horseless carriage. But it worked and, along with the Benz tricycle, heralded a new age—one that would, however, have to face significant obstacles before it could capture the imagination of the public.

Many parts of Germany were subject to speed limits as prohibitive as that imposed in Britain, and in some provinces self-propelled vehicles were forbidden entirely to use the public roads. In France there were no such restrictive laws, and the French, already in the grip of the bicycle craze, were notably open to mechanical novelties. By 1890 two French companies, Panhard et Levassor and Peugeot, were manufacturing and tentatively marketing cars powered by Daimler engines built under license by

Panhard. In 1891 Emile Levassor built the first vehicle with a front-mounted motor—a 2.5 hp Daimler V-twin—driving the rear wheels, thus introducing the format that would eventually become standard for modern cars, replacing the horseless carriage layout.

Benz meanwhile had found a French agent, Emile Roger, and began selling tricycles in France. In 1893 Benz introduced the four-wheel Victoria, and business picked up so spectacularly that by 1894 he was able to sell 572 machines, giving him the industry lead. Most of these automobiles were sold in France, and it was in France that the first organized test of comparative automobile performances, the Paris–Rouen Trial of 1894, was held. It was sponsored by a Paris daily paper, *Le Petit Journal*, which offered a reward for the vehicle that covered the course most efficiently, with regard not only to time but also to safety, cost and ease of handling. A De Dion–Bouton steam tractor—driven by Comte Albert de Dion, noted fencer, gambler and boulevardier—was the first to arrive in Rouen, having covered the course at an average speed of 11.6 mph. This was not a race, however, and the jury awarded the De Dion second prize, naming the Panhard and Peugeot gasoline-driven cars the co–first prize winners, judging them more practical vehicles. De Dion quickly saw the writing on the wall and went on to build highly efficient internal combustion engines (he had made experimental models as early as 1889), which powered his own cars and others built by new concerns such as Renault and Delage that were early entrants in the French market.

De Dion was one of the aristocratic enthusiasts who organized the first true automobile race, from Paris to Bordeaux and back, a distance of 732 miles, which was staged in June 1895. The weather was good, and from the first Emile Levassor established a lead in his two-cylinder Panhard and gradually pulled away from the pack, which included twenty-three machines powered by internal combustion engines, thirteen by steam engines and two by electricity, along with an assortment of motorized bicycles and tricycles. Levassor left Paris at noon on June 11 and bowled along the *route nationale*, cheered on by thousands, arriving at Bordeaux at ten-thirty the following morning. Disdaining the services of a relief driver, he drank a glass of champagne at the wheel, turned the Panhard around and entered Paris by the Port Maillot just two days and forty-eight minutes after leaving. The public acclaim was unbounded. In a little over forty-eight hours Levassor had proved the practicality of the automobile.

Levassor's claims to fame, then, are considerable. Not only did he design the first front-engined car, but he also won the first organized race and helped establish the automobile's viability. Unhappily, he also has the distinction of being motor racing's first fatality, dying of injuries suffered at the wheel of one of his own cars just two years after his triumph in the Paris–Bordeaux–Paris event.

A primitive factory for horseless carriages, c. 1905. *Bettmann Archive*

Chapter 2

RED CARS
AND
REDOUBTABLE
BUGGIES

*S*teeped in the heavens and hells of a more innocent age, William Blake confronted the Industrial Revolution in its infancy and cursed its "dark satanic mills." Alone in many of his opinions, Blake was far from unique in deploring the blights upon pristine landscapes caused by smokestacks and smelting kilns. Forced by circumstance into the vanguard, British writers from William Wordsworth to Thomas Love Peacock heaped bitterness and scorn on a form of progress that belched fumes into air, until then innocent of anything more sinister than the odor of cow dung and the smoke of bonfires, and leaked poison wastes into rivers once alive with pike feasting on minnows and frogspawn. Men of conscience lamented the endless hours of drudgery spent by underpaid workers beside fiery blast furnaces and tunelessly chanting cotton gins. They composed tracts in defense of children and animals sent down into underventilated mines to bring up the tons of coal consumed every moment by the insatiable monster that was irrevocably changing the face of the planet.

Yet the Industrial Revolution had other aspects too. There was a poetry, captured by painters like Turner, in the paddle wheelers that cut silver swaths across rivers and estuaries from the Firth of Clyde to the Mississippi. There was a pugnacious bustle that matured into a muscular vigor about the locomotives, celebrated by artists like Monet and writers like Zola—that hauled chains of varnished coaches along ribbons of polished steel, bringing brief fame to obscure towns like Stockton and Darlington in England, certifying the importance of rising centers like Chicago, eating up the miles between hundreds, then thousands, of communities where distance had been judged in terms of the mileage a good horse could cover between sunup and sundown.

And the Industrial Revolution brought a new generation of toys, from mass-produced lead soldiers to cameras to player pianos. Ludwig the Mad of Bavaria, Wagner's patron, isolated himself in a world of elaborate lifelike automata, humanoid robots that would accompany him on railway journeys and sit in his box at the opera. Frank Woolworth, founder of the dimestore chain, entertained guests at his Fifth Avenue palazzo by "performing"—he sat at the keyboard and activated the controls—at an enormous mechanical pipe organ whose music was augmented by special effects such as thunder and lightning.

In Europe, the blight and novelties alike were superimposed upon a long established patchwork of tightly woven national cultures. If certain areas such as the British Midlands and the Ruhr were dramatically transformed by the satanic mills, most regions—those that consumed more than they produced—were able to integrate the newfangled products of the age into the established fabric of society. Or so it appeared at first. Later it would seem that the vine was choking the host tree, but in the first phase the new middle class, itself created by the manufacturing industries, welcomed the arrival of cheap cuckoo clocks, affordable machine-turned facsimiles of Chippendale chairs, electroplated cutlery and molded-tin picture frames, not to mention the very real benefits of such practical gadgets as the flushing toilet.

In America the situation was somewhat different. Even the cities of the Eastern Seaboard were relatively young and thus especially prone to being shaped by the tools and toys of the Industrial Revolution. More significant, most of the continent was still wide open and thoroughly unmade. In Europe the railways linked established urban centers, pulling regions closer together. In America the railway barons began unfurling tentacles of steel out into the wilderness, creating new communities overnight. To promote these new communities, the railways offered low fares, steamship passage included, to bring immigrants from Inverness and Ulm, from Christiania and Cork, to the north woods of Minnesota and the prairies of Kansas. The immigrants carried with them their cuckoo clocks and machine-turned Chippendale chairs, their electroplated cutlery and their molded-tin picture frames. As they prospered they bought factory-made Irish lace from the general store or decorated their walls with chromo-lithographed reproductions of Alpine views. These products of the industrial age took on a poignant cultural significance in their new settings. To a resident of Stuttgart the cuckoo clock in the parlor was simply a domesticated echo of the great animated timepieces in the church towers of the Black Forest. To the immigrant from southern Germany that same cuckoo clock became far more potent. It might be shoddy in its workmanship and tawdry in its stenciled decoration, but it stood for an entire way of life, left behind but unforgotten. West of the original colonies America was empty, both physically and culturally. Settlers were desperate for both tools and tokens of the worlds they had left behind, so the products of the Industrial Revolution were rushed in to fill the vacuum. Peddlers, go-getting merchants and the Sears, Roebuck catalogue made sure that the flow of goods never ceased.

In reality, of course, it was only pockets of the vacuum that were filled (along with the merchants' tills). Catalogues might bring patent-pending civilization to Cody or Kalispel, but there were still vast unpopulated spaces out there beyond Boot Hill, and those open spaces were an invitation to move on, especially now that the railroads had provided an easy means of transportation, whether you paid your fare or rode the boxcars. Some might be content to settle down among the cuckoo clocks, but others, having uprooted themselves once, found it easy enough to uproot themselves again and again. The frontier closed just as the first Industrial Age reached its apogee, but the wanderlust continued, and America, especially west of the Appalachians, remained a continent populated to a large extent with restless men: gamblers, gandy dancers, mule skinners, migrant farmers, prospectors, rootless Civil War veterans and others of no fixed abode.

It was against such a background that the automobile came to the American landscape, and the landscape dictated to a substantial extent the way the car would evolve and be perceived in North America. Special physical conditions would demand special (though not necessarily superior) standards of performance. More important, the cultural imperatives involved were significantly at variance with those existing in Europe. Americans and Europeans alike would enjoy a love affair with the automobile, but the parties would conduct it in their own ways, making different demands and sacrifices, and seeking different forms of ecstasy. Only when it came to disillusion would they find themselves united.

Disillusion was a long way off, however, when F. W. Lambert inaugurated the automobile age in America, driving his gasoline-powered tricycle on the streets of Ohio City, Ohio, in 1891. There are other claimants to the title "America's first motor vehicle builder," and certainly several experimenters were at work on automobiles by 1891. It seems likely that at least two or three models were functional before 1893, but until compelling evidence is presented to the contrary there is little reason to suppose that Lambert should not be given credit for this first. He had hoped to produce his tricycle in quantity and offer it to the public, but the prototype was destroyed by fire, after several successful runs, and he took no further part in the development of the industry, refusing even to seek credit for his pioneering contribution.

Because of this the brothers Charles E. and J. Frank Duryea, bicycle mechanics of Springfield, Massachusetts, have often been considered the first American car builders; they constructed their initial motor carriage, a crude, one-cylinder affair, after reading about European experiments, probably including those of Benz, that appeared in *Scientific American*. The article about Benz was published in 1889, but it was September 21, 1893, before the Duryeas were ready to unleash their brainchild on the citizens of Springfield. The Duryeas differed from Lambert in their persistence and fundamental grasp of self-promotion, qualities that have won for them, in many history books, the sole credit for bringing America into the automobile age.

Charles was the fast talker of the family, and the idea of building a horseless carriage seems to have originated with him. Without Frank, however, he would never have succeeded. Frank had the practical mind and sure hands of a trained toolmaker, and he possessed a dogged disposition that was the opposite of his brother's mercurial temperament. In January 1892, Charles took his plan to a Springfield financier named Erwin Markham and persuaded him to put up $1,000 in return for 10 percent of future profits. The brothers rented a second-floor loft above a manufacturing company, installed a cheap second-hand buggy there and began to build a primitive one-cylinder engine that, according to Frank, resembled a cast-iron pipe with a flange at one end to which the cylinder head would be bolted. Everything, from the ignition system to the transmission, had to be built from scratch and without benefit of plan or model. The buggy had to be strengthened too, to support the weight of the engine, and by September all the money was gone.

Characteristically, Charles took off for Illinois, planning to make his fortune in the bicycle-building business. Frank stayed on in Springfield. He starved and became so ill that he was hospitalized, but by February he had the motor working. He mounted it in the buggy and demonstrated the contraption for the benefit of the owner of the

Very possibly the first true American automobile was this gasoline-powered tricycle built in Ohio City, Ohio, by F. W. Lambert, who tested it successfully in 1891. © *1992* Automobile Quarterly

loft building. The motor started, all right, and Frank engaged the belt drive, but he was unable to return the car to neutral. Slowly, the buggy took off, dragging Frank behind it, until it crashed into a wall. Luckily, the landlord was amused.

Although the vehicle moved, Frank realized that the motor was far too primitive to be practical on the roadway. He went to Markham and told him he would have to build an entirely new engine. Markham put up more money and Duryea set about constructing a marginally more sophisticated motor, this one featuring, for example, a wet-cell-battery–powered ignition system in place of the alcohol burner he had used to heat a copper ignition tube in the original model.

By September the modified horseless buggy was ready and Duryea and Markham had it towed to the outskirts of town under cover of darkness, not wanting the first road

test to be observed by unnecessary and potentially scep-
tical witnesses—though they did ensure that a reporter
from the local paper was present. With Frank at the tiller
(modified from bicycle handlebars), three men pushed until
the engine caught and the buggy began to roll forward
under its own power. It continued rolling until it encountered a low curb, about six inches high, then came to a
dead stop. Other road tests were somewhat more successful but demonstrated to Frank that the belt-drive transmission devised by his brother was not adequate to his
needs. He persuaded Markham to part with one more
check—bringing the total investment to about $3,000—and
offered to work without salary till the job was complete.

With that money, Frank converted the buggy to an all-
metal transmission system, but he was still not satisfied
with the engine and was convinced that only a two-
cylinder version would be adequate. Markham was not
prepared to put up further funds, but the modest success
of the vehicle in its original form had attracted enough
attention to interest another investor, H. W. Clapp, who
saw the commercial potential of a successful horseless
carriage. He provided enough money for Duryea to build
a two-cylinder motor, then attempted to whet the appetites
of other moneymen.

In July 1895, potential investors sent a Mr. Slater, a
hard-boiled steam engine expert, to inspect the Duryea
machine and take a ride in it. With Frank at the tiller and
Slater in the passenger seat, the buggy negotiated a hilly,
wagon-rutted, eighteen-mile circuit through the Massachusetts countryside. Slater was impressed. So were the
potential investors, and in no time the Duryea Motor
Wagon Company was formed, with Frank and Charles—
freshly returned to the fold—as partners. Frank drew up
plans for an improved model, which he called the Buggy-
aut, and by the end of 1896 thirteen had been produced.
The American automobile industry was a reality.

The Duryeas' fame was ensured in 1895 when a two-
cylinder model driven by Frank won the first important
American automobile race. Organized by the *Chicago
Times-Herald* and highly publicized, this race was held

under horrendous conditions over fifty-five miles of slick, icy roads. The Duryea completed the course at an average speed of about 5 mph (having been slowed by an accidental detour from the official route and an enforced pause for repairs, which involved waking a sleeping tinsmith to forge a new sparking device). Of the five remaining entrants, only one, a Benz imported from Europe, succeeded in finishing.

In 1896 the Duryeas were the first to take an American car abroad, sailing for England to participate in the London-to-Brighton rally, which had been organized to celebrate the repeal of England's red flag law. Their prestige was now such that they were able to find a ready market for the vehicles, which were still made laboriously by hand in their Springfield shop. Duryea might have established itself as the first great American marque, but before long the brothers quarreled over which of them deserved primary credit for their innovations and so the partnership was dissolved and their later contribution to the evolution of the automobile was negligible.

Such quarrels were not uncommon among the American pioneers. Elwood Haynes, an engineer employed by the Indiana Natural Gas & Oil Company, went into business with Edgar and Elmer Apperson, of Kokomo, Indiana, and with them developed a one-cylinder car that made its first run on the Fourth of July, 1894. These partners built sound automobiles and enjoyed a good deal of success with various models of the Haynes-Apperson, but they too eventually fell out over who had contributed what to their pioneering efforts. (In addition, Haynes felt he should have been given precedence over the Duryeas, arguing that he had started work on his car first.) Haynes and Apperson became separate makes and both were manufactured in Kokomo until well in the 1920s.

Another pioneer was Hiram Percy Maxim, son of the inventor of the Maxim machine gun. After graduating from MIT, the younger Maxim went to work for the American Projectile Company in Lynn, Massachusetts. There he experienced a stroke of inspiration, conceiving of the idea of a motorized carriage, apparently without having any knowledge of other innovators in either Europe or America. He was aware of the existence of the internal combustion engine but, interestingly, given his technical background, had never seen one when he was first smitten with his brain wave. After obtaining a second-hand Columbia tricycle, manufactured by the Pope Manufacturing Company of Hartford, then America's premier producer of pedal cycles, he went to see an Otto engine in operation. (Like many such engines, it was being used to power a pump.) This was in 1892, and now Maxim began to experiment with internal combustion, starting at the most basic level imaginable by igniting small quantities of gasoline in cartridge cases. It took him three years to rig his tricycle with a fully functional one-cylinder engine, but when he had the vehicle running he attracted the attention of Colonel Albert Pope of Pope Manufacturing, who invited Maxim to head up a new motor carriage department. Maxim accepted, and thus began one of the first attempts at full-scale automobile production ever made in America, but it did not develop along quite the lines he had imagined. Colonel Pope was one of many Americans who was dubious about persuading customers to "sit over an explosion." Maxim was permitted to build a few vehicles powered by internal combustion, but the bulk of Pope's early production was dependent upon electric power and in its first two years of existence the new Pope division sold an impressive 500 electric carriages. These were powered by heavy accumulator batteries (weighing as much as 750 pounds) and were both quiet and remarkably speedy. The problem they faced was that they could travel only a relatively short distance—typically forty or fifty miles—before the batteries needed recharging, a shortcoming that has continued to hamper development of this otherwise promising form of traction.

Nor was electricity the only alternative to gasoline. Steam was the classic power source of the Victorian age, and its use in self-propelled vehicles was well established when Francis E. and Freelan O. Stanley went into business in Newton, Massachusetts, in 1897, producing the first of their famous Stanley Steamers. The contribution of the

Stanley brothers, along with other steam advocates in both Europe and America, was to produce a steam engine that was light enough to mount in a carriage-size vehicle. Kerosene or gasoline was burned to heat the boiler, and these motors, operating at pressures of up to 600 pounds per square inch, were highly efficient, but they had drawbacks. It required at least twenty minutes for early Stanley Steamers to work up a head of steam. The White Brothers of Cleveland, manufacturers of classic steamers, introduced a flash boiler in 1901, an improvement that permitted a head of steam to be produced more rapidly, but still the thermal efficiency of the steam engine never matched that of the internal combustion engine, and the steam engine required much more frequent service. In the end steam cars could not compete, and the same was true for electric cars. Both alternative systems survived the early years of the automobile industry, but from the first it was clear to most people that the internal combustion engine was the logical way to go.

Many of the American pioneers of the automobile first encountered the internal combustion engine as an adjunct to farm machinery, and this was probably the case with Henry Ford, who had maintained farm machinery for a living before building his quadricycle and driving it through the streets of Detroit on June 4, 1896. (He was not the first to introduce the automobile to the Motor City, having been preceded by three months by another inventor, Charles Brady King.) That same year, in Cleveland, Ohio, Ransom Eli Olds put his first car to the public test. It was the immediate predecessor of the celebrated curved-dash Oldsmobile—the "merry Oldsmobile" of Tin Pan Alley fame—which was the first production car to really capture the public's imagination. With the curved-dash Olds, a motorized buggy with tiller steering, an American had developed a car that would remain in production for several years and sell in the thousands (more than 12,000 were purchased between 1901 and 1904). It was a significant achievement and announced that the pioneering phase of automobile development in America was at an end.

During that pioneering phase, the automobile embodied the best and worst aspects of the Industrial Revolution. For some it was a monstrosity, a mobile satanic mill spewing exhaust fumes and menacing cattle and pedestrians alike, yet it shared in that poetry of self-propelled power embodied by the steamboat and the transcontinental locomotive, and the rich who could afford it certainly regarded it as an elaborate mechanical toy. What was missing, for the time being at least, was the one aspect of the Industrial Revolution that appealed most to the American collective psyche, which, as the rest of the world had discovered, was ultimately pragmatic. This is not to say that Americans were lacking in imagination or a sense of fantasy, even awe, but American society had grown up with a puritan notion of perfectibility that was at odds with the relative fatalism of most European cultures, especially those in areas dominated by Catholicism. The Puritan ethic preached that the soul was perfectible through prayer, persistence, self-denial and mortification of the flesh: the Calvinistic mechanism of redemption. If the soul was perfectible, then certainly man's artifacts and offices were subject to infinite improvability. Americans, after all, had with the sweat of their brows, and virtually overnight, forged a constitution and a form of government that was, surely, preferable to the near feudal systems of the Old World. The United States in the nineteenth century was heir to the rationalism that had dominated Western thought in the eighteenth century. The founding fellows of England's Royal Society and France's Encyclopedists had sewn seeds that had borne fruit in America, where cities were laid out along rational lines and doctors were already espousing the revolutionary idea that diseases were something to be treated rather than suffered. Europeans, in thrall to a tradition that could be traced back to the Greeks by way of the scholastic philosophers of the Middle Ages, tended to treat knowledge as something of value for its own sake. Americans wanted knowledge to be useful. An American industrialist might display great taste in building a collection of art, then bequeath it to the community that had been his instrument for the accumulation of wealth, with the understanding that it would serve to improve that community. Not a few American museums were incorporated as educational institutions, the notion being that a utilitarian purpose would place them on a higher plane than that occupied by a mere repository of beauty. Sermons came readily to the lips of the men who razed forests and plundered the landscape of its ores.

So those early horseless carriages were intriguing and amusing, but they were not yet useful. To serve a purpose in the great American scheme of things they would have to become much more reliable and they would need proper highways to run on. There were those, of course, who believed in their perfectibility from the outset, but the main thrust of Yankee ingenuity, in those last years of the Victorian era, was directed toward another form of transportation with greater promise of immediate utilitarian return. This form of transportation is of interest here because it was to have a significant impact upon patterns of highway growth.

The mass transportation of passengers within cities began in Paris in 1819, when horse-drawn omnibus service was inaugurated. The omnibus was introduced to New York in 1831, and it was soon realized that a more comfortable ride could be provided by horse-drawn carriages with flanged wheels running along rails laid on stone ties in the middle of the street than with traditional wheels running on cobblestones. This was the beginning of tram or streetcar service, which quickly became popular on both sides of the Atlantic. Other means of power—steam and cable—were introduced to replace horses, but not until electricity was successfully used as a power source did streetcars truly come of age. The man who made this possible was Frank Julian Sprague, a former assistant to Thomas Edison, who in 1888 successfully electrified a twelve-mile stretch of streetcar line in Richmond, Virginia, solving a number of tricky engineering problems in the process. His electric trams derived their power from a single overhead line by means of a pole, at the tip of which was a wheel—a "trolley"—that maintained running contact with the power line. So successful was his system that it was almost universally accepted, and Sprague-type street cars began to appear around the globe. At first they were limited to established urban thoroughfares, but soon they began to reach out to suburbs and to link neighboring towns, often running along private rights of way, and so the interurban trolley was born. The term "interurban" was first used in 1892 to describe a two-mile line in Indiana, but the first true interurban, by general consensus, was the fifteen-mile trolley route between Portland, Oregon, and Oregon City, which opened for service in February 1893.

The possibilities of electric trolley systems were quickly evident to men of enterprise. In linking existing towns and suburbs they were able to provide more frequent service than could practically be supplied by the railroads, and they could be made to push out from existing urban centers to give access to virgin areas suitable for development. The potential was tremendous. A group of investors might, for example, purchase a parcel of land five or ten miles from a city center, obtaining it for a song because of its poor access to the center. By running an electric trolley line to that parcel of land, however, they could increase the value of the property many times, in some instances even before the trolley line was built—and this often provided funds for investment in the transportation system. A single moderate-sized city might provide several such opportunities, and land-hungry families proved eager to snap up lots in the new subdivisions. Local governments, happy to see the expansion of their fiscal base, were only too pleased to grant rights of way that in many cases, eventually, helped to define future highway patterns.

Interurbans were to become a presence in many parts of the country by the early years of the twentieth century. In the Northeast, for example, it was possible to ride from Shawmut, Maine, to New York City using only the electric trolley. A ferry across the Hudson then permitted continuous service (though with many changes) as far south as Delaware City, Delaware, or as far west as Newville, Pennsylvania. But it was in the Midwest and West that the interurbans had their greatest impact. The largest of all the electric suburban transportation systems was the one that grew up in the Los Angeles region, a system that determined many of the growth patterns—and hence, highway patterns—of what was to become the nation's quintessential automobilized city.

Los Angeles' future prosperity had been virtually guaranteed in 1876, when the first Southern Pacific train rolled into town, linking the growing pueblo with the transcontinental railroad and thus the rest of the country. Nine years later, the Atchison, Topeka & Santa Fe Railway arrived to provide stiff competition, and a fare-cutting war ensued: at one memorable point round-trip tickets from the Midwest were selling for one dollar each. By then Los Angeles already had horse-drawn trolleys and cable cars, and by the late 1880s these were being replaced by electric trolley lines. Typically, these were built by opportunistic entrepreneurs whose business ethics were not always the most scrupulous. For capitalization they tended to call on property owners who were willing to provide subsidies in return for services in the hope of making a profit on their real estate. It gave these lines a marginal existence, and by the turn of the century trolley tracks connected downtown Los Angeles with Santa Monica on the coast and Pasadena to the north. It was at this point that Henry E. Huntington came into the picture.

Henry Huntington was the nephew and right-hand man of Collis P. Huntington, most vigorous of the Big Four, the Sacramento entrepreneurs who had established the western end of the transcontinental railroad. When Collis died, in 1900, Henry expected to inherit leadership of the Union Pacific–Southern Pacific combine, but he was outmaneuvered by Edward H. Harriman. Instead, having married his uncle's widow, he moved to San Marino, just outside Pasadena, and began to build the estate—now the Huntington Museum and Library—that would be the center of his new empire.

Huntington seems to have been genuinely infatuated with Southern California and upon relocating there pronounced Los Angeles the city of the future, citing its climate, its agricultural fecundity and its ideal position to take a lead in Pacific trade. A practical man, he put his considerable fortune where his mouth was, buying up large parcels of land throughout the region and meanwhile incorporating the Pacific Electric Railway as a tool with which to develop these holdings. Unlike the early promoters of trolley lines in the area, Huntington was not undercapitalized and as a veteran of the railroad wars he was an expert in negotiating rights of way. A likable man, as tycoons go, Huntington seems to have married his acquisitive instincts to an authentic streak of civic altruism, taking real pride in the services he was able to contribute to the community. In his days with the Union Pacific–Southern Pacific he had been a functionary, however elevated, and the executor of his uncle's wishes rather than an innovator. The Pacific Electric was his to shape and build, however, and he set to work with formidable energy, writing to his mother that he was never happy unless he had something to grade.

The PE was incorporated in 1901, taking over the existing Los Angeles & Pasadena Line and the Pasadena & Mount Lowe Railway, a famous scenic route that ended with a cable car ride to the top of Echo Mountain, high in the San Gabriels. Almost immediately Huntington set about transforming the Pasadena Line from narrow to standard gauge, permitting larger passenger cars and, more important, allowing for the interchange of rolling stock with the established steam railroads. Simultaneously, gangs of Mexicans were set to work on grading new routes, the first to go into service being the Long Beach Line, which opened July 4, 1902.

This inaugurated a decade of extraordinary activity and by 1911 the PE tracks connected Los Angeles with the ocean at several points, connected the major beach towns, ran south as far as the citrus orchards of Santa Ana, served sections of the San Fernando Valley, and provided extensive service to the burgeoning San Gabriel Valley, reaching out as far as San Bernardino. Eventually more than a thousand miles of standard-gauge track, complete with overhead wires and a network of PE-owned power stations, knit the Greater Los Angeles area together. Plying these tracks were the famous Big Red Cars, the open vehicles of the early days quickly giving way to comfortable, enclosed, high-speed cars comparable with the cars pulled by intercity express trains and furnished with bathrooms and other conveniences. On busy routes, three or four of these cars could be coupled together, and in the heyday of the PE commuters could travel between downtown LA and San Bernardino in 105 minutes, a time that accommodated frequent local stops yet still compares favorably with what can be achieved today by automobile in rush-hour traffic. In many areas, such as Hollywood, riders could transfer to the narrow-gauge yellow streetcars of the Los Angeles Railway Corporation, also controlled by Huntington, for local rides.

At first the Big Red Cars traveled through bean fields and orange groves, stopping at simple wood or stucco stations that served undeveloped subdivisions. These consisted of a few shingled bungalows set among a grid of empty lots, sidewalks and street furniture already in place—the landscape familiar to the world as the background of Mack Sennett's Keystone Comedies. Needless to say, many of these subdivisions belonged to the Pacific Electric Land Company, and Huntington did everything possible to attract potential home buyers to its holdings. He had, for example, purchased considerable acreage in Redondo Beach and drew huge crowds there on weekends by building a palatial bathhouse with three "plunges," and laying on all kinds of entertainments, including George Feeth, the first California surfer, imported from Hawaii. With his massive redwood boards as long as a racing scull, Feeth was keeping alive a sport that at that point had almost died out, even in the islands. This lone missionary would train a whole generation of West Coast surfers, but in the meantime his feats, which must have seemed tantamount to walking on water, served in 1907 to bring potential purchasers into contact with PE-owned lots within sight and sound of the Pacific breakers. Hundreds were sold at a tidy profit to Huntington and his associates.

Weekend jaunts to Redondo Beach, or to the mountains, helped give the Big Red Cars an almost sybaritic image. Certainly they were used by commuters, but they were also employed for pleasure. For miles the PE tracks skirted the ocean, and tourists could take the 175-mile Orange Empire trolley tour, which looped through the citrus fields and vineyards that covered vast areas between the still tiny satellite towns. A shorter circular route popular with visitors and locals alike was the so-called Balloon Route, which the PE took over from the former Los Angeles Pacific Company. Starting from downtown, this carried the sightseer through Hollywood to Santa Monica, then, by way of Venice, to Redondo Beach and back through Culver City. Another sightseeing route visited the San Gabriel Mission and Busch Gardens, then returned to downtown by way of the famous Cawston Ostrich Farm in South Pasadena, one of the most popular tourist attractions of the period. On New Year's Day, scores of trolleys converged on Pasadena for the Rose Bowl Parade, and for special occasions—weddings and funerals—the wealthy could hire deluxe cars, like the *Poppy* and *El Amigo*, fitted with lounges and kitchens just like the grandest Pullman cars.

Natural rivals: automobiles and interurban trolley cars of the Pacific Electric Railroad. *American Stock Photos*

Needless to say other factors contributed to the growth of Los Angeles, but the PE's impact must not be underestimated. Between 1900 and 1910 the population of Los Angeles County rose from 170,000 to 504,000, and most of these newcomers were dependent to a greater or lesser extent on the Big Red Cars and the smaller Yellow Cars. In 1911 Huntington sold out his interests to Harriman and the Southern Pacific (with whom he had been forced to form an alliance). He retained control of his streetcar systems, but it was through his structuring of the PE that he made his most lasting contribution to the evolution of the region. Communities like Manhattan Beach, Watts and Azusa owed their prosperity, if not their very existence, to the PE. The routes forged by the Big Red Cars virtually dictated the area's growth patterns so that in the future the highways would be obliged to first duplicate, then eventually replace, the PE's routes. It is instructive to study a modern freeway map alongside a map of the old PE system. The parallels are inescapable. In the San Gabriel Valley the San Bernardino Freeway matches the old San Bernardino Line, while the Foothill Freeway (Interstate 210) retraces the route of the former Glendora Line. South of downtown the Long Beach Freeway has been substituted for the Long Beach Line, the Harbor Freeway for the San Pedro Line. The Santa Ana Freeway runs a little to the north of the former Santa Ana Line, the Santa Monica Freeway approximates the route of the Venice Short Line, and the first freeway to be built, the Pasadena, closely follows the route on which PE service was inaugurated in 1901. In some places the freeways actually occupy the rights-of-way originally established for the interurban cars.

It was much the same story all over the country, in Seattle and Cincinnati, Minneapolis and Indianapolis. Suburban land speculation went hand in hand with investment in electrified trolley systems. Those interurban systems helped shape the cities and thus, to a large extent, dictated future patterns of automobile traffic. But in creating new suburbs the interurbans helped foster an upwardly mobile class of Americans—akin to the old middle class, yet discernibly different—that would soon demand private transportation as a proper adjunct to house ownership.

The rise of the automobile meant that the prime of the interurban was very fleeting, perhaps undeservedly so. Nostalgia has invested the trolleys with a patina of legend, but even at the time they were regarded with affection, as is evident from Fontaine Fox's *Toonerville Trolley* comic strip. However checkered the intentions of their sponsors, the interurbans were a remarkably rational form of transportation, one that singularly suited America's image of itself at the time. Electricity had promised clean energy; the trolleys were clean and did not spew fumes into the atmosphere. They were noisy, it's true, but in a cheerful kind of way, and there was something appealing about traveling with a group of one's neighbors, whether to work or on an expedition to see the desert in bloom. Trolleys facilitated travel between dormitory towns and centers of employment, yet at the same time they fostered a sense of community.

But even in early photographs of the trolley cars—ladies in Edwardian dresses stepping gingerly aboard, boys in knickers watching from the curb—automobiles often appear, gasoline-powered buggies darting across the right of way like cheeky sparrows. There is something antisocial about them, something lacking in respect. By comparison, the trolley cars, modern though they may have seemed at the time, look like old-fashioned embodiments of civic virtue.

This is especially evident a little later, in silent movie comedies, many of them made by anarchic rebels on the run in Hollywood, ready to dash for the Mexican border at the first sign of camera-smashing goons employed by the motion picture patent holders back East. Men like Mack Sennett may not have thought of themselves as anarchists, yet their humor was essentially antiestablishment and it frequently expressed itself in terms of automotive lunacy, with cars teetering on the edge of the Santa Monica Palisades, the Coast Highway a sheer drop below, or stalling on the interurban tracks only to escape destruction by a Big Red Car at the very last second.

The PE trolleys played an unwitting role in many early Hollywood two-reelers, being forced into service not as villains—they were too friendly for that—but as clumsy instruments of doom, lumbering vehicles whose fate was determined by the rails they were forced to run upon while the cocky automobile was free to break all the rules of polite society. Those Keystone Kops two-reelers and Fatty Arbuckle shorts were harbingers of things to come, early warnings that the automobile would defy reason as it took possession of men's minds and souls.

The interurbans represented rational, pragmatic America. In linking established communities and enabling the development of new dormitory suburbs, they belonged to the America that believed in family life, neighborliness, settling down and maturity. The automobile was always a threat to this kind of stability. True enough, the notion of the family car and the car as a way of linking workplace with home was established early on. But the car also represented restlessness, the itch to move on still existing beneath the placid surface of a nation that worshiped stability, yet was not prepared to give up adventure and mobility just because the frontier no longer existed. American heroes, after all, were not settlers. In those early Hollywood westerns, the leading man—William S. Hart or one of his imitators—rode into Dodge City or Tombstone, took on lawlessness, made the streets safe for the townspeople, then rode off into the sunset. No staying put for him. The greatest real-life American hero of the day, Teddy Roosevelt, was just such a gunslinger, staying in town (Washington, D.C.) just long enough to put the nation straight, then taking off for new adventures.

For young Americans at the dawn of the automobile age, the horseless carriage stood for adventure. It was a symbol of individual freedom in a world that was being tamed at a pace that was frighteningly rapid. Especially out West, where squabbles had been settled by six-shooters just a generation earlier, civilization had arrived with the suddenness of a mudslide. As late as the 1870s Los Angeles had been a notoriously violent frontier town, home to famous bandits like Tiburico Vasquez. A quarter of a century later, boosters were portraying it as the Athens of the Pacific and peaceful families from Iowa and the Dakotas were establishing homes in Glendale and Pomona. Seldom, if ever, had a hick town grown into a major regional center so rapidly, and now the interurbans of the Pacific Electric helped that regional center grow into a city of national consequence in a matter of a dozen years.

The population just grew and grew, but it was a population without roots. Ninety percent of the people who rode the Big Red Cars had grown up somewhere else, and their parents or grandparents had already moved west before that, either from Europe or the Eastern seaboard. Some of them were tired and finally ready to settle down with the cuckoo clocks and the Irish lace, but many were still restless and suspicious of stability.

Settlers and rootless alike, they were ready for the automobile. It promised precious personal mobility to the restless, and it permitted the settlers to believe they had not given up freedom of choice entirely. The dichotomy is still apparent in car advertising today and it has colored the entire American experience with the automobile.

Early American automobiles were often quite compact, as is the case
with this 1902 runabout driven by its manufacturer, Walter C. Baker.
Bettmann Archive

Chapter 3

SELF-
STARTERS

While American pioneers were still busy with horseless buggies—tiller-steered carriages with engines mounted under the driver's seat—European manufacturers were forging ahead with considerably more sophisticated vehicles that bore a growing resemblance to the modern automobile. The buggy type was not unknown there, but increasingly Europeans favored the Panhard-Levassor layout with the motor up front and rear-wheel drive, guidance sometimes being by way of a steering wheel rather than a tiller. Introduced in 1898, the steering wheel, was one of Emile Levassor's remarkable contributions to automobile design, having been conceived by him shortly before his untimely death. European automobile builders and enthusiasts were also quick to embrace such improvements as pneumatic tires, which came into favor after Edouard Michelin mounted Dunlop tires on the car that he and his brother entered in the 1895 Paris–Bordeaux–Paris race. The Michelin brothers made sixty-five tire changes during the race, but by employing detachable rim flanges of Edouard's design they were able to make these changes rapidly and with relatively little difficulty, solving a problem that had till then deterred motorists from abandoning hard tires. The Michelins opened their own tire factory in Clermont-Ferrand and soon became Dunlop's chief rival, though the German firms Metzeler and Peter were significant competitors.

By the beginning of the new century, well-engineered, progressively conceived cars were being built in several European countries. Fiat and Isotta-Fraschini were founded in 1899, two years before Ettore Bugatti, then twenty, showed his first car at a Milan automobile show. Spyker, which for a while dominated the London taxi market, built handsome automobiles in the Netherlands starting in 1902, while the first representative of the aristocratic Hispano-Suiza marque rolled out of a Barcelona workshop in 1904. British manufacturers were taking advantage of the repeal of the red flag law, and by the turn of the century firms such as Lanchester were making handsome vehicles, as advanced as those of all but a handful of their continental rivals. It was the French and Germans who continued to lead the way, however, with names like Panhard, De Dion, Renault, Peugeot, Adler, Benz and Daimler very much at the fore. The world's total production of automobiles in 1903 was estimated at 62,000 vehicles, France building almost half of them.

Perhaps the most remarkable cars built in the first half decade of the twentieth century were those designed between 1901 and 1905 by Wilhelm Maybach of Daimler Motoren-Gesellschaft AG, automobiles that resulted from a visit to the Daimler factory by Emile Jellinek, a wealthy Austrian enthusiast who was hoping to convince the company to build a lighter, faster, more powerful model. As it happened, Maybach had a number of new ideas on the drawing board, innovations he was waiting for an opportunity to try out. These included a four-speed gate-change gearbox, mechanically operated inlet valves, a honeycomb radiator and a pressed-steel chassis, all revolutionary at the time. Jellinek was impressed and told Maybach that he would place an order for three dozen cars incorporating these improvements on the sole condition that the resulting vehicle should be named for his elder daughter, Mercedes.

The result was the Mercedes 35, which was unveiled during the festivities of Nice Week, 1901, an ideal occasion, since the new car immediately caught the attention of the entire *haut monde*, from Europe's still untaxed aristocrats to the cash-laden offspring of American robber barons. In the post-Levassor mode, the 3050 cc, 35 hp four-cylinder engine was mounted at the front and the car featured a low-to-the-ground box-section chassis, which, along with a short wheel base and wide track, offered much better road holding than had been the norm, and with it greater comfort. Coachwork came in several luxurious styles, of which the open *Tourenwagen* version was perhaps the most popular. In full road trim the Mercedes 35 was capable of about 50 mph. Stripped and tuned for racing it was considerably faster, and in April 1902 the American enthusiast William Vanderbilt drove one at a speed of 69 mph (111.106 kph), then a world record for gasoline-powered automobiles.

For the moment the Mercedes outstripped all competitors in terms of both refinement and performance, and it was snapped up by well-heeled motorists from both sides of the Atlantic. The mellifluous Mercedes name seems also to have helped ensure its fame, and in 1903 Maybach and Daimler came out with a more powerful and still more luxurious version, the celebrated Mercedes "Sixty," equipped with a 9236 cc, 60 hp engine which gave it a performance that would shame some automobiles built three quarters of a century later. With its lack of a windshield, its four foot-operated pedals, its outside gearshift and brake levers, it was not easy or comfortable to drive by present-day standards, but it was nonetheless an extremely modern car, right down to the use of a gas pedal instead of a manually operated accelerator. Its influence would be felt for years and is very much apparent in, for example, the Rolls-Royce 40/50, the famous Silver Ghost, which was the first of the British marque's great luxury cars. This classic was introduced in 1906 and remained in production, with relatively minor changes, until 1925.

The fact that the Mercedes "Sixty" was such an advanced vehicle should not be taken to mean that, even as late as 1903, Europe had entirely accepted the automobile. This masterpiece of engineering, capable of speeds that would be appropriate to the modern freeway or autobahn, was in fact restricted in many places to a pace more suitable to the bicycle, or even the pedestrian. In Switzerland, for example, a speed limit of 4 mph applied to all built-up areas, while 15 and 20 mph limits were commonplace.

This was a world where farmers as a matter of course drove cattle and sheep along roadways, and where pigs and chickens often wandered at will across rights of way. Needless to say the typical Touraine farmer did not appreciate discovering that his prize porker had been reduced to *charcuterie* beneath the wheels of an errant Minerva or Darracq. Nor was he entirely happy when his horse reared and bolted after being terrified by a noisy Renault *voiturette*. He did not care one bit for the clouds of dust left behind by a speeding Peugeot. Nor, for that matter, did the citizens of Paris, accustomed to uncontested jaywalking—or at least to the familiar warnings given by horse-drawn carriages and omnibuses—take kindly to this new hazard to pedestrians. One Parisian, a Monsieur Hugues Le Roux, took exception to being struck, apparently without major injury, by a car, and responded by informing the prefect of police that he intended to furnish himself with a handgun and use it on reckless drivers. His letter found its way into several newspapers and caused the editors of *La Locomotion Automobile*, the world's first car magazine, to announce that motorists might be forced to arm themselves with machine guns in self-defense.

In its less frantic moments *La Locomotion Automobile* did much to neutralize autophobia, and in this it was joined by various automobile clubs that united motorists to lobby in favor of their chosen toy. In England the Automobile Association was organized specifically to hire teams of bicyclists who would warn motorists of speed traps. The Royal Automobile Club, meanwhile, sponsored a series of tests which demonstrated that a car, properly handled, was safer than a horse-drawn vehicle, especially in emergency stops. Test after test showed that at comparable speeds the car could be brought to a halt in half the distance or less of that required by the horse-drawn competition.

Such pragmatic tests may have played their part in legitimizing the role of the automobile, but political clout was probably just as significant. Early car owners were wealthy and often well connected. In Europe, royal patronage was not uncommon. King Alfonso XIII of Spain drove an Hispano-Suiza—appropriately, an Alfonso model —on a record-breaking run from San Sebastián to Madrid. If the monarch is a motorist, could the people long resist the motor car? At a slightly lower level, there were plenty of European petty aristocrat automobile enthusiasts who were used to riding roughshod over local magistrates and law enforcement agencies.

At this point in history the car in Europe had a distinctly upper-class cachet. Certainly there were makers like Fiat, Renault and Vauxhall who looked to the middle-class market, but the innovators were the *grandes marques* like Daimler, Rolls-Royce, Isotta-Fraschini and Horch, which catered to what became known, ironically, as the carriage trade. The United States would have its *grandes marques* too, but their role would be secondary to that of organizations such as Ford and General Motors. Except for an occasional visionary, like the Englishman Herbert Austin, few in Europe seriously thought about anything as radical as a car for every family. The general public in Europe did become involved in motoring early and enthusiastically, but as spectators rather than as owners. Automobile racing and speed records caught the fancy of the man in the street and he eagerly devoured news of these powerful new machines and the men who drove them at risk to their lives.

At first there were two basic kinds of contests: city-to-city races of the Paris–Bordeaux–Paris type and out-and-out speed trials, in which a car was pitted against the clock over a measured kilometer. Briefly, steam cars and electric cars dominated this latter category, a torpedo-shaped electric hot rod, *La Jamais Contente* being the first to break the 100 kph barrier. The city-to-city races were tests less of speed than of endurance and reliability, though one should not underestimate the daring of the drivers who sat with little protection above flimsy fuel tanks and thrashing chain drives that could cut a man in two just as effectively—and more permanently—than any illusionist at the Théâtre Robert-Houdin.

The 1903 Paris–Madrid race was a turning point in demonstrating the dangers of this kind of event. Ten people and innumerable farm animals were killed before the race was stopped at Bordeaux. Among the dead was Marcel Renault, one of the three brothers who had founded the Renault company, which had made its reputation by winning highly publicized city-to-city races. More significant, perhaps, half the dead were spectators, and it became clear that free-for-all racing on the public highways was doomed, though a few later events such as the Paris–Constantinople race in 1905 and especially the Peking–Paris race of 1907 continued to attract great public attention. Prince Scipione Borghese won the latter in a 35/45 hp Italia, covering the course in sixty days and at times driving along the roadbed of the Trans-Siberian Railroad.

By then, however, the emphasis had shifted to closed-circuit road races; crowd control was more manageable and spectators, in some cases at least, enjoyed the advantage of seeing cars speed past several times, since many of these events were conducted over multiple laps of a relatively short course. The Circuit des Ardennes had been inaugurated in Belgium even before the tragedies of the Paris–Madrid race, and in 1905 Count Vicenzo Florio sponsored the famous Targa Florio over a mountainous circuit in Sicily. That same year the Royal Automobile Club, faced with parliamentary opposition to road racing in England, organized the Tourist Trophy races over another mountainous course in the self-governing Isle of Man, and in 1906 the Automobile Club de France staged the first Grand Prix at Le Mans. The result of these closed-circuit races, which depended on skill and handling as well as sheer speed, was the evolution of a distinctly European style of sports car, agile as well as fast, dashing and always fun to drive. Indeed, each of the major producing countries evolved its own variant on the style so that Britain, over the decades, would offer its MGs and Jaguars, France its Delages and Bugattis, Germany its BMWs and Porsches, Italy its Ferraris and Alfa Romeos. Some of these marques did not come to full prominence till half a century later, but the philosophies behind them were established by the experience of early closed-circuit racing.

In this period, too, tracks designed specifically for high-speed driving were first constructed. In 1907 Hugh Locke-King built a 2½-mile speed oval on his estate at Brooklands in the south of England, with scientifically angled curves that permitted a car to be driven at continuous speed without deflection of steering. Brooklands remained in use till after World War II, and its key legacy may be the test tracks used by most of the world's leading manufacturers. So far as racetracks are concerned, however, the tradition of Brooklands evolved chiefly in America.

It did not take long for Americans to be bitten by the speed bug. William Vanderbilt first snatched the timed-kilometer record away from the electric car, driving a French-built gasoline-powered Mors. The Vanderbilt name was preeminent in early American racing circles, since the family sponsored the celebrated Vanderbilt Cup races, which turned the villages of Long Island into a carnival of speed on summer weekends in the first part of the century. A carnival of speed but also a spectacle of carnage, since these races resulted in numerous accidents and several deaths involving drivers, mechanics and spectators. The crowds—as many as 500,000 for the 1910 race—were notoriously unruly, breaking down fences and crowding the roadway to the point where fatalities were almost inevitable. After 1910 the citizens of Long Island had had enough and future Vanderbilt Cup competitions were held in Savannah (site of another famous road race), Milwaukee, San Francisco and Santa Monica.

But the real future of American racing was to be found at the Indianapolis Speedway, a 2½-mile Brooklands-style bowl built by a group of local businessmen and opened for racing in 1909. The site itself was significant, for the heartland of America would define many of the nation's attitudes toward the automobile. In fact, though, the track came close to closing almost as soon as it opened. Its original gravel surface began to break up after just a few races, but the investors decided to persevere and paved the oval with more than three million bricks; since then it has remained in continuous operation. The first 500-mile race was run in 1911.

The most celebrated name in the early history of American car racing was Barney Oldfield, who came to fame as the pilot of one of the most significant cars in the entire history of the American automobile. Without it the evolution of the industry might have been different, though nothing could have been less like a production car than Henry Ford's "999" special, built in 1902 as a pure speedster. With a four-cylinder, 80 hp engine, it was a spare, stripped-down ancestor of several generations of hot rods and dragsters.

The "999" had already won every race it entered when Oldfield was given the chance to drive it in 1902. Burly, hard-drinking and foul-mouthed, Oldfield was the Babe Ruth of the dirt track. Although he had experience as a bicycle and motorcycle racer, it seems he had never actually driven an automobile of any kind up to that point. On his first day in the "999" he negotiated the Grosse Pointe track with such abandon that he was immediately selected to pilot the Ford special in a race against the current champion, Alexander Winton. "This chariot may kill me," he told Ford, "but they will say afterwards that I was going like hell." Going like hell, Oldfield beat Winton and in doing so broke the existing American speed record by completing the five-mile race at a fraction under 60 mph.

A few weeks later, Oldfield drove the "999" to a world record for the mile, covering the distance in 1:01 minutes. Two years later, Ford himself, looking for more publicity, took the "Arrow," another special, out onto a frozen lake dusted with cinders and covered the measured mile at an extraordinary 91.37 mph, yet another world record.

The significance of the "999" and the "Arrow" is that their successes brought Henry Ford the fame that enabled

TOP: Henry Ford's 1896 Quadricycle, photographed several years later with Ford at the tiller. *National Automobile History Collection, Detroit Public Library*

BOTTOM: Located on Mack Avenue in Detroit, this was the original home of the Ford Motor Company. In 1903, more than 1,700 cars were built at this plant. *UPI/Bettmann*

him to form the Ford Motor Company in 1903, with a capitalization of $100,000, and to promote his early models. He was now ready to turn his back upon racing and build a car for the people. And the people were ready. Motoring in America had faced the same kind of public outcry as in Europe—in Michigan, police actually fired their weapons at speeding automobiles—but acceptance was setting in as people began to realize the enormous potential of motor vehicles. If racing aroused the public's interest, endurance runs and reliability trials won its admiration and trust. In 1903 three separate parties made automobile trips from San Francisco to New York, each taking about eight weeks to cross the continent, and the following year Charles Jasper Glidden began his celebrated Glidden Tours, reliability tests that pitted standard production cars against routes carefully planned to test the mettle of both car and driver. These acquired such prestige that manufacturers attempted to subvert the rules by entering specially adapted cars posing as stock models, and commercial abuses became so rampant that Glidden discontinued the Tours in 1914.

Meanwhile, between 1900 and 1910 motor vehicle production in the United States mounted from 4,000 per annum to 187,000. Total car registrations grew from 8,000 to close to half a million. The American car industry was on its way, but almost before it started, it had to endure a major trauma in the form of the Selden patent.

George B. Selden was a gifted engineer who had designed, but not built, a gasoline-powered automobile in 1879, the year he applied for a United States patent. His design combined a three-cylinder engine (which was built and tested) with many of the other characteristics that later became standard features of the horseless buggy—clutch, steering gear and so forth. Normally his patent would have been granted in 1881 and would have expired in 1898, but Selden kept it pending for sixteen years by filing amendments to the original application. The consequence of this was that the patent—No. 549,160—was finally issued in 1895. Four years later he sold his patent, for $10,000 and 20 percent of any future royalties, to a consortium of Wall

Street investors headed by William C. Whitney and Thomas F. Ryan. The following year the new patent holders, acting as the Electric Vehicle Company, filed suit against the Winton Motor Carriage Company, then the largest U.S. manufacturer of automobiles, claiming patent infringement. The potential ramifications were enormous, but matters were apparently resolved in 1903 by an out-of-court settlement whereby Winton and other manufacturers were to pay a small royalty—1.25 percent on the list price of each car—which was to be divided among Selden, the Electric Vehicle Company and the newly formed Association of Automobile Manufacturers. This organization was simply a front for a cartel of established manufacturers who now took advantage of the patent suit by attempting to use it to shut out upstarts and unwelcome competitors in general.

These upstarts and competitors included Henry Ford, just going into business, and Ransom E. Olds, whose company had now established a prime position in the industry. They and other American manufacturers banded together, along with foreign interests such as Panhard and Levassor, to fight the Selden patent, a battle in which Henry Ford, at least in the eyes of the public, assumed leadership. To most Americans it seemed to be a matter of Henry Ford, the self-made man, pitted against the establishment, and the suit did much to enhance his image. The court case dragged on till 1911, when an appeals court settled in favor of Ford, acknowledging in part the validity of the Selden patent but ruling that Ford had not infringed upon it. By then Ford had become the dominant force in the American motor industry, the Ford A of 1903 having been succeeded by the revolutionary Model T of 1908.

Under Ford's leadership the U.S. industry took on a character very distinct from anything that existed in Europe. Indeed, car building in Europe was not so much an industry as a craft, the great marques specializing in hand-built automobiles that combined engineering innovations with traditional values derived from coach building. There were similar craft shops in America, of course, but very early on American businessmen saw the possibilities of large-scale production—not necessarily along the assembly line model—in which many units would be sold at a relatively low profit.

One of the great early entrepreneurs was William "Billy" Durant, a former Flint, Michigan, carriage maker who took over Buick in 1904 and turned its fortunes around. Durant's theory was that in the burgeoning market it would be a mistake to concentrate on just one model line. Instead he saw the future in the form of a large, broadly based company that produced many models for all sectors of the market, so that if, for example, luxury car sales faltered the slack could be taken up by production of commercial vehicles. In 1907, Durant, along with Benjamin Briscoe of Maxwell-Briscoe, attempted to assemble Buick, Maxwell-Briscoe, Reo and Ford into a single combine. The plan almost succeeded, but Henry Ford demanded $3 million in cash, and R. E. Olds responded by insisting upon the same cash deal for Reo. Unable to raise that much ready money, Durant and Briscoe backed off, but the following year Durant incorporated General Motors; he brought Buick, Cadillac, Oakland (which would become Pontiac) and Oldsmobile under this umbrella, along with various parts suppliers and engineering support concerns. Durant had overreached himself, however, expanding much too rapidly and thus placing the company in financial jeopardy. It was rescued by a syndicate of bankers who placed Charles W. Nash, an able businessman, in charge of the combine.

It was Henry Ford who towered over the industry during this period of rapid expansion. As is well know, Ford was a Michigan farm boy of Anglo-Irish and Dutch descent. He displayed an early aptitude for mechanics and as a young man found employment installing and repairing small steam engines used to power agricultural machinery. Those may have been the happiest days of his life; even at the height of his success his idea of a grand outing was to go on a threshing picnic. Every September he would round up friends and family members and find a farm where he could set up one of his old Westinghouse steam engines, fire it up and thresh some clover while onlookers ate sandwiches and ice cream. Ford would sometimes say that he hated farm life, but he was in every way a product of that Midwestern agricultural world, sharing its values and prejudices, relishing its worship of hard work and joining in its deep-rooted suspicion of Easterners and Jews.

While working as an engineer with the Detroit Edison Company he turned his attention to the use of the internal combustion engine to power horseless carriages. Much given to self-mythologizing, he would later claim to have built and run his first automobile in 1892. All the evidence, however, supports the contention that his initial success— honorable enough—was the quadricycle, first tested on Detroit's Bagley Avenue in 1896. In 1899 he entered the automobile manufacturing business as chief engineer and minority stockholder in the Detroit Automobile Company. Philosophical differences with his backers, who lacked his vision and commitment to the idea of a universal car, priced for the masses, led him to strike out on his own, using racing successes to help launch his new Ford Motor Company. From 1919 onward it would be wholly owned by its founder and his son Edsel.

For practical reasons (and because of pressure from his backers), Ford started by producing medium-priced automobiles, but he was really marking time until he could find the means to produce a people's car—a vehicle he often referred to as a car to help the farmer. New production methods would be required to build such a car, and those methods would need to be grounded in levels of technological precision that were unthinkable for most people, even in so progressive an industry. That such precision was achievable was demonstrated graphically in 1908, both by the first production Model T's and by a very different kind of American car, Henry M. Leland's luxurious Model K Cadillac tourer.

European luxury cars of the period were custom-built to the extent that one Lanchester, say, might vary in subtle ways from the next, even in the mechanical components. In 1909 three Model K Cadillacs were driven to the Brooklands track in England. They were taken apart and the parts were placed in a single pile. Ninety components were removed at random and replaced with spares from the manufacturer's London agency. The stack of components was then thoroughly mixed up before being handed over to Cadillac mechanics to reassemble into three vehicles, presumably different entities from those brought in earlier. The three "new" cars were then driven on the Brooklands track for 500 miles without mechanical problems. European motoring experts were stunned. Clearly, American manufacturers had not only caught up with their European rivals but in some ways had surpassed them.

Ironically, a European innovation was a key factor in allowing Henry Ford to perfect his people's car. Vanadium steel, a lightweight alloy, was already in relatively common use in the Old World but was almost unknown in America. European manufacturers employed vanadium steel to lighten their cars for racing, without loss of strength. Ford used the same material to produce a lightweight chassis that could still take the punishment of unimproved roads, such as the dirt tracks of rural America. Working closely with his chief engineer, Harold Wills, the Wizard of Dearborn supplied his pet project with a newly designed 2898 cc four-cylinder, water-cooled engine that produced 24 hp at 1800 rpm. Ignition was by means of a flywheel magneto operating in an oil bath, and the transmission employed an ingenious two-speed, pedal-operated gearbox that required a degree of athletic ability to engage. Lubrication was by means of a "splash" system that depended on the flywheel's throwing oil onto the bands of the transmission, the surplus flowing down a tube to the front of the engine where it splashed over the other moving parts. The radically basic nature of the design can be illustrated by the fact that in early versions the Model T had no gas gauge as such. If a driver wanted to know if he had enough fuel to make it home from market, he had to stop the car, raise the cushion of the driver's seat, unscrew the gas cap and insert into the tank a special wooden ruler, issued without cost by Ford dealerships and marked out in gallons. In the absence of such a ruler a stick found by the roadside would permit an approximation. Beyond that, though, the car was virtually indestructible, the moving parts being protected from the elements by an envelope of thin metal sheeting. Ford had thought of just about everything. The high ride of the car meant that it could handle rough terrain, but if a Model T owner did get stuck in a mud hole he could often "rock" the car out of the mire by skillful manipulation of the gears, which permitted a driver to go from forward to reverse as a continuous action (the epicyclic gearbox also eliminated the then common problem of stripped cogwheels). The magneto system meant that a Model T, when properly tuned, could start and run without a battery.

The Model T was intended to be maintained and repaired, as far as possible, by the owner. The machinery was kept deliberately basic (though not primitive), and two or three generations of young Americans came to know the inner workings of automobiles by diving beneath the hood of a Model T. If cars were sexy—and from the earliest day command over these infernal contraptions seemed to carry an erotic charge—then the Model T was the proverbial farmer's daughter of a thousand commercial travelers' tall tales. This farmer's daughter was no Hollywood sex goddess, but she was wholesome and she surrendered her most private secrets to the young swain who was not afraid to tinker with her petcocks or grind her valves. The Model T was the first conquest for many an automotive Don Juan. He might graduate to racier cars, endowed with more seductive bodywork, but the knowledge he had gained out back of the barn, beneath the hood of his Tin Lizzie, would always stand him in good stead and protect him against the wiles of automobiles that depended more upon the allure of chrome trim than upon the lasting satisfaction of sound engineering.

Tin Lizzie, it should be noted, was a nickname that came to suit the Model T only as its long production run came to make it seem anachronistic. In 1908 no one would have felt embarrassed at being seen in a shiny new gray roadster (the "any color as long as it's black" policy came later). Set it alongside a Rolls-Royce 40/50 of the same period, or a Mercedes "Sixty," and a definite family resemblance would become apparent (though there would be no doubt that the Ford was the country cousin). The Model T was very much a car of its time and such a classic that, like the 40/50, it could remain in production for almost two decades. There were refinements over the years, of course, and the Model T came in a variety of styles of bodywork, but the most popular version was the tourer, an open car furnished with a folding fabric top and roll-down isinglass curtains in case of a change in the weather (isinglass was a transparent and flexible form of gelatin). The lasting success of this variant was due to the poor condition of the roads that prevailed through the period of the Model T's popularity. A fully enclosed car would have been welcome on winter mornings in Kansas or Iowa, but solid glass-fitted windows would have been shaken to pieces by the rutted and potholed terrain the vehicle was often asked to negotiate.

This Model T roadster was built in 1916, two years after Henry Ford introduced assembly-line production to his Highland Park plant.
Bettmann Archive

HIGHWAYS TO HEAVEN

The Model T is well known as the first assembly line–built car, but that applies only to vehicles built from 1914 on, though some components were put together by moving assembly line a year earlier. The history of assembly-line production dates back to the early years of the Industrial Revolution, the French, the British and the Swedish making notable contributions to its development. Later, continuous-flow assembly techniques had been used in America by firearms manufacturers like Eli Whitney and Samuel Colt, and had also been applied to the fabrication of other items such as clocks and sewing machines. America was certainly leading the world in this field when Henry Ford came into the picture, but nobody had applied assembly-line techniques on the scale he envisioned.

After the fact, and characteristically, Ford would tend to claim all credit for the introduction of mass production for himself. In reality it may not have been his idea—one of Edsel Ford's schoolteachers, Clarence Avery, may deserve title to that claim, and the Studebaker plant in Detroit was experimenting in the same direction at an earlier date. In all fairness, though, once the notion was planted, Henry Ford pursued the logic with enthusiasm, imagination and even a touch of genius. With his hand-picked team he looked into such models as the systematic packing line that Sears, Roebuck had developed to deal with the complexities of a large-scale mail-order business. It is well known that he took note of the mechanical conveyers used by Chicago meatpackers to carry carcasses along what has properly been described as a disassembly line. In 1911 Ford moved his operation into a new plant at Highland Park, Detroit, and there conveyor belts and other accoutrements of mass assembly were introduced under the direction of Ford's production boss, Charles Sorensen, popularly known as "Cast Iron Charlie." The 1908 Model T had sold for $850 in its basic touring car version. By 1914, the first year of assembly-line manufacture, the price had dipped to $490 (it would eventually drop below $300). That same year more than a quarter of a million units were sold. Eventually production of the Model T would reach a volume of 10,000 a day. By 1927, when production of the Model T finally ended, more than 15 million had been sold.

Henry Ford had made Detroit the auto manufacturing capital of the world, though many of the 15 million Model T's were assembled in distant branch factories from parts supplied by Detroit. Ford plants also opened in other countries. In England, Model T's were being manufactured as early as 1909. Charles Chaplin, in *Modern Times*, was one of the first to take public note of the drudgery and dehumanizing aspect of the production line, but for many years Henry Ford was looked on as a public benefactor, because of both the utility of his product, the Model T, and the high wages he paid (a minimum of $5 a day in 1914, raised to $6 a day by 1926) and benefits he offered his employees, such as hospitalization. Unionization and Ford's poor judgment would eventually change the public's image of the great man, but by World War I his name was one to be conjured with around the Western world, and he had made a unique contribution toward America's becoming an automobile-reliant nation.

Also crucial to this was the rapid development of the American crude oil industry, spurred by rich strikes in Texas, Oklahoma, California and elsewhere. Previously the oil industry had been profitable chiefly by supplying kerosene for lamps. Now, just as kerosene markets were threatened by gas and electricity, the automobile offered a new and potentially far more valuable market. At first the oil industry had difficulty in keeping up with demand for petroleum and prices rose sharply. New oil strikes and improved refining techniques turned the situation around, however, and after World War I the oil producers were able to keep pace with the expansion of the automobile manufacturers. Rubber, too, became a crucial commodity as tire companies like Firestone and Goodyear tried to satisfy the needs of the growing army of motorists. All of this made Wall Street very happy, and after an initial period of suspicion the financial community did everything it could to encourage the acceptance of the automobile; car industry stocks were listed on the New York Stock Exchange for the first time in 1911.

By World War I the American car was second to none in quality, except perhaps where high-performance engines were concerned, and was already somewhat distinctive in character. Francis Picabia, an artist and notable connoisseur of automobiles, visited New York in 1913 on the occasion of the Armory Show, the exhibition that introduced America to modern art. A wealthy Parisian of Cuban extraction, Picabia was one of the stars of the Armory Show—he was the only European artist to make the transatlantic crossing—exhibiting near-abstract works that shocked critics and spectators almost as much as the exhibition's *succès de scandale*, "Nude Descending a Staircase," by Picabia's friend Marcel Duchamp. Picabia and Duchamp, progenitors of the Dada movement, would establish their place in art history partly by eroticizing machinery, much as the Midwest farmboy subconsciously eroticized the innards of his Model T. For his "definitively unfinished" antimasterpiece, *"The Bride Stripped Bare by Her Bachelors, Even,"* Duchamp devised a seriocomic mythology of mechanistic arousal and seduction. Picabia, during his Dada period, was especially fond of devices such as employing spark plugs and pistons to suggest sexual organs. In fact, no one in the world of high art has ever made more effective metaphorical use of automobile plumbing than Picabia, who was the first person to understand its humorous potential. At the time of his arrival in New York, however, he was a relative innocent, a typical European car enthusiast who already had owned a long succession of luxury vehicles. (He was given to teasing contemporaries like Picasso and Braque when in the first flush of success they bought modest Renaults.) Picabia was impressed by New York—by its skyscrapers, the electric signs of Times Square, Manhattan's smartly turned-out shopgirls—but he was especially impressed by American cars, testing them to the limit on the still rustic roads of Westchester County and picking up at least one speeding ticket in the process. Above all he was enchanted by the self-starter.

The self-starter was just one of several American innovations of the period, but it was a significant one. Until

In 1921, a New York driver hand-cranks her Model T Ford.
Bettmann Archive

then all cars had been started by hand cranking (as some continued to be for another thirty years), a tiresome, physically demanding and even dangerous method. As the engine began to turn over, the starting handle could take on a violent life of its own, one that caused many a broken thumb or fractured wrist. Occasionally hand-crank accidents actually took lives; this was the fate of Byron Carter, manufacturer of the Cartercar, and it was this mishap that caused Carter's friend, Henry Leland, to make up his mind to develop a mechanical starter. Leland was the head of Cadillac, the direct successor of Henry Ford's original Detroit Automobile Company, which was already establishing itself as an important luxury marque. Leland called in

Charles Kettering, an inventor who had designed a motor for the electric cash register. This motor capitalized on the idea of delivering short bursts of power and Kettering quickly realized that the same principle could be applied to the starter motor. Self-starters were installed in Cadillacs from 1912 on and shortly after were made more reliable by the starter drive developed by Vincent Bendix.

This innovation that so impressed Picabia prevented hundreds of injuries and also helped make the automobile attractive to thousands of people, especially women, who had previously been intimidated by the new means of transportation. It is hard to grasp now just how radical the concept of the self-starter was, but the fact remains that it revolutionized the industry. Eventually even Henry Ford was convinced that it should be offered as a feature of the Model T.

European manufacturers—with some distinguished exceptions—were still aiming at the sporting motorist, or at the carriage trade where chauffeurs were taken for granted. American manufacturers—whether producing Model T's or Cadillacs—were convinced that the car was for everyone. It was acknowledged, certainly, that some buyers had more money than others, and would demand a greater degree of luxury, but the same principle applied whether you had $400 to spend or $4,000.

Beginning around 1905, specially tailored finance schemes had become commonplace, bringing car ownership within the reach of many Americans. By the early teens, manufacturers and owners alike agreed that the automobile should be simple to operate, comfortable, efficient and easy to maintain. It could be sporty or elegant or even flashy, but only if the primary requisites were met.

That cars were sexy was tacitly understood but acknowledged openly only by a few radicals like Francis Picabia.

New York's Grand Central Parkway, one of the limited-access highways that set the standard for driving environments between the two world wars. *Bettmann Archive*

Chapter 4

ARTERIAL
AUGURIES

*I*n 1907, four years before Francis Picabia picked up his Westchester speeding ticket, ground was broken for the first stretch of the Bronx River Parkway, a highway that would set standards for the next three decades. This project was a by-product of a scheme undertaken by New York City and Westchester County to clean up the Bronx River, which was then fouled by industrial waste and domestic sewage disposal, its banks home to shantytowns as well as the kind of unregulated advertising signs that would soon crowd the edges of American highways. A sixteen-mile-long corridor of land was acquired, a modern sewage system was installed, and a new course was cut for one section of the formerly polluted river, the banks of which were transformed into a landscaped public recreation area through which the parkway was threaded.

The parkway's immediate models were Ocean Parkway and Eastern Parkway in Brooklyn, conceived in the nineteenth century by Frederick Law Olmsted and his associate Calvert Vaux. While these were intended for horse-drawn traffic, they established a principle of driving for extended distances through narrow ribbons of parkland that through careful plantings would provide ever-changing vistas. Along the Bronx River, this principle was adapted to the needs of motorized traffic, a forty-foot-wide roadway being divided into four lanes that snaked gracefully between new plantings and carefully preserved old trees, passing here and there beneath discreet overpasses and across handsome bridges. The entire length was paved; the decision to do so was made at a time when there were just a few miles of paved highway in the entire nation, outside of major cities.

Only a handful of urban and suburban areas, such as Wayne County, Michigan, had ambitious road improvement schemes. The first concrete road had been built in 1893 in Bellefontaine, Ohio, but the paving of highways by local authorities and private concerns did not begin in earnest till around 1905 and then progressed quite slowly. As late as the end of 1914, there were fewer than 13,000 miles of paved highway in the entire country.

Completion of the Bronx River Parkway was interrupted by World War I, but when the full length was opened in 1923 it was judged to be the handsomest motorway in the world. In addressing the problems of the modern limited-access highway, primarily through the elimination of grade crossings, it predated Mussolini's first autostrada, which opened in 1924. By successfully dealing with the challenge of combining road building with landscaping, it set standards for the future that were soon picked up by the designers of other New York area highways such as the Saw Mill River and Hutchison River parkways. The Bronx River Parkway suggested that driving could be an aesthetic experience. That the aesthetic values of the parkway, imposed by well-meaning planners, were rooted as much in the eighteenth century as the automobile age did not yet present itself as a problem. By any standards, the Bronx River Parkway must be counted as a remarkable achievement.

If you were a farmer in Vermont, or a small-town grocer in Indiana, such progress was merely academic (and it must be remembered that the rural and small-town population was statistically and economically far more significant than it is today). Though many Main Streets were being resurfaced, often with bricks, the chances of being within 100 miles of a paved highway were slight. As far as country roads were concerned, the best that could be hoped for was that they were maintained up to rural free delivery standards. RFD was the official governmental expression of the right of every American, no matter if he lived in the remotest hamlet or sharecropper's shack, to be assured of postal service. Thus he should be able to order goods, whether a wheelbarrow or a length of cambric, from Montgomery Ward or Sears, Roebuck and be guaranteed that the local roadways would permit prompt delivery. Often this meant little more than the occasional appearance of a team of mules pulling a device called the King drag, which scraped the dirt roadbed free of ruts. A split-log frame shod with a steel scraping blade, the King drag was a remarkably useful tool, but a single rainstorm could easily undo its good work.

Naturally these rural dirt roads were built to accommodate the leisurely pace of the horse and wagon. Typically they were tree-lined and often featured sharp right-angled turns where the rights-of-way followed the edges of properties laid out according to the section system by the U.S. Land Office. As country dwellers were converted from car haters to car owners, largely by the Model T, these roads were gradually modified; in many places one of the first changes to occur was the elimination of right-angle turns in favor of gentler curves that would accommodate the speed of the automobile. Stands of trees that had once fulfilled a boundary function were now isolated in the corners of fields, beginning the subtle changes that the automobile would impose on the rural landscape. Where the surface remained unimproved, the car brought new problems. The metal-shod wheels of a buggy or farm cart tended to produce ruts that, while a nuisance, at least lined up with the progress of the vehicles forced to deal with them. In dry weather, the pneumatic tires of automobiles tended to dislodge soft patches of dirt or gravel, creating not only clouds of dust but also transverse ridges and hollows that made for an extremely uncomfortable ride and were not subject to the blandishments of the King drag.

Many such roads would not be improved until well into the second quarter of the century. Prior to World War I there were substantial areas west of the Mississippi where there were no highways at all. The beginning of a national highway program was presaged, however, by the initiative taken by a group of businessmen who, around 1912, began to promote the idea of a coast-to-coast route, to be known as the Lincoln Highway; it would link New York with San Francisco by way of Philadelphia, much of its length along the scenic path that is now occupied by Interstate 80. Heading the association formed to sponsor the highway were Henry Joy of the Packard Motor Company and Carl Graham Fisher, an auto headlight manufacturer and one of the founders of the Indianapolis Speedway. It was their notion to build this transcontinental route with private backing. They quickly attracted the interest of the Goodyear Tire Company, clearly an interested party. Next they sought the involvement of entrepreneurs in cities and towns along the proposed route—Akron, South Bend, Chicago, Cedar Rapids, Council Bluffs, Cheyenne, Salt Lake City, Reno, Sacramento—to build and improve sections of the highway that would serve the business needs of the various communities. Where an insufficient population base made this impossible, as in parts of Utah and Nevada, the association itself provided funds to establish a basic graded right-of-way. All this took time, but by the onset of the Depression the Lincoln Highway was either paved or improved throughout almost all of its 3,384 miles. Many sections were paved at a relatively early date and this did much to educate local authorities to the need for quality motor roads.

Much the same can be said of other national and regional highways that followed. Additional transcontinental routes developed after World War I included the

National Old Trails Road, from Washington, D.C., to Los Angeles; the Pikes Peak Ocean to Ocean Highway, from New York to San Francisco; the Yellowstone Trail, from Plymouth Rock to Seattle; the Lee Highway, from Washington, D.C., to San Diego; and the Old Spanish Trail, from St. Augustine, Florida, to San Diego. North-South routes included the Atlantic Highway, from Maine to Florida; the Dixie Highway, from Lake Michigan to Florida; and the Pacific Highway, from Vancouver, British Columbia, to the Mexican border. Construction and improvement of these routes was greatly facilitated by the Federal Highway Act of 1921, which refined earlier legislation permitting the federal government to provide financial aid for road building. Individual states and counties continued to plan and build the roads, but now they did so with the assurance of assistance from Washington. This marked the beginning of a rational interstate system; 200,000 of the approximately 300,000 interstate miles built by 1928 benefited from the infusion of federal funds.

Even as late as 1923, however, when the Lincoln Highway was finally completed with federal funds, long-distance travel could still be something of an adventure. Motorists had graduated from the days when conditions made it necessary for drivers and passengers alike to hide behind goggles and wrap themselves in leather armor, but it was a foolhardy adventurer who set out on the emerging web of interstate roads without ample spares and tools, along with an inner-tube repair kit, a hand or foot pump and a couple of planks to place beneath the wheels, should the car become mired in mud or snow. It was always advisable to carry an auxilary container of gasoline because gas pumps were sometimes few and far between.

At first gasoline was sold by general stores, smithies facing extinction, and bicycle repair shops that had extended their business to include car maintenance. The first gas station proper—conceived as an entity unto itself—seems to have opened in St Louis, Missouri, in 1905. Grandly called the Automobile Gasoline Company, it was actually a one-man operation devised by a gentleman named C. H. Laessig who had concocted his own home-made pump from an old water heater, a measuring gauge and a length of garden hose. The first commercially built gas pump, the Bowser Self-Measuring Gasoline Storage Pump, appeared the same year. Based on existing kerosene pumps, it was a simple suction (plunger) device operated by hand lever. Soon came underground storage tanks and "visible" pumps with transparent containers that permitted the motorist to see the quantity of fuel he was being sold and thus to be sure he was not being cheated. Often these pumps were highly decorative, and almost all were topped by the colorful glass globes advertising specific brands—Betty Blue Wonder Gas, Old Trusty, Diamond Nitro—that are now so prized by collectors. Since curbside filling caused traffic delays (it was banned in Detroit as early as 1914), drive-in stations with their own filling courts quickly gained popularity. Starting around 1913, big companies like Gulf, Texaco and Standard Oil began to plant gas stations on corner sites around the land. Initially, though, most of these were confined to busy urban and suburban neighborhoods and the open road continued to hold its perils.

If the motorist managed to survive the many pitfalls of the open road, there was still the problem of simply finding his way once he ventured beyond city limits. Signposting was notoriously inefficient, when it existed at all, and road maps were virtually unheard of in many areas. By the late 1890s automobile manufacturers, tire companies and other interested parties, such as isolated resorts, had taken to issuing road guides. These were not maps as such, rather sets of sequential instructions dependent on the driver's alertness and an accurate odometer. A typical example might instruct the motorist to leave town by way of the suspension bridge, proceed 1.3 miles to the Unitarian Church, then turn left and drive 2.7 miles to a stone farm with a red barn and a water tower, then cross the railroad tracks, and so on until the desired destination was reached. Some of these guides were illustrated with photographs showing useful landmarks. Motorists who belonged to auto clubs frequently kept charts, mileage

Early highway signs often demanded a motorist's full attention, as in these examples photographed in Wisconsin, c. 1925.
State Historical Society of Wisconsin

readings and practical notes while making intercity journeys, and copies of these informal guides were made available to other members.

Proper road maps were issued by George Walker of Boston starting in 1900, but these, though accurate, covered only a handful of well-traveled routes. Rand McNally, already known for its railroad maps, soon entered the road-map business and took to assigning numbers to highways to make them easier to identify, even setting up its own highway signs to assist the motorist. From 1920 on, one state after another, beginning with Wisconsin, began to

assign official numbers to its roads, making Rand Mc-
Nally's task infinitely simpler. By then, gas companies—
Gulf was the first—were giving away free maps at their
stations, a practice that continued for half a century.

Rand McNally produced its first national road atlas in
1924. The earliest to survive is from 1926 and it makes for
fascinating browsing. The cover shows an open touring
car parked at an overlook in a national park, apparently
Yosemite, while high above on a rocky ledge an Indian
carves trail-blazing graffiti into the cliff face. Inside the
covers, before the maps are reached, is an abundance of
useful information and advice, beginning with a cata-
logued description of national parks and monuments administered by the National Parks Service, the Department
of Agriculture and the War Department.

Under the heading "Equipping the Car" come the following suggestions:

> Carry a tire pump in good order and a good jack, also
> a small piece of plank 2 x 8 x 18 inches, to use as a
> base for the jack in soft ground. Tire chains are nec-
> essary equipment; some extra cross chains should be
> in the tool box. Carry a rope for towing, a collapsible
> bucket, one upper and one lower hose for radiators,
> with clamps, box of cup grease, a spout oil can and
> a can of extra lubricating oil.

Another section, titled "Things Worth Knowing," includes the following gems:

> Butter, oleomargarine and cocoanut butter are excel-
> lent for softening road tar for easy removal from fend-
> ers. . . .

> Women drivers of motor vehicles should be given spe-
> cial consideration—and watching.

The map section is divided into state maps and vicinity
maps, the latter providing more detailed information for
seventeen major urban areas. The state maps are organized not alphabetically, as in modern road atlases, but

by contiguity, so that Maine, the first map, is followed by New Hampshire, then Vermont, and so on. In these maps, roads are divided into four categories: paved, unpaved (graded and drained and provided with low-type surfaces such as clay, gravel or, at best, waterbound macadam), graded (graded and drained but not surfaced), unimproved roads (i.e., dirt tracks).

The driver traveling about the Northeast or the upper Midwest, would find himself well supplied with paved highways, which by then linked even moderate-sized communities in these regions. In Florida and California, too, he would often find himself running on asphalt or portland cement, and he would see numerous bulldozers, graders, pavers and straightedges at work creating new, modern roads. Elsewhere the picture was very different.

The Deep South was poorly served as far as roads were concerned. The entire state of Mississippi could boast only about 200 miles of paved road, and it was possible to drive diagonally across Louisiana, along the Jefferson Highway, from New Orleans to Shreveport, a distance of about 300 miles, and see less than a dozen miles of paved road. Nebraska had virtually no paved roads west of Lincoln, and the situation in Kansas and Oklahoma was not much better. Texas was showing good progress, especially near the major cities, but Arizona and New Mexico could manage only a couple of hundred miles of paved road between them. Most backward of all, perhaps, were Wyoming, with barely 50 miles of paved highway, and Montana, with a single stretch of paved road serving (with one small break) the 25 miles between Butte and Anaconda.

Between the Mississippi and the Sierras even the main arterial roads were unpaved for the most part, and it's easy to imagine how motorized tourists from the suburbs of Peoria or Milwaukee could feel like adventurers as they headed west for Yellowstone or Yosemite, passing through towns and hamlets with names like Spotted Horse, Ten Sleep, Wapiti, Yellow Jacket and (prophetically) Lolita City, rolling along at a stately 20 miles an hour between rows of telegraph poles, the gravel crunching beneath a new set of Firestones purchased for the trip and flying off

into the mesquite to disturb jackrabbits and prairie dogs.
It took only a little imagination for such tourists to fancy
themselves spiritually linked to the pioneers who had
forged the Oregon Trail, or the cowboys who drove herds
of cattle across the plains. The West was still pretty wild.
Sunset magazine reported a problem with discarded cans
as early as 1913, but the great sights, when you reached
them, were not yet overrun by Winnebagos and tourist
buses. You had them to yourself or else shared them with
a few like-minded motorists.

Already, however, there was more lining the interstate
highways than just telegraph poles. For a 1928 novella,
The Man Who Knew Coolidge, Sinclair Lewis invented a
character named Lowell Schmaltz who climbs into his
tourer and sets off for Yellowstone Park. He has only driven
a short distance, however, when he becomes so fascinated
with the roadside architecture—food stands and souvenir
stalls in the form of wigwams or ten-gallon hats—that he
abandons all thought of reaching his intended destination.

Exactly where this species of twentieth-century commercial architecture originated is impossible to say,
though Coney Island probably had its influence through
anthropomorphic buildings such as the giant wooden el-
ephant that served as an amusement palace. Such architecture became especially associated with the city of Los
Angeles, and it is conceivable that as a roadside phenomenon it started there and spread out along the Interstate
highways. More probably, though, it was spawned along
rural routes and quickly invaded Southern California,
which provided a hospitable environment that permitted
it to proliferate locally before it was re-exported to the rest
of the nation.

In any case, the notion that a building could be both
a shelter for a commercial enterprise and an advertising
sign was particularly well adapted to the needs of auto-

In the 1920s and 1930s zoomorphic architecture—as in these examples
from southern California—was often used to attract the attention of
passing motorists to hot dog stands and other roadside
businesses. TOP: *Henry E. Huntington Library and Art Gallery.*
BOTTOM: *American Stock Photos*

mobile culture. A business located in a city dependent on pedestrian traffic could attract customers with modest signs and attractive window displays. The pedestrian, after all, has the time to browse. A business located along a highway must attract the attention of motorists traveling at 30, 40 or 50 miles an hour. As such businesses crowd ever closer together, the need to make a visual statement becomes more and more important.

The first step, then, in commercializing the roadside landscape was to festoon structures with ever larger and more garish signs. By night, supplementary electric signs were often used, and by World War I these had achieved considerable sophistication, having reached their first flowering in New York City, where Broadway was already dubbed the Great White Way. As chain outlets and franchises—gas stations were the first—began to appear along the highways, the motorist learned to keep his eyes skinned for familiar signs that could afford to be more subdued. Initially, however, most roadside businesses were Mom and Pop affairs, and each had only one chance to attract the attention of the passing driver. Thus some enterprising merchants went beyond the notion of installing ever larger signs and actually transformed the entire side or facade of a building into a giant billboard. (Advertisements had, after all, been painted onto the sides of buildings well before the automobile era. It was just a matter of not wasting space.) From the building as billboard it was a relatively short step to conceive of a fish restaurant in the form of a boat or an ice cream stand in the guise of a giant cow. Merchants also capitalized on cartoon versions of indigenous styles, adobes in the Southwest, for example. Soon, roadside diners also began to make their lasting mark on the highway landscape.

The diner had its origins in the lunch carts that were popular in American towns and cities in late Victorian times. The early lunch carts were simply horse-drawn kitchens that stopped on street corners and sold five-cent sandwiches—fried egg and onion was a favorite—from a counter, much as an ice cream truck dispenses its wares today. In 1884, a Worcester, Massachusetts, bartender named Sam Jones had the idea of building a lunch wagon that was large enough to permit customers to enter and sit at the counter on stools, a big improvement during the long New England winters. Another Worcester resident, Thomas Buckley, began to manufacture this new type of wagon in quantity, exporting hundreds of them to other cities. A few years later, as the streetcar companies turned to electrification, old horse-drawn cars were bought up and converted into lunch wagons. Around the turn of the century, however, there was a movement to ban mobile lunch wagons from many communities, the chief arguments against them being that they interfered with traffic and, because of their low prices, attracted an undesirable element. In order to get around this problem, lunch wagon owners sold their horses, rented cheap plots of land and mounted their vehicles, shorn of their wheels, on a raised foundation of railroad ties. The modern diner was born.

Once the diner was fixed in place, there was no need for it to be limited to the size of a lunch cart, and it seems probable that at this period a few actual railroad dining cars were pressed into service as roadside diners. Almost from the outset, however, the classic diner was built from scratch, the first major manufacturer being Patrick "Pop" Tierney of New Rochelle, New York, who went into business in 1905. Tierney is the man who is credited with bringing the toilets indoors. The compact restaurants he built resembled railroad dining cars, partly by design (railroad travel was still glamorous in this period, and the dining car offered the obvious model for anyone wanting to squeeze a restaurant into a small space) but also because they were made to be transported by rail to their final destination and thus had to be built to dimensions that would allow them to fit on a flatbed freight car. Other manufacturers, notably Jerry O'Mahony of Bayonne, New Jersey, were soon in competition with Tierney and the result was ever more eye-catching diners, trimmed with neon and clad in quilted, chrome-plated steel.

Initially, diners made their appearance on the outskirts of towns and on vacant urban lots, but soon they began to creep out along the highways, where they were extremely effective because their appearance announced their utility. They effortlessly achieved the high visibility that the wigwams and stucco cows were frantically striving for, at the same time providing an emotionally charged instance of one form of transportation appropriating both style and content from another, more venerable form. Ironically, the streamlined trains of the thirties, with their shiny metal flanks, would actually seem to be paying tribute to diner architecture. Dinner in the diner afforded motorists one of the benefits of railway travel without compromising their independence of movement.

Billboards predated the automobile age. They had existed in city squares, along railroads, and even on river banks where intensive pleasure or commercial traffic justified their relatively low cost. If they were not created by the automobile, however, they were created for it. Angled for maximum visibility from the highway, they were an effective means of reaching the motorist, whether they advertised meals and lodging available five miles down the road or a newfangled refrigerator, whose utility was unrelated to highway travel. From the beginning there were complaints that such hoardings were eyesores, but judging from old photographs, many early billboards had great charm and it is a minor tragedy that representative examples have not been preserved.

It is said that between the wars a South Dakota restaurateur made a fortune by employing carefully worded billboards on highways converging on his roadside establishment. These billboards promised free ice water with every meal, a luxury then taken for granted only in high-toned big-city eateries. This roadside guarantee must have proved irresistible on humid summer days along U.S. Highway 16, as thunderstorms built above the Black Hills.

More famous by far were the Burma-Shave signs, which began to appear on U.S. highways in the mid-twenties. A successful Minneapolis insurance man named Clinton Odell was ordered by his doctor to find a less stressful line of business. Along with a chemist acquaintance, he made the curious choice of developing a brushless shaving cream, named Burma-Shave because Burma was where some of the ingredients came from. Attempting to market the product door to door proved every bit as wearing on the nerves as the insurance business. Then, in 1925, Odell's oldest son, Allan, had the idea of installing signs alongside highways leading into the city: not conventional billboards but sequences of half a dozen minibillboards that together would make up a jingle promoting the efficacy of their product. DOES YOUR HUSBAND / MISBEHAVE / GRUNT AND GRUMBLE / RANT AND RAVE? / SHOOT THE BRUTE SOME / BURMA-SHAVE. Each element in the jingle was placed fifty paces from the next so that motorists traveling at 35 miles an hour would absorb the entire message in about eighteen seconds, being set up for the punchline by a predetermined time/space relationship. HE PLAYED A SAX / HAD NO B.O. / BUT HIS WHISKERS SCRATCHED / SO SHE LET HIM GO / BURMA-SHAVE.

There was always a touch of humor to the Burma-Shave signs, and the motoring public loved this in an age when advertising tended to be ponderous and often downright hectoring. EVERY SHAVER / NOW CAN SNORE / SIX MORE MINUTES / THAN BEFORE / BURMA-SHAVE. The final Burma-Shave sign in each sequence was painted in script with a little underlined flourish.

The result of this wit was that Burma-Shave took off like a rocket, first in the Minneapolis–St. Paul area, then all over the country. For a while Clinton and Allan Odell wrote all the jingles themselves, but later they turned to an annual contest, in which they paid $100 for each verse accepted. The response was enormous and was judged by a committee headed by Clinton, who was ever vigilant for inventive but off-color entries. By World War II there were as many as 7,000 sets of jingles distributed around the country, and even after the war Burma-Shave continued to be a roadside presence for more than a decade until television advertising and overfamiliarity led to the disappearance of the clever red signs.

Another roadside presence, one that antedated Burma-Shave signs and most other manifestations of roadside culture, were the auto camps that began to appear before World War I, then evolved into, first, auto courts or motor courts, which eventually came to be known as motels. Auto camps were initially a consequence of the fact that automobiles were perceived to leak money. In the earliest days farmers could count on motorists paying handsomely for a team of horses to drag a bogged-down vehicle from a ditch or mud hole. (It was not unheard of for farmers to camouflage mud holes with branches, after the manner of an animal trap, in order to ensure customers.) Later the owners of general stores found that it paid to sell gasoline because the motorist who stopped for fuel was also likely to buy bread, coffee and other basic provisions. Some such merchants, and also town councils seeking to attract business to their community, began to offer campgrounds with

By the mid-1920s, motor courts had begun to offer shelter to motorists in many parts of the country. *Culver Pictures, Inc.*

barbecue-style fireplaces, picnic tables and primitive washroom facilities. Competition forced operators to improve their campsites and eventually some offered the additional comfort of rude cabins as an alternative to the rigors of tent life. So it was that the auto court was born, influenced perhaps—especially as the idea spread—by the bungalow courts that were becoming popular in Southern California. Paul Lanchaster, writing in *American Heritage*, has suggested that the first such court may have been the municipally owned one that opened in Douglas, Arizona, in 1913.

The motor court phenomenon was well established in the West and Southwest by the mid-twenties, and from there it spread to the Midwest and other parts of the country, especially tourist areas like Florida. As competition increased, facilities improved and the motor courts became less like glorified campgrounds and more like hotels. (In the early days it was common for the motorist to supply his own bedding.) At the same time they retained their informality and convenience. Motor tourists had tended to avoid hotels because these generally clustered in town centers, near railroad stations. The cheaper types forced one to rub shoulders with unsavory characters such as traveling salesmen, with their Gladstone bags, noisy laughs and tasteless jokes; and the better types often called for a degree of formality that was not welcome after a long, dusty day on the open road. Auto courts were convenient on several counts. They did not require the motorist to negotiate crowded city centers, full of clanging street cars; they did not require the fuss of tipping or dressing for dinner; and they afforded privacy. The motorist simply paid his fee—usually about one dollar in the twenties—then parked adjacent to the assigned cabin and unloaded his party, an arrangement that appealed not only to tourists but also to couples seeking anonymity for whatever reason. (The motor court's promise of privacy was another factor contributing sexual nuance to the burgeoning automobile culture, amplifying the car's intrinsic value as a reasonably secure if uncomfortable trysting place.) Because the motorist paid in advance, he and his party could depart discreetly without checking out, after a sound night's sleep or a stolen hour on a rented mattress.

And so the auto courts proliferated along the highways, clusters of log cabins, saltboxes and, inevitably, wigwams; soon it was impossible to travel far without coming across a U-Drive-Inn, a Cozy Court, or a Lucky Motel. The word "motel"—originally spelled "mo-tel"—was coined in 1925 by James Vail, proprietor of a San Luis Obispo, California, establishment that still exists. This was such a felicitous neologism that its use spread rapidly and by the middle of the Depression it had gained almost universal currency.

If motels came to have a slightly unsavory reputation because of the battalions of Mr. and Mrs. Smiths who signed their registers, the same was true of certain roadhouses, another phenomenon that flourished during the twenties. Roadhouses were somewhat more substantial and plush cousins of roadside diners and food stands. Some of these establishments aspired to a night-club atmosphere and featured hot or sweet music to attract customers away from their prime ribs or walleyed pike and onto the dance floor. Visiting Europeans were astonished to find that dance-mad Americans would actually get up in midcourse if lured from the table by a medley of fox-trot favorites.

Doubtless roadhouses would have sprung up anyway, but passage of the Volstead Act in 1919, which ushered in Prohibition, made them especially attractive. If a restaurateur wanted to serve illicit alcohol, it was safer to do so outside the city limits, where law enforcement officers were relatively thin on the ground and likely to be preoccupied with issuing speeding tickets. At worst there were fewer people to pay off, and a well-situated establishment could post lookouts capable of spotting a raiding party at a distance that would permit early warning.

In contrast to the garishness of most roadside businesses, the roadhouses were often quite grand and even tasteful—Stratford-upon-Avon half-timbered was a popular model, evoking the tradition of the coaching inn. While most represented relatively innocent attempts to sidestep what was perceived as an absurd law, mob influence transformed some into decidedly unsavory spots, fronts for gambling, prostitution and other rackets. Indeed, the image of the roadhouse goes hand in hand with the image of armed convoys of Mack Trucks and four-wheel-drive Jeffrey "Quads" transporting kegs of beer and cases of bathtub gin from the Canadian border or from some illicit still. As the newspapers and Hollywood quickly discovered, these convoys were frequently waylaid by rival gangs that had converted Franklin roadsters and Buick phaetons into gunships.

Motorized crime was an occasional occurrence before World War I, but it took Prohibition and the rise of hoodlums like Al Capone to give it a focus. There is reason to believe that Prohibition might have been enforced much more effectively had motor vehicles not evolved by then to a relative degree of sophistication. Had the Volstead Act been passed twenty years earlier, it can be imagined that convoys of horse-drawn drays would have made a relatively easy target for law enforcement agencies, especially on the dirt roads of the turn of the century. Five-ton trucks on macadamized roads were another matter.

Of course bootleggers adopted the automobile as an important adjunct to assassination. Whether there were many running battles between fleets of cars bristling with tommy guns is a matter for conjecture, but Hollywood certainly made such encounters seem like a commonplace of the gangster lifestyle. As for the armor-plated Packards and Cadillacs favored by chieftains like Capone and Johnny Torio, these were real enough, nor was it an accident that the St. Valentine's Day Massacre took place in a garage. The automobile even made its mark on the patois of crime. Mafia torpedos, discussing the elimination of a rival, talked of "taking him for a ride." The phrase may have originated with a Harvard graduate laboring in the celluloid vineyards on behalf of Warner Brothers, but the professionals out in the field knew a good hard-boiled line when they heard one.

What euphemistically has been dubbed organized crime was not the only sector of the outlaw world to embrace the automobile. Everyday bank robbers and stickup artists appreciated the advantages offered by eight-cylinder engines and improved highways when it came to making an escape. The car actually gave rise to a new species of criminal, the getaway driver.

John Dillinger, on his rise to the title "Public Enemy Number One," staged one of the more imaginative bank robberies by combining the effectiveness of the motor car with the glamour of Hollywood. Renting a movie camera, he mounted it on a tripod in an open car on whose side had been stenciled the legend PARAMOUNT PICTURES. Accompanied by another car full of armed gang members, the "camera car" drove into a sleepy Midwestern town where the gunmen went about their normal business, robbing the local bank. The "camera car" remained outside the bank with a "cinematographer" cranking the rented Mitchell. Passersby assumed that a pretend bank robbery was being filmed for a Hollywood movie. The gangsters emerged from the bank, freshly laden with wads of bills, and made their getaway, the whole thing being "filmed" by the "camera car," which remained in hot pursuit.

Dillinger was just the most famous of the free-lance gangsters who used the automobile to terrorize the heartland as Frank and Jesse James had used horses to wreak havoc in much the same territory a few decades earlier. Some of these criminals attained folk-hero status, at least in the opinion of those who did not suffer at their hands. In part this was because their use of the automobile embodied a kind of absolute rejection of civilized restraints that was a corollary of the motorized tourist's more orthodox use of the automobile to rediscover the wilderness. Urban gangsters like Capone were concerned with the Old World concept of establishing a carefully delineated territory under their control, and they pressed armed automobiles into service to protect that territory as a feudal state might have deployed archers or cavalry. Rural bandits used cars to revitalize the criminal tradition of Frontier America, striking in isolated towns and hamlets, then vanishing into the surrounding prairie in a cloud of dust. To a nation that was settling down to worrying about halitosis and keeping up with the Jones—but where Prohibition had made breaking the law acceptable—such reminders of the bad old days came like a breath of fresh air.

Dillinger's chief rivals in terms of fame were Clyde Barrow and Bonnie Parker—the Robin Hood and Maid Marion of the Bible Belt—who survived a famous motel shootout only to die in an ambushed car. They were as fond of automobiles as they were of guns and frequently took photographs of each other propped up against a stolen roadster, with weapons on display. On a number of occasions Barrow demonstrated, while pursued by the law, that he was as bold a driver as any Indy pilot, and at the height of the couple's fame he was thoughtful enough to write to Henry Ford endorsing Ford cars as getaway vehicles.

Given the chance, he enthused, he stole a Ford V-8 before he considered jump-starting any other make.

Clyde Barrow, the Robin Hood of the Bible Belt, wrote to Henry Ford to inform him that the Ford V-8 was unequaled as a getaway car.
UPI/Bettmann

Chapter 5

AMERICAN
ALGORITHMS

*B*y the time Clyde Barrow sent his fan letter to Henry
Ford in the early part of the Depression, Ford Motors was
in eclipse, though it was still a major force in the industry.
That eclipse was in large part due to Henry Ford's legendary stubbornness, combined with his almost messianic
belief in his ability to place his finger on the one true pulse
of the American people.

All this was in evidence in 1915, when Ford sponsored
a so-called peace ship (the *Oscar II* of the Scandinavian
Line) and sailed for Europe in an effort to put an end to
the Great War by means of a process called Continuous
Neutral Mediation, a high-minded concept that originated
with the Women's International League for Peace. The expedition turned out to be an occasion for farce benefiting
only a few sardonic members of the press corps, who had
a field day. Even Mutt and Jeff of Bud Fisher's well-known
comic strip managed to muscle in on the action, an intervention of some symbolic significance.

Ford, an institutional isolationist at heart (except
where industrial colonization was concerned) seems never
to have quite made up his mind about the war. After this

fling at pacifism he offered to place his entire empire at the disposal of the government in the name of preparedness. In fact, the Model T did valiant service on the Western Front and in other war theaters, and after America's entry into the war the Ford Company threw itself into new activities, such as building high-speed submarine chasers. Ford even trumpeted in the press his intention to return to the government all profits on war contracts, a promise that seems to have quietly slipped his mind as soon as the war was over.

The war was something of a turning point for the automobile industry, in both Europe and America, since it proved once and for all the usefulness of the new form of transportation. A graphic demonstration of this came in 1914, when taxicabs from the streets of Paris and private cars, some driven by luminaries as unlikely as Jean Cocteau and Gertrude Stein, ferried troops and nurses from *la ville lumière* to the front, foiling Von Kluck's drive on the capital. Later, convoys of trucks became a common sight, transporting men and supplies to Ypres and Verdun. Although the truck was almost as old as the car, it came into its own during the war, when heavy truck traffic in the United States, around munitions plants and on routes leading to ports of embarkation, did much to convince authorities of the need for improved roads. Assembly-line techniques were improved, as automakers met the sudden demand for guns and tanks as well as trucks and cars; the development of powerful new airplane engines such as the Hispano-Suiza V-8, the Liberty (based on a prewar Mercedes design), and an extraordinary V-16 monster conceived by Ettore Bugatti contributed much to the future evolution of automobile engines.

When the war was over, Henry Ford went back to business as usual, churning out thousands of Model T's day after day. Other manufacturers perceived that a new age had dawned. It had not yet been dubbed the Jazz Age, and jazz was just one ingredient in the cocktail (though a potent one), but by the dawn of Prohibition the new age was very much in place, its protagonists the flapper and the sheikh, the latter sometimes manifesting himself as Joe College.

The flapper had roots in the prewar suffragette movement (the term was being used in England at least by 1913 for fashionably emancipated young women), but it was the suffragettes' daughters who gave the term its full meaning, with their bobbed hair, short skirts, casually dangling cigarettes, and advice to "park your corset" and enjoy yourself.

The very word "park" tells us that these were children of the automobile age. Car storage had always been a problem for the motorist when he left his suburban garage behind. Gradually, businesses and municipalities supplied lots where cars could be left while the owner carried out his or her chores. Some such lots were beautified with plantings and minimal landscaping, which earned them the name "car parks"; hence the verb "to park" became applicable to automobiles, corsets, and even chewing gum.

The term "sheikh" derived from the film *The Sheikh*, one of Rudolph Valentino's greatest cinematic hits. Urban sheikhs favored slicked-back hair and tailored suits. The campus variety, however, was more given to varsity sweaters and raccoon coats, the latter perfect for keeping a fellow warm while watching Red Grange break tackles on a crisp fall day or heading for Lovers Lane in an open Stutz or, more likely, a second-hand flivver.

One of the most durable images of the Roaring Twenties is that drawn by John Held (one of the leading chroniclers of the decade) of a pair of youngsters—she cloche-hatted and sporting visibly rolled stockings, he furnished with Oxford bags and a hip flask—petting in a car beneath a starry sky. By then, the skies were alive with radio waves carrying opera selections, accordion solos, and uplifting sermons to soothe the nerves of parents as they waited uneasily in the parlor for their daughter's return. It is impossible to filter the automobile out of our received picture of the twenties. The Jazz Age was a bumpy ride in the rumble seat of a Maxwell; it was a sequined Joan Crawford, on camera for *Our Modern Maidens*, tearing along a dirt road in a Rolls-Royce Phantom; it was a Bix Beiderbecke soaking up gin in the backseat of a Reo as a C melody sax player drove his sidemen to their next gig, instrument cases and baggage strapped to the roof and running boards; it was Charles Lindbergh riding down Broadway in an open limousine with tickertape falling around his head.

Increasingly, American cars had a distinctive look of their own, much prized in the domestic market but sometimes looked down upon abroad, even by those who were suitably impressed by American engineering achievements. The use of pressed-steel components, a consequence of modern production techniques, made American cars look tinny to European eyes. Other American bad habits included such lapses in taste as brightly painted radiator grilles and an excess of chrome-plated accessories. It was largely a matter of perception, of course, which possibly owed something to European resentment at the decisive impact of America's intervention in the Great War. Yet there was a real difference, too, which became more evident as the decade progressed. It becomes very clear if you compare a British sports car of the late twenties— a Riley Brooklands, say—with a two-seat Stutz speedster of the same period. Both are low-slung, handsome, powerful cars, but the Riley is somehow more nimble-looking. It is built for the serpentine twists of the British country road, which could make a journey from your solicitor's office to the solace of the Bird and Bosun a challenge, made up equally of frequent gear changes and alertness for foxes being pursued by packs of baying hounds. The Stutz, on the other hand, seems built for outrunning motorcycle cops on a well-surfaced four-lane highway. In its standard 1928 form, the Stutz was just a shade faster than the Riley, but the Riley could manage 80 mph with a four-cylinder 1087 cc engine, while the Stutz relied on a hefty 4735 cc eight-cylinder power unit. Needless to say, the Stutz was much heavier than the Riley, and this too was characteristic of American sports cars (or sport cars, as they were usually called in the United States at the time). In fairness it should be noted that racing versions of the Stutz did well in European competition and that the Stutz was certainly the safer car to drive: it was far more solidly built and was fitted with hydraulic brakes on all four wheels, a very advanced feature for the period. If these failed to keep you out of trouble, the windshield was made of shatterproof safety glass, another American innovation.

Other high-priced American marques in the twenties were: Pierce-Arrow, till it ran into financial problems, Auburn, Marmon, Jordan—with its famous "somewhere West of Laramie" ad—and the magnificent Model A Duesenberg, a close cousin of the car that won the 1921 French Grand Prix, an American first that raised many eyebrows. The Model A was also built in other versions, as an elegant brougham, for example, and in this category it joined such luxury models as the Packard Twin-Six, Cadillac and Lincoln V-8's, and the American-built Rolls-Royces assembled in Springfield, Massachusetts. Rolls-Royces were made under license in Springfield between the wars, till reduced demand during the Depression forced closure of the American plant. The American-built cars were virtually identical with the British models, but featured left-hand drive and occasionally differed in engineering detail. Bodywork was always custom-designed, as was that of British-manufactured Rolls-Royces of the period.

The real news, however, was the adoption of production-line techniques by Ford's competitors, with the result that the American public was offered interesting and modestly priced alternatives to the Model T. An early and initially successful entry into the contest was the Willys Overland, which sold for around $800 immediately after the war and offered a degree of comfort and convenience that was a cut above that found in the Model T. The Essex, manufactured by the Hudson Motor Car Company, sold in the same price range and in 1922 revolutionized the market by introducing a fully enclosed and weather-tight sedan version for just $100 more than the basic tourer. Far more significant in the long run, however, was the emergence of first General Motors, then the Chrysler Corporation, who together with Ford would make up the big three of the auto industry.

In 1916 Billy Durant briefly regained control of the General Motors Company, which now reorganized as the General Motors Corporation, but his inability to keep a tight rein on financial matters undid him again. He was ousted once more when General Motors, like several other car manufacturers, found itself on the verge of bankruptcy during the slump of 1920–21. (A factor in this slump was a rise in the growth of used-car sales, which for the first time cut into the market for new vehicles.) GM was bailed out by a DuPont–Morgan consortium which installed Alfred P. Sloan to run the company; he held the title of president from 1923 on. If Henry Ford was a visionary who wore blinkers much of his life, Sloan was a gifted organizer who kept his eyes and ears wide open. One of his first moves was to strengthen GM's relationship with its retail outlets, offering dealers terms that were considerably more advantageous than those given by Ford. By establishing a strong relationship with the dealer, Sloan encouraged feedback between retailers and the various GM divisions that supplied them, so that division heads were able to gain a clearer picture of customers' requirements and whims. Adept at delegating responsibility, Sloan gave his division heads the freedom to respond to the demands of the marketplace.

The Chevrolet Division—deriving from the company originally founded by Durant and Louis Chevrolet, a pioneer racing driver—was placed in the hands of William S. Knudson, formerly one of Ford's top aides. When Knudson took over, Chevrolet was perhaps the weakest arm of GM, competing rather unimaginatively with Ford and other manufacturers of modestly priced cars such as Essex, Overland and Dodge (whose copywriters coined the word "dependability" to describe its primary selling point). Knudson knew as much about modern production techniques as anyone in the industry, and he encouraged his designers to be innovative—not to the extent of scaring customers off, but by attracting them with the latest conveniences and with styling that approximated the look of more expensive products. Like Fiat in Italy and Citroën in France, who were European pioneers of mass production, Chevrolet turned its back on Ford's basic black and began to make a feature of brightly colored coachwork, made possible by the arrival on the market of new, durable, quick-drying, synthetic enamel paints. Prior to the appearance of these synthetics, black had been the only color that dried rapidly. Some colors had taken as long as two weeks to dry and then had required multiple applications. After Duco introduced the new synthetics, color became practical as an option in low-priced cars and GM was quick to take advantage of this, placing a fresh emphasis on style and chromatic variety intended to appeal especially to women, now a significant sales factor as more and more families became two-car households. Under Knudson's leadership, Chevrolet rapidly made inroads into the basic Model T market, and then began to reach out beyond.

Other GM divisions followed a similar course, with Cadillac leading the way. This pragmatic approach began to coalesce into a styling philosophy after 1927 when Harley Earl, a West Coast custom car designer, was called in to style the La Salle, conceived as a smaller and less expensive but still up-market stablemate of the Cadillac. Earl modeled the original La Salle on the aristocratic Hispano-

Icons of the Jazz Age: a dapper gent in a raccoon coat and a cloched flapper in the rumble seat of a handsome 1928 Chrysler.
Bettmann Archive

Suiza, achieving the look of a custom-built car in a moderately priced production vehicle.

Alfred P. Sloan was sufficiently impressed by the La Salle to put Earl in charge of the specially created and quaintly named Art and Color Section which would coordinate styling for all GM divisions. Understandably, Earl encountered resistance from some established division bosses, but the success of his policies, combined with his physically intimidating presence, gradually pushed opposition aside and soon Chevrolets, Oldsmobiles, Buicks and Oaklands (just then transmuting into Pontiacs) began to sport flashy two-tone bodywork and rakish white-wall tires, till then thought suitable only for luxury marques like Cadillac and La Salle.

Earl was on his way to becoming the most influential car stylist of all time, his prestige and power at GM being confirmed in 1937 when the Art and Color Section was reorganized as the Styling Section. By then new manufacturing techniques dictated that GM divisions must share certain major body parts. Yet each division had to retain its own visual identity and to this end Earl set up divisional studios within the Styling Section where, behind locked doors, Buick designers would struggle to make their cars look different from Oldsmobiles and Chevrolets even though body units were to a large extent interchangeable.

Earl oversaw all this and at the same time institutionalized the notion of making each year's model just a little different from the last, thus promoting the commercially useful concept of built-in obsolescence. Under his tutelage the automobile industry became a branch of the fashion industry.

Even before Earl established his fiefdom, however, the policies instituted by Sloan and Knudson at GM had their impact elsewhere in the industry. Prompted by his style-conscious son Edsel and other advisers, Henry Ford finally saw the writing on the wall, and in 1927 production of the Model T was halted after more than 15 million had been built. Ford actually closed down production for six months, then brought out his handsome yet slightly stodgy Model

A with a 40 hp, four-cylinder in-line engine and a conventional three-speed gearbox. It sold well, but Chevrolet promptly countered with a six-cylinder car that retailed in the same price range.

Nor was Ford's only competition coming from General Motors. In 1921, Walter Chrysler, former railroad mechanic and GM executive, was called in by a group of bankers to run the troubled Maxwell Motor Car Company. In 1925 it was taken over by the newly organized Chrysler Corporation. Maxwell provided Chrysler with a sound engineering team but inadequate manufacturing capacity to suit his ambitions, and so in 1928 he took over the Dodge Brothers Manufacturing Company, a healthy, well-respected firm put on the market by the founders' heirs. Dodge's superb sales network and extensive production-line manufacturing facilities gave Chrysler the opportunity to enter the low end of the market, which he did in 1928 with the Plymouth, a new line intended to go head to head with Ford and Chevrolet. It managed to do this with considerable success. Like Sloan, Chrysler met the challenge of adapting to a rapidly changing market. Few of his rivals had the imagination or means to match him, and by the onset of the Depression, famous makes like Peerless, Reo, Franklin and Hupmobile were being slowly pushed into oblivion as the Big Three came to dominate the market.

Henry Ford no longer stood alone, and GM would soon outstrip his plants in productivity, but he remained a formidable presence in the industry. It should be acknowledged that he had a very definite constituency that remained doggedly faithful to him and his products. It must be remembered, too, that the Jazz Age, as portrayed by the artist John Held and the writer F. Scott Fitzgerald, hardly touched the lives of millions of Americans. They glimpsed it when they went to the movies and were familiar with its real-life cast of playboys and debutantes, showgirls and bootleggers, gridiron heroes and dubious evangelists, from the pages of the yellow press. They discussed the doings of Babe Ruth, Texas Guinan, Mayor Jimmy Walker, the Prince of Wales and Aimee Semple

Model T's ready for delivery to Ford showrooms, 1925.
Bettmann Archive

McPherson. They heard the hits of Jerome Kern and George Gershwin on their Atwater Kent radios. But none of this had a profound effect on the routine drudgery of their lives.

For every American couple that left a speakeasy as the milkman began his rounds, there were many more who rose with the first cock's crow to perform the same chores their parents and grandparents had performed. The one thing that distinguished these early risers from their parents—whether they worked on a farm or clerked for a booming chain store like J. C. Penney—was that they probably owned a car, and many were prepared to settle for a used Model T. This was the world celebrated in Frank King's *Gasoline Alley* comic strip, which began in 1918 and came of age in 1921 when the foundling, Skeezix, was discovered on Uncle Walt's doorstep. *Gasoline Alley* was a success because it was firmly grounded in real life. It began by making fun of the foibles of small-town car owners, but quickly King discovered that the car had become so integrated into American life that he had unwittingly provided himself with a springboard from which to launch a continuing narrative of much broader appeal.

Perhaps the most famous social study of the twenties was *Middletown*, by Robert and Helen Merrell Lynd, an investigation of changes in everyday life in Muncie, Indiana, between 1890 and 1924. One thing discovered by the Lynds was that by the end of this period few families in Muncie were prepared to do without their automobiles. By the end of 1923, they disclosed, there were 6,221 passenger cars in the city, one for every 6.1 persons "or roughly two for every three families." Of those 6,221 cars, 41 percent were Fords.

Doubtless many of these cars were put to purely practical purposes, but the Lynds discovered that they were most appreciated as instruments of leisure. Church attendance was down on fine Sundays because it was more agreeable to visit a nearby lake. A labor organizer protested that "the Ford car" had harmed union causes because members preferred being out on the open road to attending union meetings. The car was enabling working-class families to take vacations—if only long weekends—that had never been possible before. The women were especially vehement in the automobile's defense. A mother of nine informed the Lynds that she would rather do without clothes than give up the car, while another housewife said she'd go without food rather than have the family lose its wheels.

Such people were not yet subject to the wiles of Harley Earl. They required basics and these came most frequently in the form of a Ford Model T. That constituency was probably shrinking as the twenties progressed, but it was kept alive for a while longer by the onset of the Depression.

Before then, automobile ownership had reached every level of American society, even the poorest. The twenties saw the arrival on the scene of a new kind of indigent: auto tramps. These were homeless individuals and even families who traveled the country looking for seasonal work and living out of battered cars. One step up the ladder from auto tramps were the likes of the Snopeses, William Faulkner's family of redneck gypsies who took up residence in Yoknapatawpha County the way that roaches infest a kitchen, the black shells of their battered Model T's enhancing their insectlike image. At the other end of the social side, the fall of Fitzgerald's Jay Gatsby is precipitated by a car crash, while Merton Gill, the Candide-like hero of Harry Leon Wilson's *Merton of the Movies*, achieves his apotheosis on the pages of *Silver Screenings*, where he is shown posing with his wife in their high-powered roadster.

But the real changes in the twenties were occurring in the mildly fashion-conscious middle class world that was patronizing such makes as Chevrolet and Plymouth. These were the same upwardly mobile families that were also modernizing their homes with refrigerators (General Motors had acquired Frigidaire), washing machines, vacuum cleaners and phonographs, often bought on the installment plan. By 1929, 60 percent of all car sales involved installment payments, and the Lynds' ground-breaking Muncie study revealed that it was not uncommon for a man earning $35 a week to spend $35 a month on the family car. By 1929 the United States manufactured 85 percent of the motor vehicles built anywhere, and there were 26,500,000 cars, trucks and buses on the American road.

One notable shift in car usage was that increasingly automobiles were being employed to give access to cities and towns rather than as a means of fleeing the urban environment. Where early motoring had been conspicuously recreational, new patterns were more complex. For example, men who had taken advantage of the railroads or the interurbans to move their families out to the suburbs now chose to use their cars to commute to their jobs back in the cities. Salesmen increasingly made use of cars, whether traveling from town to town or within a given city, and the number of trucks and delivery vans rose sharply in the postwar years. (In 1915 there were 12,148 commercial vehicles in New York City; by 1920 there were 83,746.) More and more, too, rural families and suburbanites used their cars to come into town seeking entertainment, most typically a night at the movies.

This increase in urban motoring was offset to a partial extent by the gradual disappearance of horse-drawn traffic from the streets. At a certain point the mixture of motor vehicles and slower moving horse-drawn vehicles was itself a major problem, but this began to ease after World

War I. Another factor inhibiting the free flow of motor traffic was the continued presence of electric street cars and interurbans where they shared the public thoroughfare. Most cities had ordinances, similar to modern schoolbus laws, that required automobiles to halt when a trolley car was loading or unloading passengers. Streetcars also enjoyed the right of way over automobiles, and the tracks themselves could be a nuisance, especially in wet weather. On the other hand, the physical presence of the streetcars, with their fixed trajectories, helped prevent some latterday abuses such as double parking.

Well before World War I it had become apparent in certain busy cities that a code of traffic regulations would be needed, along with the necessary signs and street furniture to make enforcement practical. It is indicative of the laissez-faire attitude that once existed that the first painted

Detroit's first stoplight, introduced in 1914. *Motor Vehicle Manufacturers Association of the United States, Inc.*

center dividing line did not appear until 1911, in Michigan. (Indeed, despite drivers' preferences for the right-hand side of the road, left-hand drive did not become standard in American cars till around 1908.) Other novelties included the traffic island, introduced in San Francisco in 1907, the electric traffic signal, first seen in Cleveland in 1914, and the NO LEFT TURN sign, which made its debut in Buffalo in 1916.

The world's first systematized traffic code—it covered just two pages—had been introduced in New York in 1903. Based on the results of a soundly practical study by William Phelps Eno, it imposed a degree of common sense and courtesy on the chaos of Manhattan, establishing rules for passing, yielding right of way, and so forth, and setting down basic hand signals to warn other motorists of one's intentions. Eno's fame was such that he was invited to Paris to install his system there, which he did to much acclaim, and gradually his ideas spread both in America and the rest of the world. Even at the onset of the Depression, however, uniformity was a long way off. An article bylined H. H. Sawyer in the February 1930 issue of *The American Mercury* pointed out that there was tremendous inconsistency even with regard to so basic a matter as hand signals, which varied not only from state to state but sometimes from city to city. Sixteen states had no code at all regarding hand signals, while a dozen had no speed limit (though Utah limited maximum speed to 30 mph). Most surprising of all, twenty-eight states did not require a driver's license of any sort at this period, while South Carolina permitted twelve-year-olds to operate motor vehicles. If traffic regulations varied from place to place, the same was true of the means used to enforce them; for instance, while some cities already employed electric stoplights, others preferred a system of mechanical semaphore arms. The traffic control tower that stood for a good part of the twenties at the intersection of Fifth Avenue and Forty-second Street was a Manhattan landmark almost as famous in its day as the Woolworth Building. Twice the height of the then popular double-decker buses, this tower was an ornate metal structure that J. C. Furnas, in *Great*

Times, recalled as resembling "a Parisian pissoir high on four skinny legs." Police officers sat in the elevated observation post, which afforded them a fine view of developing traffic jams, and operated batteries of signal lights located at the summit of the tower. Eventually, however, it proved to be more of a traffic hazard than anything else and was torn down to be replaced by automatic signals.

The accuracy of the pissoir description notwithstanding, that traffic control tower also had the air of something out of Fritz Lang's 1927 science-fiction film *Metropolis,* or borrowed from one of those fanciful visions of the future so popular with magazines and newspapers in the first quarter of the century. These visions tell us something about how Americans of the period envisioned the evolution of motor traffic, consigning it to twenty-lane parkways and soaring elevated highways linking giant, ziggurat-topped blocks in an ever more vertical city; dirigibles drifted overhead, biplanes banked beneath cloud-kissed Venetian bridges and autogyros rained like autumn leaves upon rooftops and penthouse landing pads. There is a strange sameness about these projections of the future, whether conceived by an architectural visionary like Hugh Ferriss or portrayed by Winsor McCay in his *Little Nemo* comic strip. All these predictions were predicated on the belief that the future was represented by the vertical city, such as New York or Chicago, this notion being fueled by the relative novelty of the skyscraper, and reinforced in avant-garde planning circles by the influence of Le Corbusier and other European architects and theorists. In reality the automobile was making the idea of the vertical city obsolescent, except, as in Manhattan, where the pressure of real estate values made it a necessity. The automobile ensured that the future would rest with the horizontal city, though sometimes that horizontal city would come to be organized around a cluster of high-rise buildings, symbolizing the future as imagined by Raymond Hood, Mies van der Rohe and the creators of *Buck Rogers.* Frank Lloyd Wright, a prophet of the horizontal city, thought that the occasional mile-high building might be permitted by way of vertical punctuation.

As is well known, everything's up-to-date in Kansas City, and that was certainly the case in the twenties, with a notably corrupt political machine firmly at the helm, bootlegging on the grand scale, a thriving red-light district and a burgeoning jazz scene that would give the world Count Basie, Lester Young and Charlie Parker. Physically it was already one of those horizontal cities that pointed the way to the motorized future, knit together by a dozen railroads and a well-developed interurban system, stock-yards, industrial zones and pleasant residential areas grouped around the modestly scaled skyscrapers of the established downtown area. The automobile was as big a force in Kansas City as elsewhere; here, as all over, it was spawning a good deal of uncontrolled, anarchic roadside development. This both piqued the interest and offended the delicate aesthetic sensibility of J. C. Nichols, an entrepreneur who saw the need for a suburban shopping area to serve the needs of refined car-owning families, with which, he supposed, Kansas City was plentifully supplied. The result was the Alhambraesque Country Club Plaza, which opened in 1922 and was described as a shopping village, where exotically styled stores were set among parking lots planted with shrubs and shade trees. It was even supplied with its own White Eagle filling station.

Country Club Plaza differed from earlier suburban shopping developments such as Market Square, built near Chicago in 1916, in that it was almost entirely automobile-dependent. In this respect it was an important ancestor of the modern shopping center and was quickly followed by other car-oriented shopping villages such as Highland Park, in Dallas, and Westwood Village in Los Angeles.

Los Angeles, as will be discussed in the next chapter, would rightly be perceived as the prototypical horizontal, motorized American city, the most spectacularly expanding urban entity that was, as a matter of course, able to incorporate shopping villages, drive-ins and free-form commercial strips into a fabric that was at the same time urban and suburban. Elsewhere such manifestations of highway culture tended to radiate out from established city centers. New Jersey, because of its proximity to New

York and its high level of automobile ownership, was especially fecund. Camden, New Jersey, is credited with presenting the world with the first drive-in movie theater, in 1933, but at least a decade earlier arterial roads such as U.S. 1 and New Jersey's State Highway 9 were developing significant commercial strips.

Similar strips, more or less abrasive, were spreading out like spokes from Akron and Albany, Oakland and Omaha, Minneapolis and Indianapolis. To drive along these strips was to run a gauntlet of naive and none-too-subtle pleas, prayers and blandishments, like finding oneself at a convention of exhibitionists. Many found it offensive, but in this first phase, unsullied as yet by big business, the commercialism of the highway must have possessed a certain innocent charm.

Tying everything together—chili stands, auto courts, hand-painted signs and lariats of neon—were the telegraph wires and utility poles, punctuation marks across the landscape that seemed to go everywhere the ribbons of highway went. They had vanished in New York City, where the blizzard of 1888 had driven services underground, but in the new horizontal cities and suburbs they were, and still are, ubiquitous, sometimes an ugly overhead tangle but often lending scale to an environment where everything else seems to be striving to distort it. And out beyond the cities, beyond the commercial strips, the utility poles come to serve for the more expansive American highway landscape some of the purposes poplar trees had served along the trunk roads of France—not providing shade but functioning as disciplined delineators, divisions of an endless yardstick, vanishing in perspective to enhance the sense of distance experienced by the motorist as he crossed the plains of Kansas or the deserts of the Southwest.

Those poles and utility wires had a significance. In many communities electricity arrived with the automobile, and though the telegraph was a product of the railway age, widespread use of the telephone came during the automobile era. The motor highway and the wires that ran alongside it were both symptoms of a shrinking world.

This drive-in restaurant in Hollywood, California, was still a relative
novelty when photographed in 1932. *Henry E. Huntington
Library and Art Gallery*

Chapter 6

AUTOMOVILLE
I

*T*he automobile made its first appearance in Los Angeles in 1897 and discovered there a hospitable environment. The pioneer vehicle was a local product built by J. Philip Erie and S. D. Sturgis. It was by no means the last car to be made in Los Angeles, for LA became an important secondary auto-assembly center; but it was not for vehicle manufacture that the city would become known. Rather LA came to epitomize automobile consumption, conspicuous almost from the first, and an efflorescence of highway cultures and subcultures by which the rest of the world would needs measure itself. It was just a matter of time before Los Angeles (then still pronounced by many with a hard "g") became the ultimate automoville.

Los Angeles had already undergone cycles of boom and bust since the arrival of the railroads, but the trend toward expansion and affluence was quite clear. Edward Doheny and C. A. Canfield had struck oil, near downtown, in 1892, and thanks to the invention of the ventilated refrigerator railroad car, California oranges, already sporting the name Sunkist, were famous throughout the country.

Rich Easterners made their winter homes in Pasadena and just up the coast in Santa Barbara, while increasingly Los Angeles became a tourist magnet, especially for Midwesterners drawn not only by the climate and natural beauties but also by events such as the Rose Bowl Parade and the annual Fiesta.

The climate brought advantages for the first automobilists in Southern California. The relative lack of rain meant that existing dirt roads were passable at almost all times of the year, only occasionally affected by mud and never by frost or snow. Even before any efforts were made at grading or improvement, it was possible to find comfortably drivable routes all over the area, whether you wished to travel from one community to another or to visit the beach, the mountains or the desert.

An early but minor setback was *Tribulus terrestris,* better known to motorists as the "puncture vine." The spiky seed pods of this desert plant caused havoc with the easily ripped tires and inner tubes of early automobiles. The plant had been relatively rare, but cars carried the seed pods to new locations, so that the puncture vine proliferated throughout Southern California and annoyed motorists until improved tires did away with this irritating problem in the thirties.

And so cars began to pour in, first by the score, then by the hundred, hauled cross-country in freight trains or shipped around the Horn. (Not until 1914 would ships steam to California by way of the Panama Canal.) Starting around 1904, a few hardy individuals actually drove to Los Angeles on coast-to-coast odysseys and the publicity garnered by transcontinental crossings inevitably directed attention to Los Angeles, the terminal point, and helped identify its name with car culture. Almost from the beginning, the twin poles of automobile culture, the paternalistic and the anarchic, were in evidence in California. The Automobile Club of Southern California, representing the former, was founded in 1900 and by 1905 had embarked upon what was perhaps the most ambitious program of signposting west of the Appalachians. While motorists in most of the country were forced to turn to unreliable maps or suspicious locals in order to find their way, those exploring Southern California could make their way to Ocean Park or Redlands without difficulty (though in thinly populated areas it was quite common for passing motorists to use road signs for target practice, pumping them full of bullet holes). In 1909 the Automobile Club began publishing *Touring Topics*, later known as *Westways*, which, along with magazines like *Sunset* and *Out West*, did much to promote automobile touring on the West Coast.

As already noted, the anarchic side of the car culture was spectacularly represented through the antics committed to film by the comedy wing of the motion picture industry, active in Los Angeles from 1907. From the outset, Hollywood gag writers and directors perceived that the car had great comedic possibilities. There was something inherently ridiculous about those early Reos, Maxwell-Briscoes and Studebakers. They could be cocky and pompous at the same time. The public was fascinated by their power and potential—which was fully demonstrated by the first movie stunt drivers—but audiences also liked to see these vehicles humiliated, sometimes to the point of destruction. As animals became human surrogates in the animated cartoons of the sound era, so cars served as human surrogates during the silent period. Having been thoroughly robbed of dignity by a bunch of actors in antique police costumes, a Pope-Toledo might be abandoned on the Southern Pacific right-of-way to be demolished by the cowcatcher of a westbound express. Those same Keystone Kops often used a specially modified "collapsible" Model T Ford, which could be squashed between two other vehicles and still continue to run, though flattened to a pancake like Wiley E. Coyote after a fall into a canyon. Or a handsome Buick tourer, guilty only of having been purchased by a movie company, might find itself rolled off the tip of the Santa Monica pier. Such acts of wanton destruction were especially powerful at a time when many members of the audience could only dream of owning a car. Like a middle-class girl who had captured the heart of Chaplin's tramp, the automobile was worshiped from afar, and the emotional investment that went along with such worship made the humiliation and destruction all the more effective. Yet ultimately the audience knew that the vehicle had no soul, and could be replaced. It might be blown up by a bomb, but, as when similar fates befell Elmer Fudd or Yosemite Sam, no permanent harm was done. Another car would replace it in the next movie.

Many of these early comedies were shot on the run, and the director often permitted the bare plot line he had been given to interact with actual events encountered by chance or by design. Thus one of Chaplin's earliest Sennett shorts was filmed at the Vanderbilt Cup auto races in Santa Monica, the comedian playing "chicken" with the oncoming cars. Similarly, when an actor or stuntman transferred, at high-speed, from a Pacific Electric interurban car to the roof of a sedan running alongside, it was not necessarily planned—especially in the very early days—but might result from a director's taking advantage of shooting on a street where the Big Red Cars ran. It can be presumed that motormen must have lodged their share of complaints, or possibly they were paid off by the film crew, or perhaps they were content just to appear in the movies. Later shots involving automobiles and public transportation, such as those in Harold Lloyd films (*Girl Shy* contains a classic sequence), were more elaborate and clearly involved collaboration by all parties concerned, but the effect was the same, with the automobile generally playing an anarchic role or else suffering humiliation. In the late Laurel and Hardy silent film *Big Business* an irate James Finlayson demolishes the heroes' car item by item while they retaliate by tearing his house apart.

For all their willingness to desanctify the car on screen, movie people took their own automobiles very seriously. Fatty Arbuckle, star of so many of those early comedies, put together a stable of cars that included a Rolls-Royce, a white Cadillac, a Stevens-Duryea, a Renault and a $25,000 Pierce-Arrow that came complete with a cocktail bar and a toilet. Not to be outdone, Sessue Hayakawa had a gold-plated Pierce-Arrow. Mae Murray's Pierce-Arrow was more modestly finished in canary yellow, but to make up for this her chauffeur and footman wore livery to match and had alternate costumes to go with her cream-and-black Rolls, as well as with the white Rolls she saved for premieres and such. Murray was not the only star to embrace this particular notion. Francis X. Bushman was attended in his lavender Rolls by servants in lavender uniforms and completed the picture by smoking lavender cigarettes. Clara Bow drove a flame-red Kissel painted to match her hair and was often accompanied by a pair of chows whose coats had been dyed the same color. Valentino, appropriately enough, favored European cars, including a cream-colored Mercedes, a custom-built Voisin tourer with a specially designed silver cobra adorning the radiator cap, and an Isotta-Fraschini with silver mountings and a walnut-paneled interior. Gloria Swanson's Lancia was upholstered in leopard skin. But possibly the most exhibitionistic car of all in silent Hollywood was the custom-built monster driven by Tom Mix, its hood decorated with a tooled saddle and a brace of steer horns. By the early twenties, places like the parking lots of Musso & Frank's in Hollywood and Baron Long's Vernon Country Club (a speakeasy popular with the movie colony) were jammed with Stutzes and Marmons, Packards and Hupmobiles, Jordans and Locomobiles, Rolls-Royces and Hispano-Suizas. Then as now, luxury automobiles were symbols of success, and the fan magazines promoted the movie star playthings for all they were worth.

Nor were movie people alone in favoring luxury cars. Many Angelenos were growing wealthy from oil, fruit packing and real estate speculation—not to mention the service industries that go along with affluence—and Los Angeles quickly became one of the nation's premier automobile markets. In fact it's possible to see that automobile ownership took on a special significance there, almost comparable with home ownership. There are interesting parallels in Angelenos' aspirations with regard to cars and homes, deriving in part from the way the inhabitants of Los Angeles utilized their cars to give a unique identity to the architectural fabric of their environment.

Los Angeles is a city of purloined cultures. Immigrants brought Old World habits and customs to many parts of the nation, but Southern California was from the first the leader in the phenomenon of third-, fourth- and fifth-generation Americans recreating aspects of other and sometimes alien civilizations at third, fourth and fifth hand. The Fiesta de Los Angeles, for example, had its justification in the city's Spanish and Mexican past, but it was enacted not by the native Mexican population but by local Anglos who dressed up as caballeros and señoritas and rode fine Arab stallions bedecked with tooled leather. Costumes and customs alike owed as much to fantasy as history, and the entire spirit of the occasion was rooted more firmly in popular novels such as Gertrude Atherton's

An auto camp in Big Pines Park, near Los Angeles, c. 1928.
Culver Pictures, Inc.

The Californians and *The Splendid Idle Forties* than in history.

Hollywood heightened the already present predilection for fantasy. The movies in general suggested that it was possible to conjure up any civilization from the past or present with a few well-chosen props, and the citizens of LA soon grew used to giant outdoor structures such as the Babylon set built by D. W. Griffith for *Intolerance* or the Arabian Nights set constructed by Douglas Fairbanks for *The Thief of Baghdad*. Sited among bungalows and modest two-story villas, such sets dominated the landscape and fired the imagination of home builders. The pantiled Monterey ranch-house style (sometimes modified to Mission style, especially for public buildings) was well established by the late nineteenth century, as were several variants on British vernacular, from half-timbered mock Tudor to crenelated fairy-tale Gothic. As the city boomed in the first decades of the twentieth century, exotic architectural idioms proliferated. Where once immigrants had remembered the old country with the aid of cuckoo clocks and lace, now their grandchildren constructed from brick and stucco fantasy versions of an Old World they had perhaps never seen, except in postcards. Towered Tuscan palazzi rose cheek by jowl with Maghrebian minarets. Cape Cod cottages, built on a grander West Coast scale, faced Norman manor houses across newly graded roadways. Elaborate chimneys copied from Hampton Court Palace rose from the crest of steep roofs cleverly tiled to resemble thatch. An entire community, Venice of America, was conceived by tobacco tycoon Abbot Kinney to adorn the shores of the Pacific with canals and colonnaded arcades in emulation of that other Venice on the Adriatic.

On a more modest scale, California also evolved a distinctive style of shingled bungalow, characterized by low-pitched roofs, open-truss porches and exposed rafter ends, that is one of the most interesting indigenous vernaculars to appear in the twentieth century. But even these delightful structures, lining the gridded streets of South Hollywood and the hillsides of Silver Lake, are often embellished with borrowed details—a pair of Egyptian columns framing the front entrance, for example. Easterners, having achieved a different stage of cultural assimilation, came to Los Angeles, smirked at the presumption and naïveté, then departed aboard the *Chief* or *Sunset Limited* for more civilized climes—unless, of course, Hollywood was offering them $1,500 a week to sit in the writers' building at Metro or Paramount. Midwesterners, on the other hand, visiting from less polished settlements and liking what they found in Los Angeles were all too willing to enter into the storybook and travelogue fantasies encountered while riding in the Yellow Cars or enjoying a Tanner bus tour. Many stayed on to cruise those same streets in Model T's or Willys Overlands. The hybrid public and domestic architecture of Los Angeles was one of the first great roadside attractions of the automobile era.

It wasn't an accident that almost all of the new buildings in Los Angeles, however humble, were furnished with garages, or at least driveways, for developers intuitively realized that car ownership would soon be as important as home ownership. Just as the home in Los Angeles was perceived as a form of self-expression—back East, even in the new suburbs, conformity was still highly prized— so the automobile was seen as more than just a means of transportation. More readily than elsewhere it was understood that a car could make a statement and that it was emblematic not only of one's present status but also, more important, of one's aspirations. In a city full of newcomers, first impressions were vital. In an automobilized city, first impressions could often depend upon the type of car you were driving.

In terms of the sheer number of vehicles registered there, Los Angeles was rapidly becoming the automobile capital of America. Scott L. Bottles has calculated that in 1915 there was one car in LA for every 8.2 residents, as against the national figure of one car for every 43.1. By 1925 there was one car in LA for every 1.8 residents, compared with a national average of one for every 6.6. In this department LA took an early lead and has never relinquished it.

Not everyone looked on this as a good thing. Outsiders in particular often found it quite disturbing, as was the case with an English couple, Jan and Cora Gordon, who lived in Los Angeles during the twenties and returned home to publish in 1930 a withering description of the city, inappropriately titled *Star-Dust in Hollywood.* If one of the great appeals of Southern California was its outdoor life, the Gordons saw this as being completely negated by the typical Angeleno's devotion to the automobile.

> The truth is, the people seemed to venture rarely into the open air. If they wished to go out, they slipped from the backdoor to the garage, shut themselves primly into a closed car, and drove away. If they wished to do the family shopping they drove into large open-air grocery shops specially arranged so that they could select their provisions without getting out of the car. If they wished for distraction they drove to the sea or up into the hills and stared at the view through the windshield.

Another frequently expressed concern, voiced as early as the World War I period and reiterated ever more stridently during the twenties, was that the morals of teenagers were endangered by easy access to automobiles. In *The City Boy and His Problems: A Survey of Boys' Life in Los Angeles,* published in 1926, Emory S. Bogardus cited many authority figures—teachers, clergymen and the like—for their belief that families were far too free in providing cars for their children, a practice that was seen to lead to a variety of crimes and misdemeanors, including truancy and hooliganism. Doubtless this concern existed elsewhere, but the affluence of Los Angeles and the easy acceptance of the car there seems to have made worries especially acute.

There was also the matter of teens using their cars, or their parents', for petting parties and worse. This was a frequent subject of discussion in Los Angeles newspapers. In 1921, the *Times* ran a story in which Captain Cannon of the county motorcycle squad said that many reports had been received of "night riders" parking alongside country boulevards and indulging in orgies. Four years later, the Pasadena police chief complained that cars had turned large parts of the Crown City into a red-light district. He attributed this to the new popularity of fully enclosed vehicles—coupes and sedans—which offered a degree of privacy not available in old-fashioned touring cars.

On another front, automobile traffic was beginning to cause considerable problems in downtown Los Angeles. Angelenos led the country not only in car ownership but also in car usage, and despite the increasingly decentralized character of the city, until the twenties the downtown zone remained the business and cultural focus of the area. In 1918 it was acknowledged by the Board of Public Utilities that downtown was becoming clogged with automobiles to an extent "relatively more intensified than in any other city commensurate with its size." By the following year, the City Council began considering a ban on parking in the city center, a proposal that caused a storm of protest from drivers and merchants alike. The immediate result was a compromise that saw the imposition of certain restrictions and also a sharp rise in the creation of commercial parking facilities. A more significant consequence was a massive program of street improvements, the Major Traffic Street Plan, to facilitate traffic circulation in and around the downtown area. This was voted on in 1924 and rapidly implemented.

At the same time, the City Council ordered a study of mass transit, which resulted in a proposal that elevated railroads should replace some street-level trolley lines in the downtown area. This suggestion was received with horror. The majority of Angelenos wanted nothing to do with these overhead spiderwebs of steel that cast the streets of so many Eastern cities into darkness. The proposal was voted down, and seen in retrospect this defeat probably sounded the death knell for traditional public transportation systems in the Los Angeles area, though the interurbans continued to operate for another three decades. Public opinion aside, experts increasingly agreed that fixed-rail mass transportation was no real answer to the area's needs because the low population density would make it financially unviable.

The railways and the interurbans had already played a crucial role by establishing a pattern of suburbs and satellite towns, but typically these were sited in flat areas of the coastal plain or inland valleys. After World War I, the automobile permitted these suburbs and satellites to expand, especially into the foothills, where developers could break away from the grid and take advantage of spectacular scenic possibilities on winding canyon roads. In Los Angeles and elsewhere, one significant way the automobile changed the American landscape was by permitting the development of hilly and even mountainous areas. Horse-drawn vehicles could climb quite steep gradients but seldom did so as a matter of routine, and the descent, without efficient brakes, was positively dangerous. The first automobiles, with their primitive gearboxes, also had problems with steep hills, but these were soon overcome—especially in the more expensive cars—and so the foothills of the Santa Monica Mountains, like other hilly areas, became fair game for developers.

Because it has always attracted moneyed and celebrated residents, Beverly Hills is not entirely typical of Los Angeles' satellite towns, yet it displays most of the essential characteristics that have determined growth in the area. The first house built there was erected by Maria Rita Valdez, who around 1840 received a Mexican land grant for much of the acreage that now constitutes the so-called "gilded ghetto." The land passed to various American owners, most notably Burton Green, who entered the name Beverly Farms when registering his claim to the property (supposedly in honor of Beverly, Massachusetts, a town he remembered with affection). Despite this name, Green hoped to find oil there. Instead he struck water—itself a valuable commodity, especially in those days before the Los Angeles Aqueduct—and so decided to subdivide the land for residential use, laying out the grid of streets that now makes up the downtown area and inviting prospective buyers to pay a visit by Big Red Car. Fortunately for Green and his partners, the new community was served by a stop, then called Morocco Junction, on the PE's Sawtelle and Hollywood–Venice lines. This helped attract buyers, and the first house was erected on Crescent Drive, near Lomitas, in 1907. Five years later, the arrival of the Beverly Hills Hotel brought resort business to the budding community. At first many guests came to the hotel by trolley, but increasingly these well-to-do patrons preferred the convenience of the automobile. Soon the PE's importance became secondary to the fact that Sunset Boulevard, though unpaved west of Fairfax, linked Beverly Hills with Hollywood and hence downtown LA. The grading and improvement of other main arteries such as Wilshire Boulevard further diminished the significance of the interurbans for the new community.

The city of Beverly Hills was incorporated in 1914 with a population of 550, but the most crucial date in its history was 1920, when the newly married couple Mary Pickford and Douglas Fairbanks moved into the groom's hunting lodge, on a hillside high above the Beverly Hills Hotel, refurbished it and named it Pickfair. Suddenly Beverly Hills was famous, and scores of movie stars rushed there to build homes, some in the flatlands laid out by Burton Green but many, increasingly, in the foothills. As soon as the city began creeping into the hills, farther and farther from the democratizing influence of the Big Red Cars, it became inevitably dependent upon the automobile, a phenomenon that was accelerated in this instance by the affluence of the new residents. Soon the community was so in the thrall of the automobile that pedestrianism was frowned upon outside the commercial zone. In the late twenties an Englishwoman staying at the Beverly Hills Hotel decided to explore Benedict Canyon on foot, and was promptly arrested for suspicious behavior, generating legends that continue to this day. The lesson was clear. If a tourist wanted to gaze at the gateposts of the stars—and who didn't?—then he needed to get his hands on a car or else take a bus tour. The chances of coming face to face with Clara Bow might be slight, but there was always the possibility of spotting her flame-red Kissel in the driveway, which in the world of auto-eroticism might well be almost as stimulating.

As significant as the automobilization of the suburbs and satellite towns was the evolution of automobilized shopping strips—an archetypally LA phenomenon. Until the early twenties the common wisdom was that the success of a commercial area depended on direct access by streetcar or interurban, and real estate prices were structured according to this theory. Starting around 1922, however, a section of Western Avenue, a north-south thoroughfare between Hollywood and Los Feliz, was developed as a shopping street with only automobile access. To the surprise of all but a few enterprising merchants, it was an immediate success and property values along Western skyrocketed, increasing "almost overnight," according to *Sunset* magazine, from $50 to $1,000 and even $2,000 per foot of frontage.

This was just a prelude to the conscious development of automobile shopping strips, of which the Miracle Mile section of Wilshire Boulevard is historically the most famous example. This boulevard, named for H. Gaylord Wilshire, a financier and socialist proselytizer who among other things once had a monopoly on Los Angeles billboards, gradually pushed west from downtown, along the former route of El Camino Real. In the mid-twenties it attracted the attention of promoter A. W. Ross, who saw the potential of a shopping street that would serve Beverly Hills and other nearby affluent communities and provide a convenient alternative to downtown LA, which at that time was still home to the majority of the fine stores, especially department stores. Since Wilshire had been zoned for residential development, Ross had to obtain variances, which even in a city as corrupt as Los Angeles in the twenties could only be done for prestigious and influential businesses. Many such businesses proved to be very interested in expanding into this new area, then thought of as suburban. What the developer had in mind was Southern California's answer to Fifth Avenue, a swank shopping street but one that would cater to the motorized carriage trade. Far from being cheap and flashy in the way of exurban motor strips, Miracle Mile would feature elegant facades built flush to the sidewalk as in a conventional pedestrian city situation. But behind these handsome buildings would be vast parking lots, each provided with easy access from the boulevard. And Wilshire would be a true automobile thoroughfare, unencumbered with trolley tracks and furnished with the city's first synchronized traffic signals.

By 1928 Ross's plan had been largely realized, and the Wilshire branch of Bullock's, which opened in September of that year, is said to have been America's first suburban department store—though its setting would now be considered urban. Featuring a separate entrance for customers arriving by automobile, it was a handsome Art Deco building with a soaring tower that at night was floodlit and visible for miles around over the endless tracts of bungalows and the nodding pumps of the nearby oil fields.

Miracle Mile represents the paternalistic side of the evolution of the Los Angeles automobilized shopping strip, soon to be copied in other parts of the city—along sections of Melrose and Santa Monica boulevards, for example— then all over the country and around the world. The anarchistic side of this same evolution is best exemplified by the unchecked growth of other automobile-dependent streets like the Sunset Strip and Ventura Boulevard.

The Sunset Strip is the section of Sunset Boulevard that runs between Hollywood and Beverly Hills. Once the site of the village of Sherman, it came to prominence because it was a major corridor that ran through an unincorporated zone—a narrow parcel of land subject to the jurisdiction of Los Angeles County but of no urban entity. Because of its unique position between the entertainment industry's commercial center and a deluxe dormitory community, the Strip was ripe for extravagant development from the twenties on. Without city fathers to oversee its evolution, that development was inevitably guided more by personal whim and mercenary considerations than by communal wisdom. At an early date the Strip became a classic example of an arterial road hemmed in by billboards, which has determined much of its character to this day. It also attracted the kinds of businesses that elsewhere were typically located on the outskirts of town—roadhouses and such whose patronage by movie stars and moguls earned national attention.

During the twenties, the Sunset Strip, by now paved, was home to several speakeasies. At the end of Prohibition, Billy Wilkerson, restaurateur and publisher of *The Hollywood Reporter*, purchased a disused "speak" and gambling den, the Club La Boheme, because he needed a wine cellar to store the wines and spirits he was importing from Europe for his Vendôme restaurant and liquor store. He then struck on the idea of opening the upstairs as a night club, and the result was the famous Trocadero, which made the Strip fashionable. The Troc's neighbors included the Clover Club, a gambling joint that was eventually replaced by the Club Seville (it featured a glass dance floor over a pool filled with carp) and eventually became Ciro's, another of Wilkerson's successful ventures. Across the street was the Mocambo, a popular night spot. Restaurants along the Strip included the Cock 'n' Bull, patronized by the British colony, the Café Lamaze and the Players Club, owned by Preston Sturges.

Valet parking was *de rigueur*, since this stretch of Sunset was thoroughly automobilized, yet in its thirties and early forties incarnation the Strip was remarkably tasteful. The Trocadero, for example, was housed first in a graceful neo-Colonial building with a striped awning and folksy weathervane (its inheritance from the La Boheme), and this theme was picked up by rows of single-story shops in the close vicinity, not a few of them sporting Regency-derived bow windows. Several Georgian-style buildings had been built there as early as the late twenties, one housing the popular Russian Eagle restaurant. When the Troc was remodeled in 1936, along eclectic *moderne* lines, it was in step with other developments along the Strip, most spectacularly the late-Deco-style Sunset Towers apartment building, which has recently been refurbished as a luxury hotel. Prior to World War II, then, the Strip did not depend upon glitz and honky-tonk to attract customers. To some extent they were drawn by the show business notoriety of spots like the Troc, but beyond that the motorist proceeding

The Sunset Strip, between Hollywood and Beverly Hills, as it appeared in the early 1940s. Photographs like this were used by the billboard company Foster and Kleiser to sell advertising space.
Henry E. Huntington Library and Art Gallery

at a respectable speed would receive from the architecture signals that said "class" as surely as an igloo beside Route 66 said "ice cream." This was achieved by modifying established up-market modes so that they could be recognized easily at 35 miles an hour. Even the billboards were attractively sited, which was facilitated by the survival of a good deal of open space along the Strip. Well into the thirties parts of it were positively bucolic, especially at the western end, near Doheny Drive, where Gates' Nut Kettle, a health-food restaurant, occupied the site later made famous by Scandia.

Elsewhere in Los Angeles a cruder but more robust architecture had made its presence felt, a vernacular in which kitsch had been raised to new heights in response to automobilized lifestyles. As noted earlier, roadside businesses demanded signs that could be read, or at least spotted, from a cruising car, so that often buildings were transformed into billboards. Inevitably, such structures proliferated in Los Angeles, as did programmatic structures built to resemble objects, animals or comestibles. Thus, instead of advertising itself with a sign representing a grand piano, one music store was built in the form of a grand piano; to make sure that no one could miss it, it was painted bright red. Similarly, a camera store had its facade designed to emulate a giant camera, the "lens" serving as entrance. The Brown Derby restaurant on Wilshire was topped with a giant brown derby hat; not to be outdone, more modest eating establishments drew attention to themselves by assuming such guises as a Zeppelin or an ocean liner, while one real estate office was built in the form of a sphinx. Literal-mindedness led to hot dog stands in the shape of gargantuan frankfurters, complete with buns and mustard, while rival entrepreneurs preferred a punning approach by selling their wienies from stucco structures sculpted to emulate a variety of canines. At the height of this phenomenon, which seems to have peaked during the twenties, examples of the genre could be found from coast to coast, but the idiom remains identified with Los Angeles, where it occurred in greatest profusion.

The natural setting for such emblematic and zoo-morphic buildings, described with disdainful gusto by Aldous Huxley in his 1939 novel, *After Many a Summer Dies the Swan,* was strips such as the eastern end of Ventura Boulevard, where what was then U.S. Highway 101 passes through North Hollywood, formerly known as Lankershim. Ventura Boulevard runs along the fringe of the Santa Monica Mountains at the southern edge of the San Fernando Valley, an area that until World War II was largely agricultural but already subject to real estate speculation and tract development. Its population more than doubled between 1930 and 1940, reaching 112,000. At its eastern limit Ventura Boulevard connects with Cahuenga Boulevard, which until the construction of the Hollywood Freeway was the chief artery between the San Fernando Valley and Hollywood, and hence with the developed Los Angeles littoral. Much of the motor traffic heading for the Valley from Los Angeles, or into Los Angeles from outlying communities like San Fernando and Van Nuys, would travel along Ventura Boulevard, as would a good deal of long-distance traffic.

In a sense Ventura Boulevard evolved simultaneously as a rural highway and an urban thoroughfare. (Parts of Lankershim, which had had Pacific Electric service until 1911, were fully developed by World War I.) Businesses served both a local population and transients, including before long motorists from Hollywood and other communities across the hills looking for the bargains that came along with the Valley's low land values.

To some extent we must rely on speculation to trace Ventura Boulevard's growth pattern, but it can be assumed that among the first businesses were rustic roadside stands offering local produce, the truck farmers' wares being advertised with hand-lettered signs like those still found across the nation from New Jersey to Oregon. Real estate offices also proliferated early, since from the turn of the century on prospective buyers, furnished with prospectuses and packed lunches, were trolleyed or bused into the Valley to snap up bargain lots. In areas like Lankershim and Van Nuys, where populations took root, the boulevard became host to groceries and hardware stores and all the usual staples of suburban life. Soon these stores began to compete for the business of transients as well as residents and in order to do so increased the size and gaudiness of their signs. Prohibition brought roadhouses to Ventura Boulevard, as to the Sunset Strip, and since much of their business was done at night they were among the pioneers in introducing electric signs to the boulevard. Electric signs were also a feature of small hotels and auto courts that catered to tourists, who were increasingly motorized and wished to save money by staying on the outskirts of the city (though Route 66, where it ran through the San Gabriel Valley, was more of a motel strip). Gas stations, also brightly illuminated at night, sought out their already traditional corner lots and the continuing cheapness of real estate attracted other automobile-related concerns —used-car dealerships, body shops, garages specializing in all kinds of repair and maintenance work. Increased

Westwood Village in 1939. Located adjacent to the UCLA campus, in what was then one of the quietest sections of Los Angeles, Westwood was planned as a commercial enclave entirely dependent upon the automobile. *Author's collection*

business naturally brought rib joints and chili stands, even a few burger outlets, though prior to World War II burgers were looked down on compared with other kinds of fast food.

Ventura Boulevard could even boast its own movie studio, Republic, appropriately enough a representative of Hollywood's poverty row.

At first these enterprises were often set among bean fields or vacant lots, but gradually the gaps were filled in with businesses of all kinds, though for some time there were open stretches between the main strip at the Cahuenga end of the boulevard and the smaller strips identified with communities such as Sherman Oaks, Van Nuys and Tarzana. The Depression may have helped the growth of strips like Ventura Boulevard because they lent themselves so readily to bargain operations, whether cut-price firearms or reconditioned vacuum cleaners. And each of these enterprises sought to draw attention to itself in whatever way its proprietors thought might work.

In its own upstart way, Ventura Boulevard approximated the ethos of a Hollywood party where everyone except for a few executives and established stars clamors for attention. The proximity of Republic Studios would make it a party thrown in honor of Roy Rogers—which would be appropriate, given his later association with the fast-food business. The executives might be equated with the gas stations owned by the big oil companies, the stars with the successful, mock-Tudor roadhouses, whose parking lots were filled with Packards and Auburns. For the rest it was a colorful crowd of talented and untalented aspirants vying for the eye of a producer: starlets trying to outdo one another in depth of décolleté but snickering at the newcomer who takes off all her clothes; good-looking cowboys trying to talk about French wines before they'd mastered English grammar; old vaudevillians telling increasingly risqué jokes; jaded writers managing to make an exhibition of themselves even as they deplored the vulgarity of the system. And always, of course, someone was prepared to fall into a swimming pool.

And so it was along Ventura Boulevard, with the motorist cast in the role of producer because it was he who had the dollar to spend. Show biz had come to the roadside, where urban culture filtered out along the highway and highway culture penetrated the outskirts of the city. Necessity, modified by imagination and desperation, became once more the mother of invention. Invention spawned a kind of communal folk art in which laissez-faire economics gave rise to an aesthetic of anarchy that, because it was not recognized as such, frightened no one except urban planners. They saw the success of Ventura Boulevard and similar strips around the nation as a threat to their honor and livelihood.

We can only imagine today what the Ventura strip was like in its heyday, because although there are people alive who remember it, that world is as lost to the rest of us as Quattrocento Florence—more so, perhaps, because a significant proportion of Florence's monuments remain. As for the Ventura Boulevard of the thirties, there is not even a significant photographic record. At the time of writing a battle is raging over the survival of a Ventura Boulevard car wash, a relatively late example of folk baroque, scheduled for replacement by a high-rise building. The residents of Studio City hope to save it so that their children will have some idea of the world that once was. This car wash is from the fifties, and the sad fact is that the monuments of the old Ventura strip have already vanished. So rapidly have things evolved—an inevitable by-product of the strip's laissez-faire character—that its landmarks are erased before they have the chance to become reputable and therefore worthy of consideration for preservation. Is there such a thing as a museum-quality taco stand?

What distinguished the old strip from the present-day one was the proliferation of highly individuated signs and structures. Between the wars, and even into the fifties, the national corporate logos were few and far between, the oil company signs being the major exception, and each individually owned business had its own distinctive advertising style, sometimes dependent on hand-painted graphics, sometimes on neon sculpture, sometimes on zoomorphic architecture, sometimes on sheer size. The result was a cornucopia of kitsch such as the world had never seen before, each item designed to attract drivers into somebody's parking lot.

Nor was Ventura Boulevard unique. Similar strips could be found from Santa Monica to San Bernardino. Yet it would be a mistake to assume that this hothouse culture was entirely typical of Los Angeles in its first automobile phase. In many cases the company that came to dominate the billboard industry, Foster and Kleiser, was careful to set its hoardings among carefully tended gardens, often framing them with clumps of palm trees. Foster and Kleiser actually boasted an in-house nursery that employed fifty horticulturists and for several years sponsored a weekly garden club of the air on local radio. Billboards were becoming more adventurous, however. Quoted in the *LA Times* (August 3, 1989), retired Foster and Kleiser artist Gino Raffaelli recalled painting the first billboard cutout that broke the limits of the basic rectangle—a seventeen-foot reproduction of Michelangelo's "Moses"—in April of 1936.

If Los Angeles drive-by advertising was increasingly imaginative, the city's drive-in and drive-through businesses attracted most attention, and imitation, around the country. Early LA drive-in restaurants simply brought roadside culture into the city. The 1929 Carpenter's drive-in at Wilshire and Vermont was built in a kind of modified Monterey style thought appropriate for Southern California. It differed from ordinary LA restaurants only in that its parking lot was in front of instead of behind the building and it had two arched entrances open to the parking lot. Other examples of that period aped Cape Cod or Oriental models. In the thirties, however, LA designers gave the world a marvelously functional jazz-*moderne* idiom in which the drive-in restaurant was conceived as a kind of gas station purveying food and drink instead of gasoline. Such buildings were sculptural signs, usually brilliantly illuminated at night, each at the hub of its own parking lot. Liveried waitresses would bring sodas and sandwiches out to customers' cars, though patrons generally had the option of eating inside at a counter that circled the kitchen as the parked cars circled the restaurant.

Drive-in restaurants were followed by drive-in shoe shines, drive-in florists, drive-in banks, drive-in movie theaters and even drive-in churches. The most pervasive example of drive-in architecture, however, was the supermarket.

The twenties had been a great period of expansion for grocery chains like the Atlantic & Pacific (A&P) Company, Safeway and Piggly Wiggly. Piggly Wiggly developed the self-service supermarket concept (originally these stores were called groceterias), but in LA this notion was married to the idea of driver convenience. From the early thirties, local chains like Sunfax, Ralph's, and Cash is King built markets, by then called "supers," plain and simple, that opened primarily onto parking lots rather than onto a street. True, the housewife did have to leave her car to shop, so that the "super" was a hybrid rather than a full-fledged drive-in, but many stores compensated for this by having neatly uniformed young men available to carry groceries out to the car and store them in the trunk. As early as 1925, Ralph's, which then had ten stores, offered a discount on goods that were driven home by the purchaser and so did not require delivery.

By the late 1930s Los Angeles had become an automobilized city like none other on the face of the planet. The interurbans and streetcars continued to provide color from another era, but the automobile was king. Nowhere is this more apparent than in the stories and novels of Raymond Chandler. This is manifested not so much in isolated passages as in the overall tenor and texture of the narratives, which have a geographical restlessness that is the very opposite of the traditional, claustrophobic country house—closed-room mystery detection genre. In pursuit of justice and morality, Philip Marlowe crisscrosses Los Angeles—occasionally venturing farther afield—in a variety of roadsters and modest coupes, noting landscapes and landmarks, winding canyons and all-night drugstores, with the kind of shorthand precision that is exactly what the owner of a drive-in restaurant or liquor store would count on from passing motorists. He seldom dwells upon features of the city his creator described as having all the personality of a paper cup, yet nothing essential escapes him, and Marlowe's motorist's eye gives these fictions their character every bit as much as the narrator's wry, wisecracking comments. As for the automobile itself, Marlowe—the ultimate skeptic with regard to LA's so-called culture—simply takes it for granted, though he cannot avoid, from time to time, a poker-faced compliment for some sporty cabriolet or streamlined sedan driven by a client or con man.

Whereas several of Chandler's early stories, written for pulp magazines like *Black Mask*, provide brilliant sketches of motorized LA in the thirties, the novels offer full-fledged tours—though the reader sometimes needs to do a little detective work of his own, since Chandler often changes place names to protect innocent neighborhoods. (Santa Monica, for example, generally appears as Bay

City.) Even out of context his prose is capable of capturing the flavor of being at the wheel of a car in automoville circa 1940:

> On the highway the lights of the streaming cars made an almost solid beam in both directions. The big corn-poppers were rolling north growling as they went and festooned all over with green and yellow overhang lights. Three minutes of that and we turned inland, by a big service station, and wound along the flanks of the foothills. It got quiet. There was loneliness and the smell of kelp and the smell of wild sage from the hills.
>
> *(Farewell My Lovely, 1940)*

Sadly, early film versions of Marlowe's adventures do not capture the LA of the period because they were shot largely in the studio. Howard Hawks's splendid 1946 version of *The Big Sleep*, starring Humphrey Bogart supported by a first-rate cast, disappoints only in that it gives few glimpses of the real city. More interesting as a record of the period is the 1944 adaptation, scripted by Chandler and directed by Billy Wilder, of James M. Cain's hard-boiled Southern California novel *Double Indemnity*, a movie that is peppered with brief documentary vignettes. Just one instance: When Fred MacMurray's insurance salesman character drives up to the house where he will meet Barbara Stanwyck, his co-conspirator-to-be, he is clearly not on a studio lot but in one of those foothill suburbs created by the automobile. The details are telling. The winding roads, though presumably relatively new, are cracked and patched, a consequence of hasty construction in a zone where mud slides are not infrequent.

That Los Angeles—the city of James M. Cain and Raymond Chandler—can still be found, but already before World War II another Los Angeles was taking shape. It was not formed by individuals fueled by Arabian Nights dreams or grass-roots commercial aspirations but was, rather, powered by corporate interests and sponsored by city fathers attempting to reassert paternal discipline over the rising tide of individualistic enterprise and whimsical chaos that had succeeded in creating a new kind of decentralized city that was both absurd and charming.

Needless to say, architects were loud in their criticism of LA's free-form development, which contained an implicit challenge to their self-importance. In December 1941, a group of Los Angeles architects and planners staged an ambitious show at Exposition Park that purported to demonstrate how LA could be remade under "ideal" circumstances. Reviewing this exhibition, *Time* magazine correctly identified its content as poppycock—"a Lewis Mumford dreamworld." Los Angeles, the reviewer noted, was likely to remain its sprawling self for some time to come.

Much more significant was a publication issued that same year by the Los Angeles Regional Planning Commission, *A Comprehensive Report on the Master Plan of Highways for Los Angeles County.* This report called for a continuation of the kind of decentralized evolution of Southern California that had been encouraged by the interurbans and the natural growth of automobile traffic. To facilitate that evolution it proposed a system of limited-access highways crisscrossing the Los Angeles basin. (In this it was responding to a similar plan offered by the Automobile Club of Southern California four years earlier.) In short, the stage was set for the LA freeway system, which would be constructed in the fifties and sixties.

Even before Pearl Harbor Angelenos could experience a couple of foretastes of that system. First to open to the public was the Arroyo Secco Parkway (later renamed the Pasadena Freeway), a between-the-wars-style limited-access highway very much in the tradition of the Bronx River Parkway. A few months later came the first unit of the Cahuenga Freeway (later part of the Hollywood Freeway), a true glimpse of things to come: a totally functional high-speed corridor with eight traffic lanes in addition to the Pacific Electric tracks that ran down the center.

These were the first steps toward a new stage of evolution which guaranteed that LA would retain its preeminence as the world's ultimate automobilized city and thus become a laboratory for the problems that would beset motorized America in the second half of the twentieth century.

Programmatic architecture alongside a Montana highway, a gas station in the shape of a tepee. *American Stock Photos*

Chapter 7

FROM DUESENBERGS TO THE DUST BOWL

*A*few salient images will forever be used to sum up the Great Depression in which America, like much of the industrialized world, languished during the 1930's: out-of-work men selling apples in Times Square; Hoovervilles housing the homeless on the outskirts of great American cities; the tattered Bonus Army routed on the streets of the nation's capital; half-starved children huddling in shacks wallpapered with cereal boxes and Sunday comics supplements; dust storms blackening the sky and stripping the land, leading to nomadic families that fled westward in beat-up cars piled high with what possessions they had been able to salvage.

It is said that when the 1940 film version of John Steinbeck's *The Grapes of Wrath* was shown in the Soviet Union, audiences had difficulty identifying with the Joads' plight. "How can these people be poor," the reasoning went, "when they own a car?" This is a measure both of how far the United States had outstripped the rest of the world in automobile production and how deeply Americans had come to rely on the automobile. The Depression, very real though it was, hardly made a dent in automobile ownership. Motor vehicle registrations did drop between 1929, the year of the Wall Street Crash, and 1932, the year Franklin Delano Roosevelt was elected to the presidency—but only by 10 percent, from 26,500,000 to 23,877,000. There was still one car for approximately each one and a half American families. The difference was that there were fewer new cars on the road. Americans held on to their pre-Depression cars or bought a car secondhand. At this time the negative image of the used-car dealer came into being. These were desperate days, and used-car sales was one of the few areas of the economy that was actually expanding. Naturally this sellers' market attracted fast-talking salesmen who were being cut loose by other industries—men who knew there was nowhere else to go. Moreover, the used car was a salesman's dream precisely because most American males prided themselves, often without much justification, on knowing something about the inner workings of the automobile. It was an example of the adage that a little learning is a dangerous thing. A skillful salesman could manipulate a customer's real or imagined knowledge of overhead camshafts and epicyclic gearboxes through a combination of flattery and the threat of embarrassment (few men are prepared to admit the limits of their understanding where the innards of cars are concerned). The salesmen could also exploit the myths that inevitably grew up around every car after it had been on the road for a while: "This model didn't sell well, but that was because it was ahead of its time."

During this 1929–1932 period, however, new-car sales slumped by an astonishing 75 percent and several of the smaller companies went under or began to founder. Names like Kissel, Moon, Pierce-Arrow, Peerless and Stutz would soon disappear from the marketplace. Other veterans of the industry sought to adapt to changed conditions. The Hupp Motor Car Company was transformed into the Hupp Corporation, manufacturing parts for other car builders and eventually expanding into the kitchen appliance field. Reo abandoned passenger-car production in the mid-thirties to concentrate on commercial vehicles, and Marmon, famous for luxury cars, went out of business but rose phoenixlike in the form of Marmon-Herrington, builder of four-wheel-drive trucks.

After his ouster at General Motors, Billy Durant had spent the twenties running Durant Motors, best known for its low-priced Star. Durant's usual problems with managing money weakened the company before the Wall Street Crash, and the Depression did the rest. In 1933 the company folded, and two years later Durant, age seventy-five, filed for bankruptcy. The old entrepreneur, most colorful of the industry pioneers, was not finished yet, however. Later that year he opened a supermarket in Asbury Park, New Jersey, then went on to promote a chain of bowling alleys aimed at the family market, a novel idea at the time and one that might have brought him leadership in this field, had World War II shortages not interfered with his plans.

The casualties were significant, and yet the car industry not only survived the Depression but actually began to prosper once more, the big corporations gaining an ever more secure hold on the market. The thirties also proved to be a notable period for American highway building, and after a pause for breath the commerce of the highway strips regained momentum and began to acquire a new veneer, however thin, of sophistication.

As for design, the thirties was a notable period for American cars; ironically, during the Depression the American luxury car reached its peak, with handsome twelve-cylinder Packards and sixteen-cylinder Cadillacs gracing the driveways of Beverly Hills and Palm Beach. Greatest of all was the stupendous Model J Duesenberg, which with its supercharged successor, the "SJ," was quite simply one of the finest cars ever built, the only American automobile ever to reach the high plane of combined engineering excellence and sheer luxury achieved by a tiny elite of European manufacturers such as Rolls-Royce, Hispano-Suiza and Isotta-Fraschini.

Fred and August Duesenberg were Iowa farm boys who grew up to build racing cycles around the turn of the century, then went on to build some distinguished racing cars, scoring victories both at Indianapolis and on the European Grand Prix circuit. During World War I they worked on the development of aero engines: the Liberty (based on a 1914 Mercedes racing car design, it became the basis for the postwar Packard twin sixes) and the formidable Bugatti V-16 engine (a direct inspiration for the straight-eight engine used in the Model A Duesenbergs of the twenties). Superbly engineered, the Model A managed to be sporty and dowdy at the same time and found only limited acceptance among the well-heeled potential customers who could afford it (about 500 were built). The Duesenberg brothers were aware that they had to modify their thinking if they were to survive. In fact, in 1926, the company did go into receivership, but fortunately was bought by the bold and ambitious young automotive promoter Errett Lobban Cord, who was already president of the Auburn Automobile Company of Auburn, Indiana, producers of elegant, up-market cars. He was convinced, however, that America was ready for a super-luxury automobile, and based on his own race driving and mechanical experience he sensed that the Duesenberg brothers, obsessed with perfection, were the people to carry out his dream.

It was part of Cord's genius that he understood his gilt-edged corner of the American marketplace. The Duesenbergs' abilities and track record would have made them ideal candidates to build a great sports car, along the lines of the Type 43 Bugatti, the Mercedes-Benz SSK (designed by Ferdinand Porsche), or the Bentley Le Mans. Cord sensed, however, that rich Americans had little use for the subtleties of such cars. They wanted performance, certainly, but in a package that was big for the sake of bigness, expensive for the sake of spending money, and as impressive to the man on the street as it would be to the automotive connoisseur. The astonishing thing is that he was able to achieve this without arriving at a product that was totally crass.

The Model J Duesenberg that made its debut at the 1928 New York Salon immediately attracted the attention of the market for which it was intended. With a 142½-inch wheelbase, it was suitably impressive, its elegant body-work (the prototype was a convertible roadster, black with scarlet pinstripes) riding on a massive, centrally lubricated chassis. Beneath the long, sleek hood was an in-line eight-cylinder, water-cooled, four-valve, twin-overhead-cam engine of 6882 cc. It was not the biggest engine around, but it was Fred Duesenberg's masterpiece, capable of producing 265 hp at 4200 rpm. Although the car weighed over 4,600 pounds (weight varied according to coachwork), it was capable of accelerating from 0 to 99 mph in 21 seconds and had a top speed of 118 mph. When the supercharged version was put on the market in 1932, all-around performance was enhanced and the top speed increased to 129 mph for a phaeton with its top lowered. In Js and SJs alike, the ride was smooth, thanks to rigid axles suspended on semielliptic springs with friction dampers. Braking was sure thanks to hydraulic brakes on all four wheels, vacuum-boosted to accommodate the car's weight and performance capabilities.

Another remarkable feature was a dashboard display that included, in addition to the usual instruments, an altimeter, a barometer, a tire pressure indicator and an oil-change indicator that lit up every 700 miles!

Like a purchaser of a Rolls-Royce in that period, the buyer of a Duesenberg took delivery—at a cost of $8,500 to $11,750—of a hand-built, factory-tested chassis that included radiator grille, hood, headlamps, fenders, running boards and the trademark "bow knot" bumpers. After that the purchaser handed his toy over to a coach builder, and almost inevitably the firm selected would be one of the *grands couturiers* of the American automobile world such as Brunn, Le Baron, Derham or Walter Murphy of Pasadena. Gordon Buehrig and J. Herbert Newport designed some of the handsomest versions—from courtly broughams and dual-cowl phaetons to sporty roadsters—while the popularity of the Duesenberg abroad led to European versions by the likes of Fernandez and Letourneur and Marchand. It is a great tribute to the logic of the Duesenberg chassis that no amount of creative panel beating could disguise its basic character, permitting a family re-

Clark Gable with his supercharged Duesenberg roadster.
Author's collection

semblance between cars as conceptually dissimilar as the short-wheelbase SSJ speedsters built for Gary Cooper and Clark Gable, and the more sedate Rollston-built "Twenty Grand" sedan.

Unfortunately there were not enough movie stars and maharajahs to go around, and Duesenberg went out of existence in 1937, having built less than 300 of the great Js and SJs, but not without having given the nation a new expression of excellence: "It's a doozy!" Meanwhile, Cord had introduced in 1929 an almost equally luxurious car under his own name, the L29, which featured front-wheel drive and is said to have been a popular, if conspicuous, getaway car in gangster circles. It was intended to compete in the Cadillac and Packard range but enjoyed only limited success, partly because its front-drive transmission was difficult to maintain and also inefficient in certain situations. (According to a possibly apocryphal story, a movie star who bought an L29 found that it would not handle the steep grades that led to his Beverly Hills home—except in reverse gear.) Later in the decade, Cord introduced his famous semistreamlined Cord 810, the so-called coffin or mobile refrigerator (a name suggested by its unusual front end appearance), which also featured front-wheel drive but was notably more efficient than its predecessor, and cheaper too. This car did not sell well either—advocates say it was too advanced—but it has remained a favorite with collectors and has become one of the symbols of adventurous American car design in the thirties.

But the Cord was an anomaly and the Duesenberg a magnificent anachronism. The most important design developments in fact emerged from the styling departments of the Big Three automobile corporations. The most significant developments for the future appearance of the car were their efforts to grapple with aerodynamic form, popularized in the press and advertisements as "streamlining." The principles of aerodynamic design had been understood in the nineteenth century, but the development

Skating star Sonja Henie poses in the revolutionary front-wheel-drive Cord 810, 1936. *National Automobile History Collection, Detroit Public Library*

of aeronautics brought this science to the fore. In the first quarter of the twentieth century the cigarlike forms of Zeppelins and other dirigibles seemed like the most futuristic shapes imaginable, and gradually the boxy, heavier-than-air machines of the Wright Brothers and other pioneers evolved into craft that, while a long way from the aerodynamic perfection of the jet era, were expressive of the principle of offering least air resistance.

In 1921 the Hungarian engineer Paul Jaray, chief of design and development at the Zeppelin works at Friedrichshafen, Germany, began to experiment with streamlined carriage work for automobiles. His designs were modifications of the "teardrop" form, which was known to be aerodynamically sound. Later, other designers such as Sir Charles Burney, in Britain, and Richard Buckminster Fuller, in America, built streamliners, while the forward-looking stylist Norman Bel Geddes proposed a variety of automobiles and buses based on the teardrop principle, often wiith appendages such as stabilizing fins borrowed from aeronautic practice.

One of the first American production cars to adopt some significant degree of streamlining was the 1934 Hupmobile, designed two years earlier by Raymond Loewy. This car retained the classic Levassor format, with the motor up front and the passenger compartment in the rear, making the "teardrop" model impractical to follow. Instead, Loewy concentrated on streamlining the details, emphasizing built-in headlights and covered disc wheels, along with a slanted radiator grille and windshield. The result was a car that may not have been 100 percent aerodynamically efficient, but gave the impression of being designed to cut through the air like a knife, something that until then had been characteristic only of race cars and a few custom-built specials.

About the same time the public's fancy was being caught by fully aerodynamic aircraft like the Douglas DC-2 (immediate ancestor of the famous DC-3) and streamlined trains such as the Union Pacific's *City of Salina*, which made its debut in February 1934. Encouraged by this, Walter Chrysler gave the go-ahead for production of what would become the Chrysler Airflow, one of the most innovative and influential production cars ever to come out of Detroit.

The Airflow did not emerge from a vacuum, for Carl Breer, Chrysler's chief of engineering, had been studying aerodynamic form since the twenties, testing models in a wind tunnel built with advice from Orville Wright. The car that made its debut in 1934 was revolutionary not only in appearance but also in chassis layout, the passenger compartment being moved forward so that the rear seat was no longer located over the back axle; the engine also was pushed forward to a location between the front wheels. This produced a notably smooth ride, while a novel frame structure that placed occupants within a cage of girders offered safety advantages that would be much imitated. As for the shape itself, it was a little like a section through an airfoil, the grille curving up into the hood, the roof curving down over the trunk. As with Raymond Loewy's Hupmobile, the headlights were built in, the windshield was slanted and the rear wheels were enclosed to below hub level in fenders equipped with "skirts." The Chrysler Airflow and its smaller but similar cousin, the De Soto Airflow, set many standards and goals for the future, but it was not sexy enough to catch the imagination of the adventurous customer who should have been its logical advocate. Unlike the Loewy Hupmobile, it did not have a prow that seemed to cut through the air. Rather, the Airflow resembled an upturned bathtub. It was aerodynamically sound, but it did not provide the motorist with a visual metaphor for speed such as he could find in streamlined locomotives. Breer had failed to grasp the expressive potential of streamlining, the fundamental notion—more rooted in psychology than in science—that a vehicle should convey a sense of speed and power even when standing still. Consequently, the Airflow failed to find a substantial niche in the market and disappeared in 1937, its demise hurried by a mini recession.

Over at General Motors, Harley Earl and his stylists were more cautious about entering the streamline age. They began to rake grilles and windshields, to blend headlights into the coachwork, to adopt "teardrop" mudguards, and to soften right angles into curves, but they introduced these changes gradually, modifying the look of Chevrolet and the other marques every model year, just enough to keep the customer's interest piqued but never to the extent of scaring anyone off. Only in 1940, with its "torpedo" bodies, did GM commit itself fully to the streamline aesthetic.

Ford, meanwhile, while faltering in some areas, had a notable success with a low-priced V-8 introduced in 1932, probably the last triumph that can be attributed directly to the erratic astuteness of the company's founder. Typically, it was mastery of production techniques that made this achievement so remarkable, the inexpensiveness of the engine being due to the development of new foundry techniques that enabled the block and crankcase to be cast as a single unit. In 1936 Ford's Lincoln Division introduced the twelve-cylinder, squatly streamlined Zephyr—probably named with the Burlington Northern's streamline train *The Zephyr* in mind—a car that has a slightly dowagerlike aspect to the modern eye but which probably seemed moderately futuristic at the time it appeared.

Aesthetically far more satisfying was the Lincoln Continental (later known as the Mark I), which appeared in 1940. Based in part on the Zephyr, it was styled by Ford design chief Bob Gregorie under the close guidance of Edsel Ford, who had returned from a 1939 visit to Europe with ideas for a new look. The Continental was intended as a one-off, custom-built special for Edsel's personal use, but its customer appeal was so readily apparent that it was quickly put into production and, with modifications, remained in the Lincoln catalogue until 1948.

Edsel Ford, who died in 1943 at the age of fifty, was an able executive whose real flair for design and understanding of the marketplace might have helped Ford match GM and Chrysler in innovative thinking. Unfortunately he found himself pitted against his father at the latter's most eccentric and intractable. As Henry Ford approached his seventies, his tendency toward megalomania, seldom far from the surface, came increasingly to the fore. He had never believed in defining his subordinates' responsibilities, so that the clear chain of command went no further than Henry Ford's own desk, and now he took to keeping his executives off-balance—his son Edsel among them—by pitting them against one another. If an executive crossed Ford, knowingly or unknowingly, he was apt to find his office padlocked during his absence and his family photographs and other personal belongings deposited in the parking lot.

In all this Ford was abetted by Harry Bennett, a former Navy diver and pugilist who had won Ford's confidence soon after World War I by thrashing a bully in the boss's presence. Bennett was rewarded by being made head watchman at the giant River Rouge Plant and also Ford's confidant. Small and muscular, with a penchant for elaborate cowboy belt buckles, bow ties and rakish felt hats, Bennett was a decidedly Runyonesque figure (improbably, he was a gifted saxophone player), and Ford loved to listen to his hard-boiled stories of life in the Navy and on the fringe of the Detroit underworld. Far from being shocked by Bennett's connections to Chet La Mare, the city's top bootlegger, Ford was delighted with his protégé's raffish ties and even awarded La Mare a contract to supply vegetables to the River Rouge canteen.

Bennett's opportunity to seize real power came in the wake of the kidnap scare that followed the 1932 snatching and murder of Charles Lindbergh's baby. Ford's fear was not for himself but for his grandchildren, including the offspring of his eldest son, Edsel, but it was Edsel who suffered most from Bennett's elevation to power because he distrusted Bennett and openly opposed him, thus becoming the new strongman's number one enemy. Bennett didn't have the clout to get rid of Edsel, but he did manage to plant seeds of doubt so that Henry Ford no longer trusted his son's counsel. Bennett meanwhile became head of the newly created Service Department, which became a virtual secret police force, an industrial equivalent of Hitler's SS and Stalin's KGB (though some might point to J. Edgar Hoover's FBI as a more accessible model).

Bennett's influence was felt most strongly in Ford's reaction to the labor unrest that plagued the auto industry in the thirties. One of his first coups came in 1932 when Communist organizers led a "march on hunger" through downtown Detroit, arriving finally at the Ford employment office. There Bennett confronted the mob, and things turned ugly as he was pelted with bricks and cobblestones. The police had seen enough and opened fire. As they did so, Bennett grabbed one of the leaders of the demonstration, using him as a shield. Four demonstrators were killed, including the man held by Bennett, and Bennett himself was knocked unconscious as he fell to the sidewalk. Rushing to the scene, Henry Ford embraced Bennett as a hero, subsequently granting him even more power. Preparing for further labor unrest, Bennett set up machine-gun towers around Ford plants and quietly built up his private army, drawing on ex-cons and hoods affiliated with Detroit's notorious Purple Gang. By the time the union wars began in earnest a couple of years later, Bennett was ready.

Walter Chrysler and Alfred P. Sloan were far from being friends of the United Automobile Workers of America, but they capitulated to the UAW after a series of sit-down strikes and the reelection of FDR, known to be sympathetic to the unions, in 1936. Encouraged by Harry Bennett, Ford—previously the paternalistic friend of the workers, instigator of the $5-a-day wage and a variety of progressive social programs—decided to fight on. Things came to a head on May 26, 1937, when Walter Reuther, Richard Frankensteen and other UAW organizers were attacked and beaten outside the River Rouge plant by goons from Bennett's Service Department. The event was photographed by journalists and did nothing to win sympathy for Ford. Even after this, however, Ford continued to oppose unionization, convinced that his workers were content with their lot and opposed to "red" union agitators. Only in 1941 did Ford finally admit defeat, when a massive walkout crippled production; Edsel Ford, the voice of common sense, was able to prevail over Bennett and instigate negotiations leading to a National Labor Relations Board election that resulted in victory for the UAW.

Despotism was not confined to the automobile industry itself, however, and the thirties saw the rise to power of men such as Robert Moses, who discovered in highway building the opportunity to impose their vision of America on the landscape; just as the Henry Ford of the Model T era had displayed legitimate vision, however, so did Moses and his fellow parkway prophets during the Depression. In a sense they simply interpreted the aspirations of America's middle class, which by now had turned its back to a significant extent on the old cities and abandoned large parts of them to poorer sections of the population—blacks, who had been pouring in from the rural South since World War I, and immigrant groups such as the Irish, Italians and Jews. White Anglo-Saxon Protestants, it was tacitly understood, did not belong in crowded tenements. God had put them on the earth to inhabit rows of mock Colonial villas, each sitting on a symbolic handkerchief of neatly cultivated land that evoked Wordsworthian dreams of rustic bliss while neatly isolating family from family in cookie-cutter domains behind picket fences or box hedges. This ideal of suburbanism was at least as old as the railroads and would reach its peak in the wake of World War II. In the thirties it was an especially potent ideal, since the Depression had temporarily created a near impenetrable barrier between those who had already attained suburban bliss and those who could only dream of flight from the inner city.

It is understandable that flight from the city seemed especially desirable in a period when efficient central heating was for the rich and domestic air conditioning virtually unknown. Less easy to grasp is the way the very real merits of urban life—its rich cultural texture—came to be totally overlooked by otherwise intelligent politicians and planners, so that an unspoken hatred of the city came to be institutionalized and implemented as government policy. These attitudes too would peak after World War II, but meanwhile they had a definite influence upon thinking about highway building in the thirties.

As has been seen, one of the first perceived merits of the automobile was that it provided a means of recreational flight from the cities, and the parkway concept, as embodied first by the Bronx River Parkway and its successors in Westchester County, was the apotheosis of this notion. Certainly commuters took advantage of these limited-access roads, but these thoroughfares had been conceived of initially to benefit the motorist bent on leisure, and it was to this end that commercial vehicles were banned from most parkways, and often still are. From the first, parkways were popular with motorists, and the concept would likely have spread more rapidly had not the notion of a limited-access road been so unprecedented in legal terms. Before it could build parkways (or expressways, or freeways, for that matter), each state had to pass enabling legislation that often met with stiff opposition, for example from municipalities that felt, sometimes justifiably, that through roads would siphon off business from their communities. Such enabling laws were enacted in New York, New Jersey and Rhode Island in 1937, in Tennessee the following year, and in California, Connecticut, Maine and West Virginia in 1939. Other states soon followed, and in 1943 the federal government passed a model law intended to standardize the concept of the limited-access highway. The freeway age had begun.

Los Angeles had its first taste of freeway living in 1940 whereas the Norris Freeway in Tennessee was opened to motorists two years earlier and the Willow Run Expressway in Michigan was already an institution when America entered the War. These superhighways were not conceived of as recreational roads, and thus differed in significant ways from the parkways that had preceded them. For the most part, though, the story of the limited-access highway during the Depression is the story of the parkway proper, and the name most often associated with the proliferation of parkways was Robert Moses.

Among the most formidable highway builders of the twentieth century, Robert Moses never learned to drive a car. A Jew, he had no taste or sympathy for the untidy life of the ghetto. More enthusiastically than any WASP, in fact, he embraced the notion of the automobile as a means of flight from the cluttered urban core. This is at least in part traceable to the fact that his first power base was as New York City commissioner of parks. The city parks themselves seem to have appalled him to the extent that they accommodated the needs of the Great Unwashed. For example, when he was given jurisdiction over Coney Island beaches he attempted to impose a code of behavior on sun and sea worshipers that might have been more appropriate to the smoking room of an exclusive London men's club. The prohibitions listed on signs that appeared along the boardwalk were so all-encompassing that the listed strictures demand reproduction in full:

> No peddling, advertising, littering, dogs or fires.
> No bicycling, roller-skating or vehicles other than baby carriages and wheel chairs for invalids.
> No newspapers other than for reading.
> No sitting on railing or steps.
> No bathing rings, rafts, inflated or buoyant devices. No masks, goggles or fins.
> No persons on beach from midnight to dawn.
> No acrobatics, ball playing, throwing of missiles or sand.
> No dressing or undressing, tents or shelters.
> No chairs or picnicking on boardwalk.
> No articles hung on signs, benches, baskets, railings, fences, ropes or umbrellas.
> No boats launched or beached.
> No fishing, flying of kites, flags or pennants.
> No digging of holes, creating hazards or committing nuisances. No bathing near jetties. (Bathing within life lines only.)

This was not the work of a man who craved cotton candy. Still it must be acknowledged that Moses did much valuable work to improve and expand the city park system, but his greatest enthusiasm was reserved for projects such as the creation of Jones Beach State Park, a recreational facility for urbanites seeking to flee rather than enjoy the city. Jones Beach has become an escape valve for the masses, but when it was opened, in 1929, it was conceived by Moses as a day-trip resort for the middle class. This implied automobile access (extensive parking was provided and access by railroad was pointedly overlooked), and as chairman of the Long Island State Park Commission Moses had the political clout to build roads.

In many ways Moses' earliest efforts were his best. Working with thoughtful engineer-designers like Clarke and Rapuano and Clarence Combs, he pushed handsome, landscaped, limited-access highways out into Long Island. Long Island was till then almost innocent of well-engineered modern roads, despite the early example furnished by the privately financed Vanderbilt Highway, which was a side product of the Edwardian era Vanderbilt Cup races. To link the city to the Long Island beaches he had already developed, Moses conceived the Meadowbrook Parkway, a superb expression of the principles first made concrete along the bank of the Bronx River. The Meadowbrook materialized as a ribbon of paved roadway running through a corridor of parkland that owed much to eighteenth-century landscape architects such as Capability Brown. The overpass bridges would not have looked out of place if set in a great English estate such as Blenheim, and, most important to the motorist, the pavement curved through the landscape gracefully so as to permit pleasant and ever changing vistas to unfold before him. Nor did this make driving merely more agreeable. The principle of limited access made the parkway inherently safer, and the studied sculpting of the right of way, along with imaginative planting, helped promote driver alertness and thus further enhanced the safety of the road.

It should be noted that the Meadowbrook, opened in 1934, predated Hitler's first autobahn and was conceptually superior. It is often claimed that the Nazi era autobahns were the first true expressways, and there is some merit to this argument—they were built to facilitate speed—but in certain ways they were decidedly inferior to the best American limited-access roads of the same period. It is said, in fact, that Dr. Fritz Todt, Hitler's general inspector of roads, wanted to build a system of highways based on the model of the American parkway. The military authorities, however, were more interested in rapidity of completion than in landscaping, and Todt was forced into compromises. Built hurriedly, the early autobahns were well engineered but tended to run almost as straight as Roman roads and consequently were far less scenic than Moses' parkways, despite the efforts of Todt's staff of "landscape councillors" (*Landschaftsanwalten*) to preserve existing stands of trees and provide new plantings. These early autobahns became known for their notoriously high incidence of fatal accidents, caused by the combination of speed and driver boredom.

Moses, for his part, brought his parkways right into New York City, notably in the form of the West Side Highway (Henry Hudson Parkway), most of which opened to traffic in 1937. In the city, however, he would run into problems he had not encountered on Long Island. An autocrat within the departments he controlled, Moses became used to ruling by fiat and never grew accustomed to the fact that the residents of densely populated urban areas were likely to object to having an expressway carved through the heart of still vital neighborhoods, or to having the historic character of their cities destroyed by grandiose schemes. This was a problem that was to come to a head after World War II, but an early instance, in which he was thankfully foiled, involved Moses' intention to build a bridge across New York harbor from the Battery Park area to the Red Hook section of Brooklyn.

It was generally agreed that a traffic link was needed between these two points, but all the objective studies showed that a tunnel would not only do less damage to the fabric of the city but would also be considerably cheaper to build. Moses' objection to the tunnel seems to have been that it would be invisible and therefore less likely to remind people of his preeminence as a power broker. The problem with the proposed bridge—apart from its cost—was that it would destroy the classic view of New York harbor and wreak havoc in the historic district at the tip of Manhattan, causing blocks of venerable buildings to be torn down and massive piers to be erected in Battery Park itself.

Public hearings were held in which opponents of the bridge clearly stated the case for the tunnel—its logic was overwhelming—and seemed to have won the day. At the last moment, however, Moses appeared at the hearings and denounced his critics as liars and worse. He produced no new facts to support his cause, but was so vehement and colorful in his attack that he won over the press (New York papers tended to be Moses' boosters at this time) and with it victory. It seemed inevitable that the bridge would be built, but as it happens the controversy had caught the imagination of Eleanor Roosevelt. She mentioned it in her newspaper column, and apparently brought it to the attention of her husband. No friend of Moses, the President set about scuttling the bridge scheme, calling upon the Department of the Navy to intervene. Under presidential pressure, the Department announced that construction of a Brooklyn–Red Hook bridge would imperil the defenses of the Brooklyn Navy Yard in time of war. It was an argument as weak as Moses' own arguments in favor of the bridge, but it bore an imprimateur that could not be ignored. The bridge was abandoned and the Brooklyn-Battery Tunnel was excavated in its place.

Moses never said so in as many words, but he seems to have believed that the city as it had been known was doomed, a European concept as inappropriate to America as the feudal tithe system.

Such a point of view saw the automobile as enabling educated and enlightened Americans (i.e., the white middle class) to spread out over the landscape into clusters of low-density suburbs while the old cities would be left to the poor—blacks, Hispanics and immigrant minorities. These groups would bear the brunt of urban renewal, which, while seldom defined, was envisioned vaguely as a matter of tearing down messy neighborhoods like Harlem and replacing slums with model high-rise blocks in park-like settings (a process that might be described as the suburbanization of the city).

Such a vision of the future found its ultimate expression in the Highways and Horizons Building sponsored by General Motors at the 1939 New York World's Fair, where the

Futurama exhibit conceived by Norman Bel Geddes was the hit of the show. Covering 35,738 square feet, this panorama contained a half million model buildings and a million miniature trees purporting to show the world of 1960. Compared with earlier Metropolis-style visions of the future it was a sophisticated and thoughtful exercise. The *moderne* high-rises were not unlike some that were actually built by 1960, and if the "teardrop" cars were a mistaken guess, the superhighways they ran on would have a place in the future that is already our past. The one thing Bel Geddes failed to recognize is the one thing he could have learned by driving through Scarsdale or Shaker Heights or Sherman Oaks: people actually like to live in buildings that resemble miniature versions of English manor houses or Spanish haciendas. They even appreciate the care and workmanship that went into nineteenth-century row houses. The man-on-the-admittedly-imperfect-street's vision of Utopia does not often correspond with that of the city planner.

Meanwhile, however, parkways continued to offer the car-owning man-on-the-street a civilized escape from the sometimes overwhelming assets of urban civilization: the motorist and his family could cruise through a well-tended landscape in his comfortably upholstered capsule. The federal government gave its blessing to this concept by backing such projects as the Mount Vernon Memorial Parkway, the Blue Ridge Parkway and the Natchez Trace Parkway, using the aspirations of the well-heeled to create jobs for their less fortunate brethren during a difficult period. As the parkways multiplied, the philosophy behind them intensified. The limited-access highways provided the opportunity to legislate away strip development and unsightly billboards. It provided the motorist with the opportunity to drive through a manicured landscape such as might be used to represent Heaven in a Sunday school Bible.

It was suburbanites who benefited most from these paternalistic visions, but it was also suburbanites who revolted against them. A drive along the Taconic Parkway might be an uplifting option for a Sunday outing, but in some ways it was all too reminiscent of the ordered life the family led on Cedar Lane or Myrtle Close. People might want to escape the inconveniences of the city, but they missed the friendly chaos of the urban streets and they found a surrogate for this in the commercial strips that continued to thrive and expand along the plebian, all-too-unlimited-access highways so abhorred by Robert Moses and his self-righteous ilk. It was all very well, up to a point, to have good taste imposed upon one's driving habits, but there was a moment at which all the well-sited plantings in the world began to pall and the soul cried out for a hint of uncensored vulgarity.

There was plenty available. A Depression-era study showed that the forty-eight-mile stretch of the Boston Post Road between New Haven and the New York State line boasted a gas station every 895 feet and an eating place every 1,825 feet. In New Jersey, U.S. Highway 1 sported close to 500 billboards between Newark and Trenton. This was mild compared with the Washington–Baltimore section of U.S. 1, a thirty-mile stretch that was found in 1943 to be lined with 2,450 billboards and commercial signs. Every 125 feet a business or residence had its own access to the highway.

In a sense, suburbanites had drawn out to such commercial highway strips a modified version of the urban clutter they had left behind, but by the late thirties the character of the strips was already starting to change, notably in the extent to which they were beginning to be invaded by the familiar names of chain stores. The success of the drive-in supermarket in California ensured that the idea would spread, and soon enough names like Safeway and A&P became part of the fabric of the suburban strip all over the country. Other chain-type businesses, such as Western Auto Supply, also found that the strip provided them with a natural home.

There were still plenty of pup-shaped hot-dog stands and log-cabin auto courts, but gradually roadside restaurants and motels were becoming more sophisticated and standardized. A look into the future was provided by Howard Johnson's, which had the distinction of being the first major restaurant chain to invade the highway landscape, though it was probably anticipated by some smaller local chains in Southern California.

The original Howard Johnson's was a drugstore and soda fountain in Quincy, Massachusetts, which Johnson purchased with $500 of borrowed money. Its early success was due to the ice cream, notably high in butterfat, which he made in the basement. Soon he was selling hamburgers and hot dogs, too, but the Depression brought financial problems; he hit upon the idea of franchising his name and products, and he persuaded a Cape Cod restaurateur to rename his establishment and buy supplies from the Quincy branch. The Cape Cod restaurant prospered and by 1935 there were twenty-five Howard Johnson's sited along Massachusetts highways. Five years later there were one hundred up and down the East Coast from Maine to Florida, each outlet featuring the same menu and—this anticipated things to come—flaunting the same unmistakable orange roof, which Johnson correctly guessed would be more effective in attracting customers than any garish sign. Johnson offered customers the certainty of clean rest rooms and uniform standards. It was a formula that worked with a vengeance.

No motel chain appeared in the thirties (Johnson had not yet expanded into that field) but the motel was changing too. The old tourist courts were still there, memorialized on film in *It Happened One Night*, but they were joined by much more substantial structures, sometimes streamline *moderne*, all glass brick and chrome, and sometimes achingly traditional. In Florida, California and the Southwest, motels began to offer swimming pools and even airconditioning, while motels with coffee shops became common all over the country. Even the names began to change, as owners reached for respectability in the form of signs that announced to motorists that they had arrived at Green Gables or Pleasant Acres.

Respectability was not easily won, however, as a faint air of disrepute hung about the very word "motel," and the business managed to earn the wrath of the nation's premier advocate of law and order, J. Edgar Hoover himself.

Motels, he asserted in a 1940 magazine article, were not merely "assignation camps"—which would have been bad enough—but also hideouts for criminals who used these facilities to prey upon the hinterland.

Doubtless there was some truth to Hoover's assertion. If the automobile had created a new kind of highly mobile criminal, then the motel offered him the kind of shelter and anonymity that facilitated his activities. As for the "assignation camp" charge, this was amply justified by a study carried out by researchers at Southern Methodist University in 1935. Graduate students in sociology rented rooms or cabins at motels and auto courts in the Dallas area and spent their nights at the window watching the arrival and departure of patrons. They also checked license plates to determine what proportion of customers' cars were registered in the Dallas area. Their conclusions were startling. At least 75 percent of the tourist court's business consisted of local couples seeking privacy in which to engage in illicit sexual acts. It was further asserted that on a typical weekend as many as two thousand such couples visited the thirty-eight motels studied. Perusal of the registers at one establishment suggested that most customers used fictitious names, and a talkative proprietor admitted to renting one cabin sixteen times in the course of a single Saturday.

Despite this—or because of it—the motel thrived during the Depression. Low rates made motels especially attractive to legitimate tourists and travelers during hard times, and their informality continued to make them an appealing alternative to the stodginess of old-style hotels in a period of rapid social change.

The motel, the drive-in, the billboard, the gas station, the diner: each was a fascinating phenomenon in its own right, each (with the partial exception of the gas station) an example of the vigor of grass-roots, laissez-faire capitalism. They had appeared beside the highways like so many weeds that quickly proliferated and cross-pollinated to create a hundred new hybrids in a kind of speeded-up parody of the evolutionary process. The whole—a still largely ramshackle fabric of signs, symbols and gimcrack structures—was far greater than the sum of its parts. It was an expression of controlled anarchy that was for many people deeply satisfying. There were plenty of grumblers, of course, but by the time of the attack on Pearl Harbor, the exurban roadside strip was a well-established presence in the American landscape, entering its third decade.

Pitted against this crude, kitschy, exciting world were the battalions of planners who sought government sanc-

A motel of the 1930s. *American Stock Photos*

tions to create highways free of glitz and distortions, express corridors running through an American Eden. The lines were clearly drawn: gleefully naive free enterprise versus well-intentioned paternalism. In 1940 the motorist could choose either, parkway or strip, but whichever he selected he was driving through a relatively innocent world that would soon come to an end.

PART

2

By the spring of 1942, the Chrysler Corporation was busy turning out tanks for the war effort. *UPI/Bettmann*

Chapter 8

BOOMTIME

For a brief period, from the autumn of 1939 to the 1941 attack on Pearl Harbor, the American car industry was not merely the largest in the world but also the only significant one maintaining a peacetime production schedule. While Mercedes and Rolls-Royce turned their attention to tanks and aircraft engines, American manufacturers continued to issue shiny new sedans and roadsters, among them classics like the Lincoln Continental, the Cadillac 60 Specials and the big straight-eight Packards with Rollson or Darrin bodywork. In May 1940, however, President Roosevelt had urged automakers to confront the need for preparedness in case of war. In this he was flying in the face of isolationists of various stripes, not least of whom was Henry Ford.

In addition to being an isolationist, Ford was, despite the success of his U.K. operations, profoundly anti-British and was an admirer of German efficiency, having as recently as 1938 accepted the Supreme Order of the German Eagle from the Nazi government on the occasion of his seventy-fifth birthday. He was hardly sympathetic, then, when in the early summer of 1940 Edsel Ford, nominal president of the company, agreed to produce 9,000 Rolls-Royce Merlin engines, the power plant of the Spitfire and Hurricane fighter planes, for export to Britain. Henry promptly scuttled this idea, ignoring protests from the United Auto Workers that he was displaying pro-Nazi sympathies. He did agree to build Pratt and Whitney engines and to help develop the jeep, since these were all-American projects, but his patience was tested again when, late in 1940, he was asked to build 200 B-24 bombers, aircraft that were nicknamed—ominously, from his point of view—Liberators, thus implying American intervention in foreign conflicts.

The request came from a deputation led by General James H. Doolittle. Ford greeted it with scorn, assuring the military experts that the war in Europe would be over before the order could be delivered. Despite this, a party led by Edsel Ford and production chief Charles Sorensen traveled to San Diego to look at the Consolidated aircraft plant, where the bomber was already in production. Consolidated was virtually hand-building the planes and producing less than two a day. Sorensen quickly grasped how production could be greatly increased by breaking the B-24 down into assembly units (wing, tail section, etc.), permitting employment of the techniques originally developed for the Model T, though on a much larger scale. He sketched out a rough floor plan of the kind of plant that would be needed and showed it to Edsel. The two of them presented the plan to the military, along with an ultimatum. Ford would produce the entire plane (not just parts) and they would require $200 million for a vast new factory. In return they guaranteed to produce 540 B-24s a month, in contrast with the 520 a year that was Consolidated's capacity.

Henry Ford was briefly infatuated with the scheme—its grandiosity must have appealed to him—and gave his approval, as did the government. A site was found at Willow Run, near Ypsilanti, and architect Albert Kahn designed what he described as "the longest room ever built." By now, however, Henry, crochety and perverse, had turned against the idea. When stakes were set in the ground to mark the building site, he sent out a team of men to remove them. When the stakes were reset, they were pulled up again. According to Peter Collins and David Horowitz in *The Fords: An American Epic*, Henry informed Edsel and Sorensen, "We're going to grow soybeans there. Build it somewhere else." Edsel and Sorensen ignored him and set the stakes once more, ordering in earth movers and steam shovels to begin work immediately. Henry was furious but backed off.

These were merely the first of a series of delays that soon earned Willow Run the sobriquet "Willit Run?" Although Sorensen's plan had been well thought out, it was not easy to implement. Aircraft production presented new problems, and by the time the project was underway the military draft was significantly eroding Ford's workforce. The Army thought seriously about having the government take over the plant, but Sorensen, living up to his "Cast Iron Charlie" nickname, faced down the brass, informing the military in no uncertain terms that Ford was not about to abdicate its authority to anyone, least of all a bunch of bureaucrats still wet behind the ears. Talk of a takeover was quickly abandoned, and by the time of Pearl Harbor, Willow Run had begun to live up to its promise. A year later, the factory was producing 365 B-24s a month, and Sorensen's original target of 540 aircraft a month was actually exceeded in 1943.

Its founder's irascibility and eccentricity aside, the Ford Motor Company's experience with the wartime economy was typical of the industry as a whole. There was a pre–Pearl Harbor period of tentative involvement with preparedness, and during this time Britain and her allies were supplied under the lend-lease program. This was followed by a somewhat chaotic phase, as automobile companies scurried to adapt their skills and facilities to all-out war production. Finally, and remarkably rapidly, the industry integrated itself fully with the war machine, often exceeding the goals that had been set for it.

Military requirements forced the automobile companies to diversify their production in ways their founders had never envisioned. At GM, for example, Cadillac production ceased in February 1942, and less than two months later M-5 tanks using twin Cadillac V-8 engines and Hydra-Matic transmissions were pouring off the assembly line. Cadillac also made parts for the Allison V-1710 aero-engine, which powered many of the finest World War II fighters such as the P-38 Lightning. These particular contracts were at least related to what automakers had been involved with before the war. It has been estimated, however, that two thirds of GM's wartime output consisted of items it had never manufactured before, and by V.J. Day the auto industry had adapted itself to turning out everything from bazookas to ID bracelets.

The one classic automobile to come out of the conflict was the jeep, designed by Colonel Arthur Herrington, formerly of the Marmon-Herrington Company, and manufactured primarily by Willys-Overland and Ford. During the war years, 660,000 of these four-wheel-drive workhorses were put into service, and their linear derivatives have retained their popularity. It is significant that the jeep was conceptually about as far removed as imaginable from the teardrop designs that designers of the thirties had envisioned for the cars of the future, and it is interesting to speculate upon the possibility that, had the war not interrupted the continuity of evolution, such teardrop cars might have become accepted as the logical successors to the Lincoln Zephyr and the quasi-aerodynamic vehicles emerging from GM's styling studios in the early forties.

In fact, the war provided designers with a half-decade-long hiatus during which they could reconsider the future of the automobile. Well before D-Day, Detroit was thinking about the cars customers would want once hostilities were over. Since most car manufacturers were temporarily engaged in building aircraft, it was understandable that car designers became fascinated with aviation technology. They were infatuated with the monocoque principle of construction used in aircraft fuselages, in which the skin of the fuselage carried all or most of the stresses normally absorbed by a load-bearing framework. When adapted to the automobile, the monocoque principle tends to produce a somewhat bulbous shape, often spoken of as resembling an inverted bathtub. The shape was well adapted to other fashionable ideas of the period, such as headlights that were fully absorbed into the front end ensemble. By war's end this shape was the almost universal ideal for American carmakers.

Smaller car manufacturers like Hudson, Nash and Frazer marketed monocoque-shaped cars as soon as postwar production resumed. For practical reasons, Ford and GM continued to use their prewar body panel dies for a couple of years and therefore avoided a full commitment to the bulbous bathtub look, though they flirted with it. By the time their divisions retooled, in 1948, Ford and GM stylists had moved away from the wartime infatuation with bulbous forms and were offering something sleeker and sexier. This was devastating for the smaller companies that were committed to the design implications of their 1946 dies and hence to a silhouette that was already obsolescent.

This is not to say that Ford and GM stylists were immune to the influence of aviation technology. Rather they began to draw upon it in a different way, more concerned with iconography than structural integrity. Before the war, automobile aerodynamics had been influenced by nonbelligerent aircraft such as the passenger-carrying Douglas DC-3. The war, however, provided the powerful imagery of fighter planes like the P-51 Mustang and the carrier-borne F-4U Corsair. These aircraft were not merely aerodynamically efficient but also expressed a vital aggressiveness that was deeply satisfying to the collective psyche of a nation at war. Deconstructed and reconstructed, this imagery would live on in the cars of the postwar world.

It is commonly acknowledged that Harley Earl, whose influence would be at its apogee in the fifties, first thought of garnishing a car with tail fins after inspecting a twin-boomed P-38 at Selfridge Air Force Base in 1941. He was equally impressed by jet interceptors such as the F-80 Shooting Star, which came into service just as the war ended. It would take time to incorporate this imagery into peacetime production cars, but the trend was apparent in the experimental models—the dream cars—built by major manufacturers immediately after the war. Typical of these was Earl's personal customized vehicle, the Le Sabre, named for the swept-wing F-86 Sabre, which was equipped with a formidable array of ducts, vents, blisters, bubbles and scoops—some functional, some not—suggestive of the air intakes, after-burners and drop tanks of jet fighters. Stephen Bayley has pointed out that this particular dream car embodied both a remarkable repertory of techno-symbolism and an obsession with orifices that would have intrigued Sigmund Freud. Although it would be the mid-fifties before these features were commonplace in GM production cars, the seeds were sewn with the Le Sabre. This vehicle was spotlighted as the GM Car of the Future in scores of auto shows and its likeness was widely featured in mass-circulation magazines. Although a one-off special, it was seen in reality or reproduction by millions of Americans and had a definite influence on the way potential customers began to think about the cars they would be driving a few years down the pike.

Nor was Earl alone in adopting this fighter-plane iconography. One of its earliest and most striking applications in a production vehicle was the bullet-nosed Studebaker, conceived by Raymond Loewy, dean of the prewar aerodynamic purists. (It should be acknowledged, however, that fighter-plane iconography itself was in all probability influenced by such thirties Loewy innovations as the torpedolike streamlined locomotives he designed for the Pennsylvania Railroad.)

In other, less visible, ways the war had an impact upon the concept of the automobile. Consider, for example, the idea of the car radio, which was to take on a significance that few can have anticipated prior to 1945. Car radios had existed since the twenties and by the thirties had achieved some degree of sophistication, but they were expensive items found for the most part only in luxury cars. During the Depression the majority of drivers were happy enough to have four wheels and gave no thought to the notion of the car as an entertainment center. Again, however, the war changed the perception of what was possible and what was desirable. Many military vehicles were fitted with radios, as were all airplanes. The idea of a radio in the cockpit—of a P-47 or a V-8 Ford—began to be taken for granted. In addition, when the war ended, radio manufacturers who had thrived on military contracts were desperately seeking new markets. They were able to take advantage of wartime advances in miniaturization and mass production, which rendered the car radio practical and relatively inexpensive. By 1949 the majority of new cars sold in America were fitted with a radio, even though all but a few model lines continued to offer it as an option rather than as standard equipment. This simple shift in car furnishings added greatly to the perception of the automobile as a personal environment rather than just a simple means of transportation.

Before all this came about, however, there was a long wartime drought when new cars were virtually nonexistent, gasoline was rationed and tires were patched till they looked like rubber crazy quilts. Still, the private car remained in daily use, largely because it was indispensable. Railroads operated at capacity and interurbans enjoyed a final moment of glory, but there was no way for many workers to commute between their suburban homes and the munitions plants or aircraft factories where they were employed except by car. And so, while leisure driving was severely curtailed and car pooling became the order of the day, automobiles remained an essential part of the American landscape.

Since few automobiles changed hands during these years, and fuel rationing was strict, American adolescents of the period had virtually no access to cars. Doubtless this made them covet them all the more, and this hunger for wheels manifested itself at a time when youth culture was entering a new and volatile phase, prompted in part by wartime dislocations of family life. Once the war was over, the ranks of actual teenagers was swelled by returning servicemen who wanted to enjoy the irresponsible adolescence they had been cheated of. The war had pulled the economy out of the Depression and young Americans had more money in their pockets than ever before. The youth market boomed, as can be seen from sales figures for products as various as Junior Miss fashions and phonograph records.

One area of the economy that benefited greatly from the newfound teenage affluence was made up of the drive-in businesses that had sprung up in the thirties. Drive-in restaurants that had once served cocktails to men in snap-brimmed hats and double-breasted suits now found that they could make more profit selling shakes and soda pop rickeys to kids in rolled-up dungarees and bobby sox. Immediately after the war a rash of new drive-in restaurants appeared, most of them geared to the saddle-shoe set, and the drive-in movie business, in its infancy prior to Pearl Harbor, began to thrive.

To get to a drive-in—or to a bowling alley, or to a juke joint on the edge of town—it was a prerequisite that someone in the gang have access to a car, and so in the postwar years the youth factor began to make itself felt far more forcibly than before in the automobile marketplace. Many young people could do no better than borrow the family De Soto on Saturday night, but increased affluence made ownership more and more of a practical goal for the young. The new cars that began to roll out of Detroit in late 1946 were beyond the means of teenagers, but in the late forties it was possible to pick up a prewar roadster or estate car for less than $100. College students made a cult of driving really ancient cars—Tin Lizzies and other jalopies of that vintage—but for most kids anything was acceptable as long as it moved. If the affordable vehicle was aesthetically uncouth, that could be rectified with a hacksaw and a coat of paint. Indeed, it was considered desirable to deprive, say, a 1936 Buick of its inherent respectability in any way possible. Cars built for six passengers were found to accommodate ten, and sober black fenders were made to serve as the background for graffiti. The solipsistic dreams of adolescence transformed functional vehicles into objects of fantasy, and guaranteed that anarchy—even, perhaps, nihilism—would continue to play a role in the automobile's future.

This late-forties publicity shot was used to emphasize the roominess and comfort of Dodge's postwar sedans. *Motor Vehicle Manufacturers Association of the United States, Inc.*

Nowhere was this more true than in the world of drag racing during its first and wholly delinquent phase. Head-to-head clashes between drivers on the public highway are almost as old as the car itself, but drag racing as we now know it—standing-start races over short stretches of straight road—seem to date from the late thirties, when groups of young enthusiasts met late at night on lightly traveled Southern California highways. Sepulveda and Culver boulevards were favorite venues and even before the war the Southern California Timing Association had been formed to organize formal races against the clock on dry lake beds in Antelope Valley. By the late forties, many of these pioneers had graduated to speed trials on the salt flats of Utah, their highly-tuned specials sometimes encased in war surplus aviation fuel drop tanks designed for use by B-29's on long-distance missions. These speedsters looked like bombs and were a reminder, on several levels, of the fact that the world had entered the nuclear age.

Meanwhile, illegal street drag racing spread like wildfire as young studs proved their mettle on the boulevards of Queens and LA and a thousand strips of blacktop in between. Nor were they playing with toys. The American obsession with size and power had led, in the thirties, to two-ton family cars equipped with formidable six- and eight-cylinder engines. In their original form, few of these cars were driven at anything close to their performance limits, but these vehicles were now falling into the hands of teenagers with an inflated sense of machismo and an underdeveloped grasp of the realities of mortality. Stripped down and souped up, these former dowagers of the car world became lethal weapons, with the casualty figures to prove it. (Then as now, many of the fatalities were from the ranks of innocent bystanders.)

Very soon, Indy-style racing got back into gear, and there was a renaissance of interest in the European sports car. Movies like *A Yank in the RAF* had made British sports cars seem a glamorous adjunct to the fighter ace's lifestyle. Now, with no more Messerschmidts to duel, "dicing" in an MG became even more attractive, especially for American ex-servicemen who had had the opportunity to admire these sprightly ragtops at first hand while stationed in Europe. Shortly after the war, MG TDs and Morgan 4/4s began to arrive in America, to be followed by Jaguar XK-120s, Austin Healy 100s and Triumph TR2s. From elsewhere came Porsches, Ferraris and Lancias, and soon there were American entries in the field, from small builders like Kurtis and even from the Kaiser-Fraser Corporation, which produced the starkly handsome Excalibur. Some people simply liked to drive an MG or a Morgan on the highway, the handling and acceleration of these cars being ample compensation for the discomfort of cramped quarters and drafty side-curtains. There was also a great renewal of interest in sports-car races and rallies, the whole field being covered monthly by *Road and Track* magazine. The actual number of European sports cars to be seen on American roads and tracks remained relatively small, but their admirers were legion, a fact duly noted by the Big Three in Detroit for future reference.

Detroit's immediate response to the altered postwar market was tempered by two factors: experience had taught the big automakers to move cautiously where styling and marketing concepts were concerned, and beyond that they would have to retool in order to set up full-scale peacetime operations. The first postwar cars from Ford and GM were modestly revamped versions of the 1941 models. (There had been no major changes for the 1942 model year, permitting the machine-tool industry to devote itself to military goals.) Significant styling and engineering shifts did not appear until the 1948 and 1949 models.

General Motors, Chrysler (now temporarily ahead of Ford in size) and Ford could not move quickly because they were so large, which seemed to hold out hope for smaller companies, and even new carmakers. Independents like Hudson, Nash, Packard, Studebaker and Willys emerged from the war in good financial shape, and for a few years their prospects seemed excellent, especially since each concentrated on a well-defined sector of the market. Willys, for example, continued to produce jeeps for peacetime use, capturing (though in much smaller numbers) the kind of buyers who had once looked to the Model T for strength and durability. By the early fifties, however, all of these independents were feeling the full weight of competitive pressure that could be brought to bear by the Big Three. In desperation, Packard merged with Studebaker, and eventually the illustrious Packard name disappeared entirely, following such distinguished rivals as Stutz and Marmon into oblivion. In 1954 Nash and Hudson combined to form American Motors, a corporation that managed to hold its own for three decades, though it never seriously challenged the Big Three.

Then there were the newcomers—Crosley, Tucker and Kaiser-Frazer—who for a few brief years gave promise of a less monolithic future. Crosley had come into being in 1939 as a spinoff of the Crosley radio manufacturing business and was dedicated to building small family cars of the type that would now be described as subcompact. To all intents and purposes, Crosley started again from scratch in 1946, marketing short-wheelbase, lightweight cars powered by sturdy four-cylinder engines that permitted the careful driver to obtain close to fifty miles to the gallon. Crosley also produced smart little pickup and panel trucks, along with a jeep look-alike inelegantly called the Farm-O-Road. These vehicles were genuinely ahead of their time. Postwar conditions produced a taste for conspicuous consumption rather than economy, and it would take the improbable success of the Volkswagen Bug to convince Americans that the small sedan had both practical advantages and its own peculiar charm. The Crosley experiment came to an end in 1952, just as the tide of VW imports began to rise.

Most short-lived of the new postwar companies was the Tucker Corporation, brainchild of brash Chicago businessman Preston Tucker, whom some have seen as a visionary, some as a prince of folly. In certain ways the automobile entrepreneur he resembled most was E. L. Cord, the Duesenberg backer, and it is possible to imagine that he might have thrived had he arrived on the scene at a time when the industry was open to freewheeling individualists. In any case, he seems to have grasped the notion that the war had ushered in a new era of car design, and gambled on the possibility of customers making a big conceptual leap and responding immediately to fresh ideas. If the Big Three had to move slowly, he reasoned, he could gain an advantage by snatching the initiative and hooking the public's imagination with radical innovations. This proved to be a disastrous miscalculation and his sporty, rear-engine entry into the marketplace scared off investors as well as customers. (Again, it would take the VW Bug to make the rear-engine layout acceptable.) The Tucker Corporation did not survive the forties.

One problem that faced all new entries into the field was that American consumers were understandably interested in resale and trade-in values, and these were difficult to establish with an entirely new product. This was one of the challenges faced by Kaiser-Frazer, a company that for a brief period appeared to be capable of making a major impact on the market. Henry J. Kaiser was one of the heroes of the home front, the man who had brought steel manufacture to the West Coast and who had streamlined the wartime production of merchant ships by adapting automobile-production-line techniques to the prefabrication of parts. At the conclusion of the war Kaiser set up in partnership with Joseph Frazer of the Graham-Paige Motor Company, and they set about conquering the family-car market. Well financed with millions of dollars of credit from government sources, they leased or purchased on favorable terms manufacturing facilities that had been built or converted for war work. This proved to be something of a problem in the long run, since such factories—even the famous Willow Run plant originally built by Ford—were not necessarily set up for the efficient production of automobiles. Nonetheless, Kaiser-Frazer soon had three models on the market and at first they sold reasonably well, more than 150,000 units being purchased in 1950. Because of manufacturing problems, however, they were being produced at a loss, and by 1953 Kaiser was out of the passenger car business in the United States, though the company remained in the industry, taking over Willys-Overland and producing jeeps and commercial vehicles at the Willys plant in Toledo.

One thing that contributed to the failure of the Kaiser-Frazer line was the fact that all three models were conventional to the point of being stodgy. If Tucker had erred in the direction of reckless innovation, Kaiser was relentlessly conservative, leaning toward the marketplace position traditionally occupied by Ford. Over at Ford, meanwhile, things were changing. Welcoming the 1949 Fords in July of 1948, Devon Francis of *Popular Science* magazine eulogized, "If this piece on the car seems prejudiced, the sin is innocent. I've driven it. It's the next thing to flying." Not only did the 1949 Ford feature many engineering improvements—a new ladder-type frame, independent front-wheel suspension, a Hotchkiss drive—it also looked new and that was all-important in the postwar world. With its lower roof line and "bustle-back" rear end, strongly influenced by the Studebaker Champion, the 1949 Ford looked forward to the second half of the twentieth century and assured potential customers that Ford could keep up with GM and Chrysler.

Changes in the Ford's appearance reflected changes in the Ford hierarchy. Edsel Ford had died in 1943, his health broken by constant battles with his father and Harry

Henry Ford, c. 1941.
UPI/Bettmann

Bennett. Ford senior, now eighty, resumed the presidency of the company, but he was lapsing into senility and was increasingly in the power of Bennett, who no doubt harbored hopes of taking over the Ford empire. But Bennett had implacable enemies in the founder's wife and Edsel's widow, who succeeded in maneuvering Henry Ford II, Edsel's son, into a position that enabled him to take over the presidency of the company in 1945. Much later, questionable business decisions and personal scandals sullied Henry II's reputation, but any honest assessment of his career must acknowledge that his initial impact on the Ford organization was almost entirely beneficial. Practically his first deed as president was to get rid of Bennett and his goons. He then called in Ernest Breech, a former GM executive, to reorganize the company along progressive lines, and gave Ford designers the go-ahead to move away from the company's dowdy stylistic tradition. His moves paid off and by 1950 Ford had regained the number two sales position from Chrysler.

This is not to say that Ford had taken the lead in styling or engineering. Rather, it began to keep pace with its principal rivals, each of which was moving away from the "inverted bathtub" look that made its debut just before the war and reasserted itself for a couple of seasons after V.J. Day. Lower rooflines became the norm, fenders were fully absorbed by the body panels and the vestigial running boards that had continued to grace most prewar cars now vanished entirely. Curves were emphasized, giving many passenger cars a somewhat bulbous appearance, though at their most striking—as in the case of Chrysler's Town & Country "woodies"—they could be both functional and graceful. Grilles became huge and toothy, like cartoon versions of the mouths of forties movie starlets. The extravagance of these grilles was a sure sign of things to come, and in 1948 pubescent tail fins appeared on Cadillacs. American car design was on the threshold of its baroque period.

Of course it was Harley Earl who was responsible for those budding fins, as well as for some of the toothiest of the come-hither grilles. GM maintained its leadership, at times commanding almost 50 percent of the market, but its postwar resurgence was not achieved without another bout of labor unrest—one strike in the winter of 1945–46 lasted for five months—which resulted in substantial gains and higher wages for UAW members. Largely because of this and similar settlements with other companies, new-car prices rose to almost double what they had been a couple of years before the war. By 1949 a typical popular family car had a base price of approximately $1,750. Popular options such as a heater and radio put the drive-home price at close to $2,000. Automatic transmission, another increasingly requested option, further raised the sticker price, but Americans, hungry for postwar luxuries, were ready to buy as many cars as the auto manufacturers could turn out. In 1949, output of passenger cars rose above the five million mark, and a million commercial vehicles were produced, the combined figure breaking the previous record, set twenty years earlier. In 1950 more than eight million vehicles of all kinds were manufactured.

The greatest sales boom in automotive history was on.

Los Angeles–bound traffic on Route 66 in the summer of 1945, a time when southern California was booming and was a magnet for job seekers from around the nation. *Bettmann Newsphotos*

Chapter 9

PIKE DREAMS

/f America's fleet of passenger cars and commercial vehicles was depleted by the end of World War II, its roads and highways had not fared much better. They had not exactly returned to the bad old days, but shortages of manpower and materials meant that they had fallen into serious disrepair. At the same time their importance as national and regional arteries was brought into clear focus by the role they were called upon to play in the movement of troops, munitions and essential goods. Looking forward to the postwar world, Congress, in 1944, passed the Interstate and Defense Highway Act, in which $1.5 billion was assigned to road building and improvement programs during the first three postwar years. This proved to be inadequate to the total task, but it did get road building off to a fast start as soon as hostilities ceased and materials became available. In particular the immediate postwar period saw many existing roads surfaced or resurfaced, so that in 1946 the mileage of hard-surfaced roads in the United States equaled that of unsurfaced roads for the first time. Astonishingly, this still left 1.5 million miles of dirt roads, a figure that would diminish somewhat during the fifties and sixties.

Very little of this first postwar injection of federal money went toward building modern, limited-access highways. That such highways were needed was no longer in question, as could be attested to by anyone who crawled between, say, Providence, Rhode Island, and New York along the narrow, cluttered Boston Post Road, which was typical of the main roads that served the nation's most densely populated areas. A startling exception to this often dismal state of affairs was the Pennsylvania Turnpike, whose 160-mile Harrisburg–Pittsburgh stretch had been opened to the public in October 1940 (its eventual length was 360 miles). Unlike the parkways of the interwar period, this superhighway was open to all classes of traffic— trucks as well as passenger vehicles—and was engineered for speed rather than landscaped for pleasure driving. In many respects it resembled the German autobahns, highly functional yet ultimately somewhat boring to drive because of its failure to provide much visual variety. When it first opened, however, it seemed like a glimpse of the future and attracted thousands of motorists who simply wanted to see how fast the family V-8 could go under optimum conditions. It quickly won the approval of truck drivers and during the war proved its worth again and again as convoys of trucks hauled the products of the Pittsburgh steel industry to Atlantic ports for shipment overseas.

There had been some doubt as to whether motorists and truck operators would be willing to pay tolls to use a turnpike when other free routes were available. As a test case, the Pennsylvania Turnpike soon proved itself an unqualified financial success, as could have been expected, given that it halved the time it took to drive between Pittsburgh and Harrisburg. Not every state was seduced by the idea of the turnpike, however. California, for example, was committed to a freeway system financed by gasoline taxes (a method of financing that could be applied more equitably there than elsewhere because of its high density of automobile ownership). It was in the Northeast that the

HIGHWAYS TO HEAVEN

toll road seemed to offer the best answer to a pressing problem. From New York to Illinois, state legislatures approved turnpikes as a way of financing the limited-access highways that were so badly needed.

The first section of the Northeastern toll road web to be completed after the war was a portion of the Maine Turnpike, from Portland to the New Hampshire border, financed with bonds secured by the promise of future revenues and opened in 1947. Turnpike building continued through the fifties, and its most spectacular achievement was the 837-mile stretch of limited access highway linking New York (Jersey City, to be precise) with Chicago by way of Philadelphia, Pittsburgh, Cleveland and Toledo. The Indiana Toll Road Commission estimated that turnpike driving enabled a trucker to save eleven hours and seventeen minutes of actual driving time on a round trip between Chicago and Jersey City, a saving that was considerably greater when you factor in sleep time and food stops. The turnpike also spared the same driver 2,339 gear changes and 696 brake applications. This was great news for the pilots of tractor-trailer rigs, rarely seen before the war, which now plied between American cities in ever greater numbers. It was good news too for truck operators who found that the cost of the tolls was far outweighed by the savings in gasoline (typically 35 gallons for that same Chicago–Jersey City round trip) and wear and tear on tires and machinery. Regular motorists also benefited from these savings in time and money. They enjoyed the opportunity to cruise at 70 miles per hour, pulling off the highway occasionally for a hamburger or flapjacks in the dining room of a clean restaurant, solidly built from local stone, its mansard roof announcing its utter respectability at the center of a neatly laid-out parking lot that took the trouble to separate trucks from private cars and tour buses.

Few people in the forties and fifties seem to have given much thought to the small towns and colorful Mom and Pop businesses that were bypassed by the turnpike and consigned to oblivion. The creation of instant backwaters was to become a pattern, and already in the first postwar road-building boom, hundreds of diners and sidewalk filling stations vanished or were reduced to operating at a subsistence level. In the South and West, however, that first generation of roadside commercial culture remained more or less intact. South of the nation's capital and west of Chicago the traveler still found himself in a highway world that had been invented in the twenties and thirties— a world that was unchanged on the surface, though its denizens, if they read *Newsweek* or *Time*, were now confronting the Cold War and the Bomb rather than unemployment and the dust bowl. It was this world that was celebrated in the archetypal book of the Beat Generation, Jack Kerouac's *On the Road.* Although the book did not appear in print until 1957, the events it describes begin in 1947. It is within the postwar penumbra that Dean Moriarty and Sal Paradise, the narrator, endlessly crisscross the country, hitchhiking, busing, or sitting behind the wheel of a drive-away Ford, driving twenty-four hours straight on a handful of bennies, pausing for a few days to shack up with a girl picked up on a Greyhound, then skidding off again through a world that is still able to give off an aura of prewar innocence even as it fills up with postwar mischief. Dean, around whom this odyssey turns, unites the worlds of the hipster and the delinquent. Denver's champion car thief, he cuts New York intellectuals down to size with his Western brand of grass-roots existentialism. Dean is at home everywhere and nowhere, and is perhaps most fully himself when he is at the wheel of a car, stolen or otherwise, bombing across the prairie or desert or performing spectacular maneuvers in a Manhattan parking lot. The automobile gives Dean his identity.

Dean, of course, takes highway culture for granted, just as he takes sex for granted, but his adventures are seen through the eyes of Sal, an Easterner and a college boy, for whom this world is completely new; it is Sal's fresh eye that makes the book such a satisfying guide to various highway subcultures during the postwar years. He notices everything—"an ornate Spanish-type motel that was lit up like a jewel"—and describes his travels in a kind of improvisational prose that was inspired by jazz but is perfectly suited to catching the rhythms of frenzied transcontinental journeys.

> In no time at all we were back on the main highway and that night I saw the entire state of Nebraska unroll before my eyes. A hundred and ten miles an hour straight through, an arrow road, sleeping towns, no traffic, and the Union Pacific streamliner falling behind us in the moonlight.
>
> I wasn't frightened at all that night; it was perfectly legitimate to go 110 and talk and have all the Nebraska towns—Ogallala, Gothenburg, Kearny, Grand Island, Columbus—unreel with dreamlike rapidity as we roared ahead and talked. [The Cadillac] was a magnificent car; it could hold the road like a boat holds on water. Gradual curves were its singing ease. "Ah, man, what a dreamboat," sighed Dean. "Think if you and I had a car like this what we could do. Do you know there's a road that goes down Mexico and all the way to Panama?—and maybe all the way to the bottom of South America where the Indians are seven feet tall and eat cocaine on the mountainside."

> (*On the Road*, 1957)

The Beats needed New York, of course: it meant the Village, Birdland, the Gotham Bookstore, friends with pads to crash in, and talk, talk, talk. Once they left the Big Apple, life started beyond Chicago, where the turnpikes ended and the West began. In *On the Road*, Sal recalls the moment when, "about thirty miles into great green Illinois," the driver of the dynamite truck he has hitched a ride with points out the place where Route 6 intersects that most legendary of all American highways, Route 66. That point is where Sal's adventures really begin.

Route 66 had already enjoyed a couple of incarnations by the time the Beat Generation rediscovered it. In the twenties, as the National Old Trails road, it had been a magnet for adventurous auto-tourists. (The number 66 was assigned to it in 1926.) In the thirties it had been one of the chief roads used by the Okies as they fled westward from their denuded farms, and it was during this decade that John Steinbeck named it "America's Main Street." In the forties and fifties and into the sixties, it became the living symbol of the open road, celebrated on television and in popular song as well as in the novels and poems of Kerouac and his contemporaries. For college students it became a standard rite of passage to spend at least one summer hitch-hiking to California along Route 66. Today if you travel from, say, St. Louis, Missouri, to Flagstaff, Arizona, the chances are that you'll fly and count your gains in frequent-flyer bonus miles. Back in the Beat era, you took Route 66, the bonus being that you learned a lot about America that you couldn't learn any other way.

A taste of this era is preserved in *A Guidebook to Route 66,* a compact volume written and published in 1946 by Jack D. Rittenhouse and recently reissued by the University of New Mexico Press. In a sequence of laconic paragraphs, Rittenhouse takes the armchair time-traveler from Chicago to Los Angeles by way of St. Louis, Joplin, Oklahoma City, Amarillo, Albuquerque, Gallup and Flagstaff, along with scores of smaller cities, towns, hamlets, trading posts and gas stations. Not given to purple prose, he provides basic, utilitarian information—"A stone picnic table here, under the trees, with a gas station nearby"—but it is sufficient to whet the appetite and set the imagination in motion, conjuring up the wheat fields and grain elevators of the heartland, the oil fields of Oklahoma and Texas, the deserts and canyons of the Southwest. Rittenhouse sketches in the scenic highspots, but his emphasis is on man-made highway landmarks such as motor courts (Arcadia, Wal-A-Pai, Kit Carson Motel, El Moderno, El Sereno, El Trovatore, Snow White, Gypsy Gardens, Have-a-Nap, Camp-On-a-Way), garages (Navaho Chevrolet) and restaurants (Green Lantern Café, Longhorn Ranch Café). The accumulation of names and brief descriptions evokes a world of boomtowns and ghost towns, unspoiled landscapes and exurban strips. It's easy to imagine leaving the Casa Linda auto court in Gallup, New Mexico, before dawn in order to arrive at the Painted Desert, as the rising sun wakens a kaleidoscope of pastels; then, after a detour through the Petrified Forest, arriving at dusk among the incipient neon and cowboy kitsch of Flagstaff, which in the late forties was still a rowdy lumber-mill town. Rittenhouse's guide is a shorthand reminder of the pleasures available to the American motorist at the dawn of the Truman era.

It might be argued that this was the dawn of the Golden Age of American motoring, when the first, picturesque phase of highway culture, typified by Route 66, was already in place, while the second, high-tech phase, represented by the Eastern turnpikes and the California freeways, was beginning to send out concrete tendrils across the landscape. For about a quarter of a century, the two phases would coexist, one offering the familiar (even if that anarchic roadside culture was only a generation or two old), the other presenting a neo-Bauhaus aesthetic of cloverleaf interchanges and soaring overpasses. Despite the evidence of what happened in the Northeast—the impoverishment of communities passed over by the new turnpikes—few drivers ever considered the possibility that the new superhighways would one day destroy the automotive Arcadia known as Route 66.

And it was an Arcadia of sorts as you hummed along the ever-changing surface, concrete giving way to brick giving way to blacktop, the Cash Box Top 40 displaced on the radio by Hank Williams and Texas Swing, KFDA in Amarillo fading as KGGM Albuquerque's signal became stronger just a few notches up the dial, Indians appearing at the side of the road, pueblos and mesas flashing by, the sun beating down on the barren beauty of the Mojave Desert, then finally the entrance into the land of milk and honey at San Bernardino, where, in 1948, two former Hollywood prop men, Maurice and Richard McDonald, opened a drive-in hamburger joint that would make their name famous around the world. Between San Berdoo and Pasadena, Route 66 became a classic exurban strip as it skirted the San Gabriel Mountains: motels, discount stores, fast-food outlets, bowling alleys and fledgling shopping centers backing onto citrus groves that stretched north to the foothills and south to the Santa Fe tracks and beyond. The final two dozen miles took the traveler to the ocean through urban Los Angeles, largely on Santa Monica Boulevard, where for a considerable distance the motorist continued to share a right of way with one of the few remaining routes of the Pacific Electric Railway.

By the late 1940s the PE was a doomed institution. It can be argued that it had in fact been doomed in the twenties, when Angelenos began to display a marked preference for the automobile. There are many people who believe, however, that its demise was at least helped and possibly sealed by a conspiracy headed by General Motors and abetted by other companies such as Firestone, Standard Oil of California and Philips Petroleum. According to evidence presented in federal court in 1949, this GM-led consortium funded transportation companies whose primary purpose was to buy up fixed rail systems and replace them with bus service. This activity was not confined to Southern California but was in fact engaged in all over the West and Midwest and involved more than a hundred transportation systems in all, the Pacific Electric being by far the largest. The court found that some parties to the alleged conspiracy, GM included, were guilty of antitrust violations leading to a monopoly in the area of bus service (the buses involved were chiefly products of GM's Yellow Coach Division).

Proponents of the conspiracy theory believe that the plot ran much deeper than this. It has been pointed out that profits from bus sales were minimal and hardly justified the pursuit of a monopoly. The real purpose of GM and the other interested companies, it has been suggested, was to destroy light-rail transportation so that local governments would be forced to turn their attentions to highway improvement, to the enormous benefit of any business involved in selling cars, tires or gasoline. This has never been proved in court, and it must be noted that however desirable the clean electric interurban seems in retrospect, the public and politicians alike had come to identify the trolley car with the decaying urban fabric that many thought should be replaced as quickly as possible. Even before the Depression, passengers were abandoning the interurbans in droves, and potential conspirators would have needed to do very little arm-twisting to persuade congressmen and council members that money should be spent on roads rather than on maintenance of what seemed like an anachronism, especially at a time when pollution was not yet perceived as a serious problem and the automobile had not been found guilty of fouling the air. There was the argument, too, that buses provided a more effective answer to the needs of mass transportation, offering a flexibility that was not available with fixed-rail systems. Buses, it was often pointed out, could operate on new expressways such as the Arroyo Seco Parkway and the Hollywood Freeway.

If there was a conspiracy, its proponents needed only to remind civic leaders of the conventional wisdom of the day. Objectively, it seems clear that the Pacific Electric and other trolley systems would have passed on without the help of GM or anyone else. In retrospect, though, it is possible to see that abandonment of interurban service had a very definite impact on some towns and neighborhoods, the most notorious example in the Los Angeles area being the transformation of Watts from a working-class Italian community into a black ghetto where the bloody riots of 1965 were ignited.

The coming of the interurbans at the turn of the century had created new suburbs, and Watts was by no means alone in being victimized by the abandonment of electric transit. For the most part, though, in LA and elsewhere, the trolley-car suburbs were well provided for by the new highways; most of these communities were now solidly established and had acquired the political clout to make sure they were not left by the wayside. And just as these streetcar suburbs began to mellow, a new brand of automobile suburb came into existence in the wake of World War II.

Sometimes called exurbs, these new developments tended to be even farther from the cities they clustered around than earlier suburbs, and their location owed little or nothing to existing forms of public transportation. Without the automobile they could not have existed. Some commentators have suggested that they were, in part at least, a response to the Bomb. Servicemen returning from Europe and Japan had seen devastated city centers, and national magazines illustrated the consequences of nuclear attack in terms of concentric circles of diminishing destruction centered on, for example, the Empire State Building or the United States Capitol. Such diagrams suggested that while midtown Manhattan might be vaporized, and the outer boroughs roasted by fire storms, Amityville, Long Island, would survive relatively intact. Yet at the same time Amityville was just close enough to Manhattan to permit a commute into the city on those blithe days when Wall Street was not nestling beneath a mushroom cloud.

There were, of course, other reasons to put down roots in Amityville—or Campbell, California; or Greenwood, Indiana; or Chevy Chase, Maryland. Except for wealthy enclaves, most inner cities continued to be plagued by the deterioration of housing and services that had become endemic during the Depression. Middle-class whites—and some working-class whites too—displayed a disinclination to share their old city neighborhoods with minority groups and sought their strictly Caucasian version of the American dream elsewhere.

The earlier flight to the well-established suburbs had made properties there very desirable and hence expensive. The typical ex-serviceman and his family could not afford to buy one of those mellow, two-story houses on a tree-lined street in Scarsdale or Evanston. Instead he looked farther afield to previously unexploited areas where developers set down single-story tract homes alongside loops and crescents of concrete or blacktop, each home hooked into the American bloodstream by an umbilical-cord driveway that terminated at a garage door or carport. So crucial was the garage to the ensemble that families seldom entered the house by the front door—which was reserved for company—normally using a secondary door that opened directly from the garage into the kitchen or dining area.

Mostly built by speculators, these postwar suburban homes—often in a debased form of the now ubiquitous

Moving-in day in a newly minted Los Angeles auto suburb, 1953.
J. R. Eyerman, Life *magazine,* © *1953, 1981, Time, Inc.*

ranch-house style pioneered in California by Cliff May—
lacked evident charm and sat forlornly on unlandscaped
lots. But they were affordable, especially to the veteran
who qualified for a government mortgage, and they were
brand-new! Time would take care of landscaping and the
community services that did not yet exist. In the interim,
there was an enormous attraction for many young families
in the simple fact that these structures had never been
lived in. The couples moving into these tract houses had

grown up in the Depression. They knew what it was like to live with in-laws, to wear hand-me-downs. It's easy to imagine how thrilling it was for the young housewife—coming from her mother's crowded kitchen, with its "Monitor-top" refrigerator, its faded linoleum and its smell of boiled cabbage—to cook for the first time in a spanking new kitchen on an electric range no living soul had ever used before.

Such domestic sublimities occurred daily and took their place, along with Tupperware parties and backyard barbecues, in a singular cultural constellation that was celebrated not only in the new suburbs but increasingly on television, the entertainment medium that came to maturity just as the exurbs came into existence. "Ozzie and Harriet," "Leave It to Beaver," "My Three Sons" and "Father Knows Best" were just a few of the shows that brought the burbs to the burbs. Even "I Love Lucy," after beginning in a city apartment, moved out to the tract-housing zone. The one thing these shows, shot in the studio, did not address themselves to directly was the role played by the automobile in the cultural and economic life of these new suburbs. ("My Mother the Car" did not debut until 1965, and even then its relationship to the actual car culture was a mite fey.) Few plots were built around car-pooling and commuting, yet the realities of this world meant that breadwinners and homemakers alike were spending more and more time in the car.

An exurban commuter might well spend fifteen to twenty hours a week just traveling to and from work. His spouse did her fair share of driving too, since in the early days of the exurbs, shops, schools and other services were generally located at a considerable remove from the new tracts. More than ever before the car had become a necessity, a tool of everyday living. Of course, there had been millions of motorized commuters before the war, but starting in the late forties their numbers took a quantum leap. For a while commute time stayed fairly constant and was sometimes actually reduced, because highway construction and improvement briefly managed to keep up with the increase in cars on the road. Even so, the commute could be slow and frustrating and it's no small wonder that car manufacturers began to put greater and greater emphasis on creature comforts to keep the driver happy under all weather and traffic conditions. As already noted, the popular option of a car radio helped make congestion more tolerable and enabled the driver to take advantage of the traffic reports that were made available by more and more broadcasting stations. Improved heating and air-conditioning systems tempered the extremes of the American climate, while power steering and automatic transmission made it easier to squeeze into those increasingly rare parking spaces and to cope with frustrating stop-and-go driving conditions.

The city dweller might see the suburbanite's life as empty (a fact attested to by reams of *New Yorker* cartoons) but increasingly the suburbanite measured quality of life in terms of driveability. In the city he found parking meters and traffic jams. The inner suburbs, only partially adapted to the automobile, offered bottlenecks and speed traps. It was only as the motorist approached the outer suburbs that he began to experience a hint of the pleasures of the open road, the automotive freedom that provided him with a cultural yardstick. He might waste much of his workday shuttling to and from work, but on the weekend he could climb into his Buick Roadmaster or Dodge Coronet and be at the beach or on a lake in a matter of minutes. Or in the evening he could pack his whole family into the car and drive to one of the inner suburbs with a movie theater or a drive-in.

The exurbs had their compensations, and to a great extent these were dependent upon car ownership and the great American highway.

The long, low silhouette and relatively understated fins of a 1957 Cadillac convertible. *Bettmann Archive*

Chapter 10

FEATS OF CLAY

*J*ames Bond's employers were able to furnish him with an Aston Martin loaded with lethal gadgets that made it capable of taking on a Red Army tank brigade. It's doubtful, however, if they could have obtained security clearance for him to visit General Motors' Styling Section, especially back in the 1950s, when next year's models were protected from public scrutiny as carefully as the next generation of ICBMs. A new chassis, a new engine, a new transmission, might be tested on the public highways disguised as a 1948 Fleetmaster. But the big secret—to be kept at all costs—was the look: the precise recipe for the aggregation of fins, vents, portholes, whitewalls and chrome that would make up the 1954 Pontiac Chieftain or the 1956 Cadillac Eldorado.

Doubtless Bond would have found a way to penetrate GM's security and enter Harley Earl's secret kingdom, and given his Old World tastes he would probably have been amused by what he saw there. If he owned GM stock, his amusement would have been tempered by profound respect, even awe.

By the early fifties, Earl and his support team had carried automobile design forward to a new phase, conceptually quite different from what had gone before. The first automobiles had been built in a purely pragmatic way, and decisions had been based on such practical considerations as how to mount an engine and drive mechanism in a wheeled vehicle that could be steered by an operator accommodated on a simple bench seat. By the time Henry Ford introduced the Model T, things had evolved somewhat, but the prototype Model T was still built in the old-fashioned way—like a wheelbarrow or a plow. Mass production demanded a different method of visualizing a vehicle. In order to produce side panels or mudguards in quantity, they had to pass through a blueprint stage. The drawing board had previously played some part in the conceptualizing of cars, but now it became crucial to the whole process. Since Ford stayed with one model for two decades, his designers had little opportunity to exploit this tool, but over at GM and elsewhere in the industry, stylists came to rely on the drawing board as a way of actually evolving designs rather than just representing them for manufacturing purposes. The engineers continued to work in three dimensions, but increasingly stylists worked out their problems in two. They moved from being igloo builders, or artists in adobe, to being the automotive equivalent of post-Renaissance architects, representing their ideas in terms of plans, elevations and perspective studies. This worked well enough until the mid-thirties, since the boxy look of the cars of the period translated well into two dimensions. Things started to change with the Chrysler Airflow, when the new emphasis on aerodynamics began to encourage a more sculptural approach.

As already noted, Harley Earl began his career as an automobile customizer. Working for Don Lee, a Los Angeles–based company, the young Earl supervised the building of one-off specials for movie stars and other members of the Southern California elite. Rubbing shoulders with show business celebrities gave him the opportunity to develop a brand of showmanship that would help him sell his ideas at GM. Standing 6 feet 4 inches, with leading man looks, he knew how to command attention. Just as important, his Hollywood customizing experience also provided him with an unbeatable apprenticeship in thinking sculpturally about automobile design.

Those custom specials were executed like metal sculptures, panels being beaten into exotic shapes expressive of the personality or aspirations of the client. At GM Earl oversaw teams of stylists seeking to express the personality and aspirations of large groups of Americans who made up the overlapping markets for the company's various divisions. From 1937 on, each of these divisions had its own production studio within the orbit of Earl's Styling Section and each studio was off limits to designers from rival divisions. Only Earl, a couple of trusted lieutenants and a handful of senior GM executives had access to all the studios. In addition to the divisional units, there was also an Advance Design Studio where "dream cars" were conceived and GM's long-term styling plans were hatched.

The studio system promoted competition and bolstered Earl's power base. Behind each closed door the goal was to style a distinctive-looking product, but the designers' freedom was curtailed both by the Advance Design Studio's styling projections and by Earl's close supervision. Each divisional studio, then, could be creative but only within the limits set by Earl's methods and taste.

Earl's approach to styling seems to have blended borrowing and bullying. He borrowed other people's ideas and bullied his subordinates into adapting those ideas to his purposes. His own general philosophy of car design was hardly profound and can be summed up in his statement that he wanted GM cars to be longer and lower. In addition he liked bigness for its own sake, possibly because he was a big man and would have felt uncomfortable in a small car. Although he possessed a fine sculptural sense, he did not sculpt or draw well and so tended to depend on verbal descriptions to get his ideas across. To make things all the more difficult for those working under him—many of whom were intimidated by his autocratic manner—he often seemed to contradict himself. Even the famous tail fins, as introduced on the Cadillac, were subjected to changes of mind on his part and were almost removed from the production car at the last minute.

If all this sounds unpromising as the basis for imaginative styling decisions, it must be stressed that most of his subordinates—even those who felt frustrated by his methods—seem to have acknowledged that Earl possessed a touch of genius. What he seems to have grasped more clearly than anyone else was that styling cars for the world's largest corporation was a very specialized category of design, dependent upon market forces and carefully coordinated teamwork. At GM, management was the ultimate design tool and Harley Earl was the ultimate manager. Under his leadership, the Styling Section developed products that were more expressive of the American psyche than almost anything else from that period.

Earl loved cars, and despite what could be taken for indecision—possibly just a means of keeping subordinates on their toes—he knew exactly what he wanted (though not, perhaps, until he saw it). He was not a Jim Brown or a Joe Namath of the design world; he was its Vince Lombardi, coaching and cajoling till he welded the talented components of each divisional studio into a winning team.

Perhaps the ultimate symbol and tool of Earl's corporate artistry was the clay model, a device that he utilized in much the same way that the storyboard was utilized by Walt Disney. In the early thirties, Disney (who was much admired by Earl) noticed that artists in his story department were illustrating the action of a planned sequence by pinning drawings to the wall. If a gag was changed, the artists would take down a couple of drawings and replace them with new ones. Disney institutionalized this idea so that every Disney cartoon could be planned out as a complete entity in advance of production. The savings implicit in this method were enormous, but beyond that the storyboard provided Disney with a means of controlling the creative process at a vital stage. He could shape a story by simply asking for changes on the storyboard and not approving the final version until he was entirely satisfied. Once the story was set in this form, the remainder of the film-making process was relatively routine. So successful was this system that it eventually spread to a large part of the movie industry, as well as to the advertising world where it is now a universal tool in the preparation of television commercials.

It was in Hollywood studios that Earl became acquainted with the idea of using large-scale clay mock-ups. There they were used to plan props needed for movies. Earl had the notion of mocking-up cars in the same way. Small-scale and full-scale clay models could be used to give a three-dimensional impression of proposed model changes at relatively little cost. Like Disney's storyboard, the clay model would give the supervising designer the opportunity to control and change form at a crucial phase. If Earl felt that a bumper assembly should be bolder, he had only to say so and wait until the work had been completed to his satisfaction.

This could have permitted a very fluid approach, had Earl trusted direct modeling as a means of change. In fact he was too much of a traditionalist for that. He liked to see styling ideas realized in two dimensions—as drawings, then templates—before allowing them to be realized in clay. Even so, the clay models provided him with his ideal tool for controlling new styling concepts.

Like the storyboard, the clay model was quickly adopted by an entire industry and had become universal well before World War II. Later design chiefs, such as Bill Mitchell, Earl's successor at GM, used it with greater fluidity, but never was it more effectively employed than by Earl in the forties and fifties. It was, for example, ideally suited to the planned evolution of styling from year to year. Earl could start with a clay model of a 1955 Pontiac Star Chief and have the studio team modify the grille, the fins, the trim, until he had a clay likeness of a 1956 Star Chief. This method encouraged changes to be arrived at gradually and organically so that while the new model would look fresh enough to excite buyer interest, it would at the same time seem familiar enough not to scare customers away. It was an approach that Earl liked to describe as a response to "the dynamic economy." Critics persisted in calling it planned obsolescence.

While the various divisional studios would concentrate on commercial evolution of this sort, the Advance Design Studio would be busy with mock-ups of "dream cars," years ahead of their time. These were featured at GM Motoramas—which, like Vegas floorshows, came complete with showgirls but featured cars as the headliners—and at other auto exhibits. One outcome of this series of dream cars was the Corvette, Chevrolet's answer to the European sports cars that were attracting so much attention in certain quarters. The Corvette appeared with considerable fanfare in 1953, with a base sticker price of $3,760. Many sports-car snobs sneered. After all, here was a car based on standard family car components that did not, in this first version, offer stick shift as an option, coming only with GM's Powerglide automatic transmission. MG aficionados reported that it handled like a sick yak.

The tough road test team at *Road and Track,* the bible of the sports-car world, thought otherwise. Reporting in the June 1954 issue, the road testers deplored the lack of a standard-shift option but otherwise found much to praise about the 'Vette. They admired its looks, found its power more than adequate and were favorably impressed by its handling characteristics, especially in wet weather. There were small complaints and it was acknowledged that the car was not suitable for racing purposes, at least as delivered directly from the factory, but the overall impression was decidedly positive: "Frankly, we liked the Corvette very much."

Performance aside, the 'Vette was one of the sexiest-looking vehicles ever to roll off a Detroit production line, the ultimate expression of Harley Earl's obsession with the airplane aesthetic: an F-100 without wings, a sublime dream boat for cruising the boulevard and making out under the stars. The Corvette sold—just well enough—on looks alone and survived to undergo the engineering changes that would make it a genuine sports car, one of America's most successful ever.

Earl's infatuation with aviation gimmickry had spread to the entire industry and was apparent not only in styling developments but even in advertising copy. "Like invisible wings," wrote a copywriter of the 1950 Nash Airflyte, "Airflyte speeds you along with 20% less drag than the average car of current design—proved by scientific wind-tunnel test." The problem was that the Airflyte stylists had not yet mastered that aviation look: the Airflyte Statesman and Ambassador models still looked like inverted bathtubs. By contrast, the 1950 "Futuramic" Oldsmobile 88—"lowest priced car with 'Rocket' engine"—had the authentic Harley Earl touch, driver and passengers being accommodated in a cockpitlike cabin behind a jaunty hood and a sculptural bumper-grille assembly that resembled the intake duct of a jet interceptor. Similar front ends could be found in Ford Motor Company showrooms—the Mercury (with Merc-O-Matic transmission) was described as having a "jet-scoop hood"—though the overall lines were a little more conservative. Chrysler Corporation, whose design team was headed by the gifted Virgil Exner, joined the battle with cars displaying notably clean lines that when combined with some jet-age techno-symbolism came to be called "the forward look."

During the period from approximately 1950 to 1953, the Big Three broke the back of the competition, and much of this victory had to do with styling. It was 1954 before Hudson, for example, came out with a car that looked as if it belonged in the same decade as the Corvette, while Nash never mastered the fifties look. Of the smaller manufacturers, only Studebaker-Packard came out with fifties designs that matched the stylistic innovations of the Big Three. Packard never approached its prewar glories, but some of the early-fifties Packards are as handsome as the Cadillacs with which they were competing. Packard was losing the battle for other reasons, however, and the marque was discontinued in 1958. Studebaker was more successful, and the company's 1953 models, along with their immediate successors, are among the classics of the period. These are sometimes described as having European style, and certainly the clean, low lines, marked by a sloping hood and a notably elegant grille, did display some transatlantic influence. The Studebaker also partook of the aviation aesthetic, in fact it was perhaps more airplanelike than anything produced by the Big Three, though this was achieved entirely with aerodynamic forms and without more than a whisper of techno-symbolism. The sad truth is that this lack of techno-symbolism and the fact that the '53 models were almost innocent of chrome cost Studebaker sales; within a couple of years its stylists, too, were piling on the bright work, though with a little less abandon than was the case at other manufacturers.

If fins and chrome are the two symbols of American cars in the fifties, chrome was the first to be used to excess. Overenthusiasm for chrome began in the late forties and continued unabated, so that by the mid-fifties some cars had shiny rear bumpers that were almost as bulbous and elaborate as the front bumper-grille ensemble. Meanwhile, chrome strip was used as a delineator wherever possible, for example along the side panels where it was often asked to perform elaborate graphic feats of emphasizing the lines of the car while providing a divider between colors in the two-tone schemes which began to achieve great popularity around 1953. Two-tone paintwork was also encouraged by the advent of the hardtop, a new body format related to the faux-cabriolet: the old sedan style was replaced by something like a convertible topped with a sporty-looking fixed roof, which when combined with a wraparound windshield was reminiscent of the bubble canopies employed on military jets. (These cars looked as if they should come with ejector seats as an optional extra.) In two-tone schemes, sometimes only this roof section was finished in a contrasting color. In more elaborate schemes, one color was brought halfway down the side panels. As for the fins, as late as 1955 these remained relatively modest—mere fairings for the taillights. Only Cadillac hinted at the extravagant inventions to come.

During the fifties Ford reestablished itself as the number two automaker in the world; uncharacteristically, this was due in part to some truly innovative design concepts, among them the Thunderbird, introduced in 1954 as competition for GM's Corvette. Like the Corvette, the first T-Birds were two-seat roadsters, but there all resemblance ends. If the Corvette was a triumph of sexy curves and techno-symbolism, the T-Bird was a sleek classic that, although by no means without sex appeal, relied on sheer elegance rather than an overt, exhibitionistic display. It had a V-8 engine that could supply close to 200 hp (the Corvette did not match this until the following year) and its handling and road-holding characteristics were generally good, if not in the Jaguar class. Ironically, it was the Corvette that was given the chance to evolve into a genuine sports car, while the Thunderbird would eventually become a boring, five-passenger hardtop. Related to the original Thunderbird in styling, but roomier and more luxurious, was the Lincoln Continental Mark II, introduced in 1956, a car that by fifties standards was an instance of understated elegance. It actually looked good in plain black trim.

The T-Bird and the Continental Mark II were like little black dresses by Coco Chanel, brought out at a time when everyone else was trying to be Christian Dior, and then some. Perhaps Dior would not have approved of such a comparison—too much costume jewelry in the Detroit styling studios—but men like Harley Earl and Virgil Exner were the world's leading automobile couturiers, and they and Dior were responding to similar fashion currents. When Dior introduced the "New Look" in 1947, its success was predicated on the sheer luxury of using extra yards of fabric to create long, swirling dresses after what seemed like an eternity of austerity and short skirts that were short not because short was sexy but because it required less material. Conspicuous consumption was a characteristic of Paris fashion houses in the immediate postwar era, and so was planned obsolescence. When Harley Earl started piling chromium onto Chevys and Pontiacs, he was expressing the same impulses that caused Dior to drop the hemline. When he changed the Cadillac from one year to the next, he was just doing what Balenciaga did from season to season.

There were two big differences. Dior, Chanel and Balenciaga had to satisfy only a few rich clients. They were producing the clothing equivalent of dream cars and, except for perfume and lucrative accessories like stockings, they were not much concerned with marketing on a large scale. They had an influence on mass-market fashion, but this influence was filtered through ready-to-wear houses, department-store buyers, etc. Designers like Earl and Exner had to succeed with a mass-market public first time out, otherwise they had a multi-million-dollar flop on their hands. The risks were aggravated by the fact that any major change in automobile manufacture involved extensive retooling. Dior depended on a relatively small number of skilled employees who could drape or sew anything he could draw, in a few hours if necessary. Car stylists, on the other hand, could not switch from the automotive equivalent of short skirts to long skirts without a considerable lead-in period. By the mid-fifties, however, yearly changes in the American automobile industry had picked up an unprecedented momentum and each division of the Big Three manufacturers was trying to outstrip everyone else in visual invention. The consequence was an efflorescence of gorgeous grotesqueries such as the automobile industry had never seen before and in all probability will never see again.

A key stage in this speeded-up evolution was the 1955 GM line, which featured such beauties as the sleek Pontiacs, shown that year in such compelling two-tone schemes as Avalon Yellow and Raven Black, and Bolero Red and Raven Black. (The use of black was especially effective, since its hint of conservatism made the contrasting color seem dashingly bold. It was also a subliminal reminder that the Pontiac provided, as its advertising copy told potential buyers, "the happiest possible meeting of smartness and utility.") Another feature of the '55 Pontiacs was "the sensational Strato-Streak V8" engine. Beginning in 1951 with the top-of-the-line Cadillac, GM had been introducing powerful new V-8's into all of its marques, either as standard equipment or as an option. Nineteen fifty-five was the year that a new V-8 (along with two all-new V-6's) reached Chevrolet, and the results were sensational: many experts nominate the '55 Chevys as among the all-time classics of the American automobile. Cars like the Two-Ten sport coupe and the Bel Air sedan were not only affordable, they were as handsome as rivals at twice the price—and were as loaded with chrome—and they could hold their own with anything on the road. Inside they were plushly appointed, and driver comfort could be enhanced by such options as full, modern-style air-conditioning. (Prior to 1955 air-conditioning had meant more or less thoughtfully placed ventilation ducts.) And they were big. For the first time in history the blue-collar worker, or the Norman Rockwellesque family man favored by Chevrolet in its advertising, could afford a car that could hack it on the highway with Lincolns and Cadillacs, and would look good doing so. It was a revolutionary concept that paid off handsomely in sales. Nineteen fifty-five proved to be a vintage business year for the entire American auto industry and broke all records with production exceeding 9,200,000 vehicles, almost 8,000,000 of which were passenger cars.

This did nothing to lessen competition, of course, and in 1957 the battle of the fins started in earnest. Cadillac had always been the leader in this area and its '57 models displayed fins that were no longer just subtle protuberances but rather insistently called attention to themselves. On some versions, such as the Eldorado Biarritz, they were pointy and rose sharply from the rear end, anticipating the look of the early sixties. In most models, however, they were carefully blended in with the rear fenders so that, although prominent, they remained an integral element in the long, flowing lines that were characteristic of cars like the Eldorado Seville and the Coupe de Ville, perhaps the handsomest Cadillacs of the fifties. The fact that these vehicles were built on a 129.5-inch wheelbase (as opposed to Chevy's 115-inch) meant that they were enormously long and thus able to accommodate substantial fins as well as formidable bumper-grille assemblies without seeming weighed down with ornament.

Other GM divisions showed substantial fin growth during the '57 model year, but it was Chrysler Corporation that really took up the challenge—on Chrysler, Plymouth, Dodge and De Soto—with fins that took off from somewhere near the rear passenger seat and overhung the back bumper. Copywriters dubbed it "the swept-wing look." There was nothing remotely discreet about these add-ons. They were sharp, aggressive and sometimes laden with attention-catching detail. The fins of the De Soto Firesweep, for example, featured sets of triple taillights that projected several inches and glowed like rocket exhausts. But if Chrysler Corporation upped the ante on rear-end styling, it did not ignore the front end, introducing during that same model year several cars—the Imperial four-door sedan was one—that featured four headlights instead of the standard two. This innovation would be copied by both GM and Ford almost immediately.

Ford's fins did not match those on the Chrysler Corporation cars in aggression, but they had a distinctive flair of their own. Typically they consisted of an almost tubular fairing, containing the taillight and projecting over the bumper and topped with a narrow, tapering finial. The fins on the Thunderbird were especially subtle, but they were already interfering with the cleanness of its lines and within a couple of years would help ruin its appearance entirely. Not surprisingly, the cars of the Lincoln Division sported the most exaggerated fins in the Ford family, though in other regards, square footage of chrome, for instance, they were less prone to excess than were their rivals at Cadillac.

The other news at Ford in 1957 was the introduction of the Edsel. Named for the man who had created the elegant Lincoln Continental Mark I, the Edsel was an overgrown ugly duckling of a car that some said was ahead of its time, meaning perhaps that they foresaw a day when ugliness would be in style. In any case, it was aimed at the midmarket areas where Ford was at its weakest. The cheaper models, Ranger and Pacer, were intended to wrestle customers from Dodge and Pontiac, while the costlier versions, Corsair and Citation, were supposed to go head-to-head with Buick, Oldsmobile and De Soto. A new Ford division was set up to produce these cars, but very little new engineering was involved, the various incarnations of the Edsel being based on existing Ford and Mercury chassis, engine and drive-train types. A few gimmicks were added, such as automatic transmission operated by push buttons set in the hub of the steering wheel, but the chief thing that distinguished the Edsel from other vehicles in the Ford family was styling.

The dashboard, for example, had an authentic high-tech aeronautics look, and the interior was in general quite handsomely appointed. The exterior was the problem. Seen from the side, the Edsel displayed lines that were almost unbelievably clumsy, especially the Citation, which featured a scooped-out rear fender into which was inserted something that resembled a misshapen ski bearing the marque's name in bold letters. The rear end was relatively inoffensive, with, in the case of the more expensive models, a sleek protuberance reminiscent of the Lincoln Continental for the spare wheel and innovative horizontal fins that merged with the trunk to form a flat top

The Edsel, coming and going. *UPI/Bettmann*

suggestive of the flight deck of an aircraft carrier. But the front end did the real damage—not that it was all bad. The twin sets of twin headlights hit the proper contemporary note, and the split sidewings of the grille anticipated the appearance of the successful Pontiac muscle cars of the sixties and seventies. It was the main, center unit of the grille that bothered most people. With its concentric, elongated, vertical chrome ovoids set off by a black background, it resembled no grille ever seen before. Searching for images, some people described it as being like a horse's collar. In a letter to Ford's PR department, a lawyer from North Dakota offered another suggestion. "It was bad enough," he wrote, "when Studebaker saw fit to design a car whose front reminds me of male testicles, but now you have gone that company one better by designing a car with a front like a female vagina."

Did other potential customers come to the same conclusion, either consciously or subliminally? Did the wrong kind of sexual overtones contribute to the Edsel disaster? (The marque survived a little more than two years.) Was that front end just too naked and provocative at a time when *Playboy* conscientiously transformed pubic areas into neutral zones with the aid of an airbrush? The answer to these questions will never be known, but what is certain is that less troublesome forms of sexual reference and symbolism were pandemic in Detroit cars of the fifties.

Despite the rise of *Playboy*, launched in 1953, commonly acceptable standards of sexuality were approximately those permitted by Hollywood, both on screen and off. The Hollywood Production Code, authored by Will Hays, remained a significant force in the 1950s. It was still a rule, for example, that if two people were portrayed on a bed together, even if cinematically married, each had to have at least two limbs touching the floor. Nor could sex even be discussed except obliquely or in the most innocuous terms. Consequently, sexual events had to be contextually implied, and sexual allure was frequently fetishized because it could not be openly expressed. Instead of the nude scenes we have become accustomed to, there were displays of silk stockings, high-heeled shoes and exotic corsetry. Breasts, buttocks and legs were emphasized by the act of partial or complete concealment. Nothing could be more characteristic of the period than the push-up bra, which served to provide a good deal of décolleté while transforming the breasts into iconic objects almost independent of the rest of the female anatomy.

As for male sexuality in Hollywood, there were a goodly number of costume dramas involving togas or tights, there was a string of Tarzan movies, and Kirk Douglas found innumerable opportunities to bare his chest, but for the most part man's body was outfitted in loosely fitting suits and slacks of the Brooks Brothers variety. Thus tailored, leading men and heavies alike relied on their omnipresent cigarettes as potent phallic emphasizers. If the plot allowed for it, the handgun played the same role, and this was especially the case in the Westerns that were so popular during the decade, on both the big screen and television.

The fetishizing of sex had become so conspicuous in the fifties that it's probably true to say that many sophisticated Americans began finding phallic and other symbols where none existed. To suggest that this could be true of the automobile, however, would be naive. It was the curvaciousness of the car's "body," after all, that made it such an object of desire, and that curvaciousness had a symmetry that was evocative of the human form, consisting as it did of smoothly conjoined protrusions, often grouped in pairs. The fins, the hooded headlights, the chromed eminences extending forward from the tumescent bumpers, all of these could be read in isolation as having a fetishistic value. But the remarkable thing about the fifties automobile was the way all these elements were put together to create an erotic whole. Doubtless there were men obsessed with fins alone, as others are obsessed with shoes, but for most people it was the ensemble that made the car such a magnet for the libido.

The late fifties Cadillac was perhaps the ultimate in fetishized sex. Advertisements for the Cadillac were aimed at the country-club set and Fifth Avenue crowd (or those who aspired to such status), but in reality the Cadillac was perceived just as readily as the car owned by sex symbols like Elvis Presley, who bought them by the dozen, and Jayne Mansfield. Jayne Mansfield not only owned Cadillacs (and died in one), she was a Cadillac incarnate. Or was it the other way around? In any case, these two assemblages of manifold fetishes had a good deal in common: larger-than-life presence, chutzpah, self-proclaimed glamour and unapologetically baroque bodywork. Mansfield's masses of peroxide blond hair could even be compared to the Caddie's acres of chrome. Some would argue that Mansfield lacked the Cadillac's class, but it's open to debate as to whether the Cadillac at this time possessed class in any traditional sense of the word. Compare the '57 Coupe de Ville with a Mercedes 300SL from the same model year—or a Bentley Continental, or a Citroën DS— and it must be admitted that the Cadillac is nouveau riche and vulgar, but vulgar in a way that is refreshingly out front and not without its own impertinent charm. It possesses, in short, much the same qualities as those displayed by Jayne Mansfield in her 1957 hit *Will Success Spoil Rock Hunter?*

It was said of Rock Hudson that he and Doris Day on screen gave off the same aura as two Cadillacs parked suggestively together on a driveway. I believe this should be amended, since while Rock Hudson may have been a Cadillac (a Fleetwood), Doris Day was undoubtedly a Lincoln Continental Mark II. Within the context of Hollywood in the fifties, Dodo, as her friends called her, was a repository of traditional values: always reliable and trustworthy, stylish without being flashy, neat, commonsensical, virtuous—a woman with the right gloves for every occasion. Within the context of Detroit in the fifties, the Continental Mark II was just such a car. Its discreetly sleek lines were the glass-and-steel equivalent of Day's crisp linen suits and cotton shirtwaists. Those suits and dresses were always cut tight around the hips to emphasize the star's pert posterior, the only hint of eroticism permitted by the studio in presenting so tomboyish an actress. The Continental Mark II had that elegant little swelling at the rear end to accommodate the spare wheel. Both Doris Day and the Mark II were at their sexiest with their rumps to the camera.

The parallels are endless—and inevitably sexist—but in the late fifties the automobile was eroticized in so blatant a way that it is impossible to ignore. The car became a sex symbol. For the male it was something to be possessed. But once possessed it was transformed into something else. Worshiped from afar, the Oldsmobile Starfire or the Dodge Sierra was desirable and inviolate. Once owned it became a luscious slave and, like any slave, however beautiful, became subject to judgment in terms of performance rather than appearance. Once he had stroked her and polished her, the owner wanted to enter her and experience the orgasm of power promised by that Strato-Streak or Turbo-Thrust V-8 under the hood. The copywriters understood this. "You really get a kick out of its quick, quiet response to your foot on the accelerator," says a '55 Chevy ad. "Behind the wheel of a Ford," responds a rival agency, "you become a new man. For under your foot lies response so eager and alive, you almost believe it's clairvoyant! This is Ford's Trigger-Torque power. . . ." Out on the highway, the vehicle is transformed. No longer a passive object of desire, its symbolism is inverted. The '59 Dodge, for example, becomes "the swift sweep of fins, the forward thrust of fenders over dual headlamps, the curving arch of compound windshield." The car as surrogate mistress is translated into the car as pretend jet fighter, a translation that involves giving a phallic connotation to protuberances and swellings that formerly read as fetishized breasts. Back home in the driveway, however, that Starfire or Sierra reverts to being an object of desire, especially for the poor lug next door who is still driving a '52 Hudson. The owner of the Starfire would quickly recall the Ten Commandments if he thought his neighbor was lusting after his wife. But nothing would please him better than the knowledge that the same neighbor was lusting after his car.

The pseudo-aeronautic aspect of car styling in the fifties was wholly self-conscious, and that is perhaps why in retrospect it seems contrived. The sexual fetishism of car styling in the fifties was largely unconscious, and this is probably why it seems so potent from a present-day perspective. It also explains why that sexuality could be so equivocal. If the gender ambiguity of fifties cars had been widely recognized at the time, Senator Joseph McCarthy would have called Harley Earl to testify before his sub-committee, and the Reverend Billy Graham might have launched a crusade to bring back those old-time, unerotic interurbans. Car sales would have plummeted.

The front end of the 1960 Ford Thunderbird. *UPI/Bettmann*

As it happened, car sales did slump in the late fifties, but chiefly because of a minirecession, aided perhaps by a change in national image that was triggered in part by the successful Soviet launching of the Sputnik satellite in 1957. The event had tremendous practical and symbolic significance, suggesting that American omnipotence might be in doubt. The megalomaniacal tendencies expressed by the automotive excesses of the fifties were called into question, but the Big Three were slow to respond, arguably because they saw the drop in sales as being a consequence of temporary weakness in the economy. Despite the fiasco of the Edsel, Ford was feeling especially healthy. A 1956 offering of Ford Motor Company stock to the public was a huge success, affirming America's belief in the company's future. It had been initiated by the Ford Foundation, which

HIGHWAYS TO HEAVEN

perceived a need to diversify its own financial base, having previously held only Ford nonvoting stock. In 1958, Ford produced its 50-millionth vehicle. The same year Chrysler reached the 25-million milestone and General Motors celebrated its fiftieth anniversary, securely in place as the world's largest corporation, with a gross income far in excess of that of many developing countries.

All three companies continued to produce large, rococo vehicles, and in cars like the '59 Dodges, the jukebox-on-wheels aesthetic reached its most extreme form. It was an aesthetic that considerable sectors of the American public continued to embrace, and customizers like George Barris were paid to exaggerate Detroit's exaggerations for the benefit of wealthy patrons. At the same time, however, the Big Three were slowly coming to sense a shift in the wind, and before the end of the decade the first compacts were rolling off American production lines. The impetus behind this move was an element of customer dissatisfaction with the ever-increasing size, cost and fuel consumption of American cars, a dissatisfaction reflected in the marketplace by a significant rise in the sale of smaller and more economical European imports.

In 1955, sales of small foreign cars amounted to a mere 60,000 vehicles, or less than 1 percent of all automobiles purchased in the United States that year. In the next couple of years, however, foreign sales began to escalate rapidly and by 1959 reached an astonishing 600,000. Participating in this unexpected boom were European companies like Renault, Hillman, Volvo and Morris (the Morris Minor became something of a cult classic). The greatest success by far, though, was that of the Volkswagen Beetle.

The Beetle was developed in the thirties by Dr. Ferdinand Porsche, designer of some of the greatest Mercedes, in response to Hitler's desire for a "people's car," a small but roomy vehicle that would have a performance suitable to the new autobahns, yet sell for the equivalent of about $400. In a sense it was an update of the Model T Ford, but Dr. Porsche's ideas were radical and he came up with an aerodynamic, rear-engined design that was hardly ravishing, yet somehow fetching. The prototype, built in

1936, already featured independent torsion-bar suspension, power brakes, rubber engine mountings and the trademark air-cooled engine. The VW was virtually perfected by 1938, with the Porsche Type 60, but production did not commence until 1945, at which time the factory was under the control of British occupying forces. The British saw little future in such an odd-looking car, and so its destiny was handed back to German management in the person of Heinz Nordhoff, a former director of GM's Opel subsidiary, who almost immediately began to explore the possibilities offered by the export market. Small quantities of Beetles began appearing in the States in the early fifties and it quickly won a devoted public. By 1959, VW was selling 150,000 units a year in the American market.

Significantly, these sales were reached without advertising, as the popularity of the Beetle depended entirely upon word of mouth supported by a growing sales and service network. At that point Carl H. Hahn, head of Volkswagen of America, decided that despite a six-month backlog of orders the company should begin national advertising, and Doyle Dane Bernbach was hired to devise a campaign that would be totally unlike any car promotion ever seen before. The initial creative team at DDB was made up of art director Helmut Krone and copywriter Julian Koenig, working closely with Bill Bernbach. The approach they devised was that of the self-deprecating soft sell, a strategy that could work only because the product they were selling had proved its quality and had already established a word-of-mouth reputation. They built on that word-of-mouth reputation, giving it a variety of humorous twists, and set about converting potential buyers who were already half convinced of the VW's virtues, yet leery, perhaps, of purchasing anything that looked so strange.

Eschewing the conventions of happy people—especially glamorous women—portrayed with shiny cars, DDB devised print and TV ads that emphasized the Beetle's smallness, practicality, economy and engineering virtues, all couched in offbeat, witty terms. "It makes your house look bigger," said one ad. "Live below your means," exhorted another. "Ugly is only skin deep," offered a third.

Each of these print ads was accompanied by a simple picture of a Beetle against a neutral ground, reproduced in black and white. No advertising campaign has ever posed so cleverly as modest. No advertising campaign has ever been more effective. Beetle sales in America climbed steadily, even when other imports fell off sharply, eventually reaching a peak of 423,000 units a year. Not that this can be explained entirely by advertising. The Beetle exacted a degree of affection from its owners that has been matched only by the Model T Ford, which it eventually outstripped in total production. More than 20 million Bugs were sold worldwide, and it is estimated that the great majority of them are still on the road.

The appeal of the Beetle can be summed up by the experience of Bill Walsh, writer-producer of *The Love Bug*, the first of a series of highly successful Disney movies that featured a car with humanoid characteristics. As first drafted, the script did not call for any specific make of car, and all that Walsh was sure of was that it should be a small car, capable of arousing "underdog" sympathy. He arranged for several small imports, including a VW, to be parked on the Disney lot beneath his office window. During lunch breaks he would stand at his window and watch how employees responded to the different cars. All of them attracted notice, but the attention drawn by the VW was of a special sort. People sidled up to it, stroked it, affectionately kicked the tires. They treated it like a friend, an intimate. There was never a moment's doubt in Walsh's mind as to which car he should cast as the Love Bug.

If the Beetle inspired affection, it also offered the public an opportunity to make a mild but pointed political statement. In the sixties the VW would become the car of choice of the counterculture, but even earlier it tended to signify a faintly leftist position, to express a disapproval of American global excesses as symbolized by Detroit's battle cruisers on wheels, and a concern with ecological issues as opposed to a glorification of conspicuous consumption. (Ironically, it was the failure of the Beetle's engine to meet later U.S. emission standards that eventually led to its demise as a leading import.)

In the late fifties, however, the Beetle was on the rise, and so was a domestic car that had been almost totally discounted by the Big Three. This was the American Motors Rambler, a relatively small, inexpensive vehicle, the brainchild of George Romney, president of AMC. Romney concentrated on production of the Rambler at the expense of AMC's more expensive Nash and Hudson lines, both of which were discontinued in 1957. The Rambler was not as small as the imports (its wheelbase was twenty-two inches longer than the Morris Minor's, but seven inches shorter than a standard Chevy's), but it was compact and it began to attract customers, especially among families looking for a second car. Eighty thousand units were sold in 1955, and by the end of the decade half a million Ramblers a year were rolling off the production line.

Following AMC's example, Studebaker began to market compacts of its own: the Scotsman, introduced in 1957, and the Lark, which followed the next year. Both enjoyed some brief success, but only until the Big Three finally came out with their own compacts—Ford's Falcon and Comet, Chrysler's Valiant and Dart, and GM's Tempest, Corvair and Chevy II. Like the Rambler, these were not small cars in the European sense. Rather they were slightly scaled-down versions of standard American cars. They sold in quantities that justified continued production. At the same time they were not such an obvious success that they could persuade Detroit of the need to move away from "full-sized" vehicles. Nor did they do much to stem the rising tide of imports, which continued unabated. The plain fact is that the American compacts were the embodiment of a compromise solution arrived at by men who for the most part were firmly rooted in the industry's past. A Corvair offered neither the quality of a Mercedes 190 nor the practicality of a VW (which it aped to the extent of having an air-cooled rear engine). It certainly lacked the sexiness of a Porsche.

Although the numbers of imported sports cars sold barely registered on the marketing charts, they were highly visible and they offered an aesthetic and a vocabulary of symbolism that was quite different from that found

Perhaps the most interesting and maligned of the first generation of American compacts, the Chevrolet Corvair—seen here in its 1960 version, which was quite capable of providing the unwary driver with adventures when taken out on a slick road. *American Stock Photos*

in American cars. Eventually, the jaunty ragtop image of the MG and Morgan was eclipsed by the sleeker appearance of a new generation of high-performance vehicles. The Porsche Speedster, the Mercedes 300 SL, the Ferrari 250-GT, the Jaguar XK-140, were lean and clean and could outperform anything else on the road. They did not impersonate airplanes, but to a significant extent they were truly aerodynamic and their designers had learned from aviation technology. They were sexy not because they were loaded with fetishistic detail, but because they were exquisite, unadorned expressions of raw power, each beautiful as a perfectly developed naked body—pliant and limber in the hands of a skilled pilot, yet slightly sinister and menacing.

Enzo Ferrari once observed, "Porsche doesn't make racing cars, they make missiles," and it is a fact that during World War II Dr. Ferdinand Porsche took time off from developing the VW to consult in the design of the V-1 rockets that rained destruction upon England. He was seventy-three when the first production car to bear his name appeared in 1948, and had little to do with the realization of this and later designs to emerge from the Porsche *Büro*. But the Porsche *Büro* attracted some of the best engineering and design talents of the period, and the Porsche marque continued the tradition Dr. Porsche had begun when designing sports and racing cars for Mercedes and Auto Union. The first competition car produced by Porsche, two years after the founder's death, was the 1953 RS Spyder, with a twin-cam engine capable of propelling the vehicle at speeds well over 100 mph. It was a veritable missile of a car—as purely functional a sports car as had ever been built—and it quickly attracted the attention of American enthusiasts.

When James Dean took possession of his Type 550 Spyder—an improved model—in the late summer of 1956, he drove it to George Barris's body shop in Compton, California, and had racing stripes added to its silver finish, along with the words LITTLE BASTARD painted on the rear end. Having just finished work on *Giant*, Dean took off on a fine September day to race the Spyder at a meet to be held in Salinas. A little more than halfway between LA and Salinas, Dean was traveling at an estimated 85 mph through the arid landscape a few miles east of Paso Robles when, at the junction of Routes 41 and 46, he collided with a black Ford two-door driven by one Donald Turnipseed. Turnipseed was uninjured, but the Spyder was demolished and Dean passed from life into legend at the age of twenty-four, his blatant sexuality and glamour forever linked to the Porsche name, the Porsche's phallic menace forever embedded in his myth.

The death of James Dean had no immediate consequences in Detroit, where fins and chromium-plated gargoyles continued to enjoy their moment of glory. But James Dean's image did not vanish with the crushing of breath from his body. The fact that he died just as he had often predicted—young and living dangerously—helped fuel a cult that sold a million posters and put a self-conscious scowl on the faces of a million teenage boys.

As an example for those who worshiped at the altar of youth, Dean in death had only one rival—Elvis, still very much alive. And if Elvis betrayed his essentially old-fashioned, hillbilly roots by his infatuation with those big ol' Cadillac dreamboats, with their fins and frippery, Dean with his Porsche was the image of sleek automotive splendor that many young Americans carried away from the flashy fifties. The baroque period was over.

U.S. 1 near Philadelphia. *Bettmann Archive*

Chapter 11

FREEWAYS AND FRANCHISERS

$\mathcal{A}$s America's automobile population rose dramatically, it became increasingly evident that an improved national highway system was urgently needed. The growth of the turnpike web was encouraging, but it left most of the country untouched, and in 1954 President Eisenhower appointed a committee to look into the matter of creating a network of modern limited-access highways. Eisenhower was not just an ex-soldier but also a former military technocrat. After West Point, he attended not only the Army War College but also the Army Industrial College. His supervision of the D-Day landings had involved overseeing engineering works on a vast scale as well as a crucial military operation. Eisenhower was not a man to be daunted by the idea of establishing a state-of-the-art highway system. Nor, given the prevailing climate of the Cold War, was he unaware of the strategic importance of such a system.

To head his highway committee, Eisenhower selected Lucius Clay, who had trained as a military engineer and was famous as the man who had supervised the Berlin Airlift. Not surprisingly, his views were very much in line with the President's. An Interstate system would have military benefits, certainly, but beyond that, it was argued, it would help stimulate the economy. Most interested parties agreed with this in principle, but there were many differences as to how these desirable results should be achieved. The Clay Committee found itself confronted with a barrage of conflicting interests forcefully presented by lobbyists representing organizations ranging from the American Association of State Highway Officials to the American Automobile Association to the Farm Bureau Administration to the Asphalt Institute.

Some of these groups wanted the maximum possible federal intervention in the road program, while others feared that such intervention would erode their own power base. Congress came up with a solution that permitted Washington to supply 90 percent of the funds for Interstate development and establish standards for their construction, while leaving administration and maintenance of the highways to the individual states. Money would be raised by taxes levied on trucks, tires, gasoline and related products, and would be channeled through a specially created Highway Trust Fund. The Interstate Highway Act of 1956 provided for the construction of 41,000 miles of toll-free highways, which included retroactive federal funding of existing turnpikes. (Theoretically the turnpikes were expected to remove tolls when they received their retroactive funding, though in fact this rarely happened; now it was argued that the tolls were needed to pay for maintenance.)

Allocation of funds was to be on a pay-as-you-go basis, so that a given year's construction would be financed by that same year's tax revenues. This did not work entirely as expected, though, and in 1958 Congress lifted the pay-as-you-go provision. By then the Highway Trust had grown into a substantial bureaucracy that answered as much to the special interest groups that had helped shape it as to the federal government. Some economists have argued that, far from stimulating the general economy, the Interstate program in fact benefited only the auto industry and those special interest groups involved in road building, while at the same time contributing to a generally inflationary climate. In any event, passage of the Interstate

Highway Act did stimulate an unprecedented boom in superhighway construction, a boom that would last for two decades.

The standards set for the new highways and administered by the Bureau of Public Roads, which possessed broad veto powers, were extremely high so that even where sections of old road were incorporated into the network to take advantage of existing rights of way, expensive improvements were generally necessary.

Roads belonging to the National System of Interstate and Defense Highways were required to have at least four lanes, divided, and to be entirely free of intersections. Lanes were to be at least twelve feet wide and there were to be ten-foot-wide shoulders at both the outer and median edges of the highway. The median itself was to be a minimum of twenty-two feet wide, except where the terrain made this a practical impossibility. Grades should not slow down trucks unduly, which would hold up traffic. In mountainous areas where gentle grades were impossible, additional lanes would be provided to accommodate slower traffic. As in the interwar parkways, curves would be utilized to enhance the aesthetics, and also the safety, of the highways, but these would be broad and sweeping so that adequate sight lines could be maintained. Similarly, blind hills were to be eliminated, so sudden rises had to be flattened out. All engineering decisions were to be based on the expectation of vehicles moving at 70 miles per hour.

Although the Interstates were not planned primarily for pleasure driving, it was nonetheless understood from the first that these highways should blend as agreeably as possible with the landscape, should provide a means of enjoying the landscape, and should be free of the kind of strip development that had become so common along stretches of the existing primary system. Every effort was made, for instance, to keep billboards away from the interstates, though in practice it was impossible to prevent them from being placed on private land adjacent to the right of way, unless compensation was paid to the owners. The Beautification Act of 1965, strongly endorsed by President Johnson's wife, Lady Bird, was only partially successful in amending this situation.

For the most part, though, the rural sections of the new Interstates did adhere remarkably faithfully to the spirit as well as the letter of the original 1956 act, so that it is possible to drive across vast sections of America today without feeling that the highway is an encroachment upon the natural beauty of the landscape. Thousands of miles of Interstate highway unwind gently across prairies, deserts and mountains without causing offense to any but the most sensitive, actually enhancing the motorist's ability to enjoy America.

Inevitably there were some lapses of judgment, but in general the sheer scale of the American landscape made it relatively easy to tuck a superhighway away unobtrusively among its folds. Problems arose where scale changes required a more delicate touch. This was often the case along coastlines, for example, where highway planners understandably wished to provide scenic drives with views of the ocean. Sometimes this was achieved brilliantly, as in Monterey and San Luis Obispo counties, California, where California's Route 1 (not part of the Interstate System) snakes gracefully above the Pacific, affording spectacular vistas of Big Sur and Carmel without in any way interfering with the grandeur of the landscape. Farther north along the Pacific coast, however, there are too many instances of highways encroaching clumsily on beach areas, some of these roads being built on landfills that have altered for the worse the relationship between land and sea. The California Highway Commission permitted the razing of centuries-old redwoods to facilitate the construction of the Redwood Freeway, while in a number of instances national and state parks have been disfigured by thoughtless routing. In general, though, the rural sections of the Interstate System can be considered a success. The real problems occurred when the superhighways approached cities and penetrated the urban fabric itself.

Motorists approaching a relatively isolated city such as Denver experienced this most dramatically. Coming from the west by way of Interstate 70, you can drive for hundreds of miles without encountering any serious obstruction while enjoying scenery as magnificent as anything the continent has to offer. This is Interstate driving at its best. Descending from the Rockies, however, the texture of driving changes rapidly and takes on a flavor that is all too familiar to the commuter, no matter where he lives. The first warning is the sudden profusion of signs designed to accommodate an increase in frequency of exit ramps. The signs are large, in order to provide information to drivers traveling at speed, so that aside from the messages they impart they also have an insistent physical presence that helps to change the landscape already modified by the buildings that begin to cluster at the sides of the highway. As feeder roads merge with the Interstate, the Interstate widens, but still the traffic becomes more dense. With downtown Denver's anonymous high-rises clearly in view by now, the driver is suddenly in Anycity, U.S.A., where the highway serves to depersonalize the approach to the urban center, especially since the suburbs in its shadow tend to be transformed into industrial wastelands or downscale residential areas drained of any of their former character. If the driver has the misfortune to arrive during the rush hour he finds himself going from the sublime to the iniquitous so quickly he may become disoriented. If, on the other hand, he is accustomed to rush hours in New York or Los Angeles, he may think he has arrived on a bank holiday.

Nowhere are the problems inherent with urban superhighways more apparent than in New York City, and the tragic reality is that many of these problems were already obvious, to anyone displaying an ounce of common sense, two decades before the passage of the 1956 Interstate Highway Act. Common sense seldom prevails, however, where there are billions of dollars to be made, especially when some of those expenditures can be presented to the electorate in terms of thousands of jobs created. The electorate is rarely reminded of the remaining billions that end up in the pockets of construction company bosses, let alone the payoffs to organized crime that have so frequently been attendant upon major construction projects. Where New York was concerned, common sense was completely neutralized by the overwhelming presence of Robert Moses, whose vision of the city was certainly magnificent but not always rooted in reality. Although not much impressed by Norman Bel Geddes as a predictor of the future, Moses resembled him to the extent that he attempted to reinvent New York as if it were a toy city such as the one Bel Geddes had created for the GM pavilion at the 1939 World's Fair. It was easy to impose a master plan on a toy city. It would have been far more difficult to compose such a plan if the well-being of existing neighborhoods and the people who made up those neighborhoods had been taken into account. Moses was not entirely indifferent to people (though at times this certainly seemed to be the case), but he assumed that implementation of his master plan, so attractive on paper, would automatically improve the lot of men, women and children—who, he seemed to believe, would have little to live for without his intervention.

By the time the 1956 act was passed, Moses had long been entrenched in a unique position of power as the head of close to a dozen city and state agencies ranging from the New York State Council of Parks and the New York State Power Authority to the Triborough Bridge and Tunnel Authority and the Mayor's Slum Clearance Committee. None of these positions was dependent upon election or reelection by the state or city's voters, a fact that led Moses to see himself—and to be perceived by a large section of the public—as above politics, and hence above corruption. But it is power that corrupts, not politics, and over the decades Moses had accumulated more power than just about any New York politician. To a large extent he was answerable to no one, his position in New York being comparable in some ways to that of J. Edgar Hoover on a national scale. As head of the FBI, Hoover, too, was a nonelected official who thought himself above politics, though not above bending the political process to satisfy his own needs. Hoover saw Presidents come and go and accumulated a secret file on each one so he could keep the incumbent in line. Similarly, Moses saw mayors and governors come and go and for the most part treated them as passing inconveniences to be bent to his will. He did not have Hoover's access to secret files, but that hardly mattered because if necessary he simply resorted to open vituperation, not caring too much if his facts were right, as long as he made his point effectively. He was respectful of Fiorello La Guardia, but held his own when the two found themselves at odds. Lesser men than Fiorello stood little chance when confronted with Moses' self-righteous and self-justifying fury.

Moses' power did not depend upon federal funding, though he was not uninterested in such funding; as an adviser to Clay's committee he managed to win himself some important concessions. But principally he was a toll road mogul whose financial base was the millions of nickels and dimes collected on New York turnpikes. In his capacity as head of the Triborough Bridge and Tunnel Authority his base was the tolls collected at river crossings giving access to Manhattan; though the New York–New Jersey connections, such as the Holland and Lincoln tunnels, were controlled by the New York Port Authority, there was still plenty left for Moses. The river tolls focused his power on the very aspect of New York area transportation that caused the greatest practical problems. Manhattan was and is the business and cultural center of both the entire metropolitan area and the nation. It was a magnet for an enormous number of people, most of whom did not sleep there. Millions worked on this relatively small island and lived in the suburbs. A sizable portion of these commuters used public transportation, but Moses had a vested interest in encouraging as many as possible to travel by car. The fact that this could only exacerbate the already horrendous congestion in Manhattan did nothing to discourage him.

Critics such as the urban theorist Lewis Mumford had long warned of the dangers inherent in policies such as those pursued by both Moses and the Port Authority, and between the wars those warnings had been borne out by experience. The Holland Tunnel had been built to facilitate automobile traffic between New Jersey and Manhattan.

Since it was almost immediately operating at capacity during rush hours, the George Washington Bridge was constructed to relieve the congestion. This was soon jammed too, and attention turned to providing a new crossing, the Lincoln Tunnel. Again the same thing happened (eventually the GWB had to be double-decked), making it quite clear that the creation of the new access routes actually generated increased traffic to the point of surfeit. The phenomenon was not unique to New York, but it was especially aggravated there because of the size of the metropolitan area and the peculiar geographic location of its center. No one could deny that improved access to Manhattan was desperately needed, or that road bridges and tunnels were called for. In retrospect, however, it is incredible that administration after administration failed to give improved mass transportation any serious priority. Some other large cities might arguably have benefited from total automobilization (though it's easy enough to quarrel with that point of view), but New York provided a casebook example of a city that should have been shielded from excessive reliance upon the automobile at all cost. Yet even there the car was declared king, and its biggest champion was the nondriver Robert Moses.

Having established his toll crossings at such points as the Triborough Bridge and the Queens-Midtown Tunnel, Moses used the revenues they generated to create highways that would connect these crossings to the farther sections of the outer boroughs as well as to Long Island and Westchester County (and hence to upstate New York

A highway construction crew at work in New York City during the Robert Moses era.
UPI/Bettmann Newsphotos

and Connecticut). In doing so he could well have provided rights of way for mass transit links, as they might have come to be needed in the future, but he resolutely refused to allow anyone to force such considerations upon him, thus setting up much of the transportation crisis New York City faces today. It was suggested to him, for example, that with little increase in cost the Van Wyck Expressway could be constructed to provide an express rail link between Manhattan and Idlewild (now Kennedy) Airport. Moses rode roughshod over this proposal, with the result that Kennedy Airport still suffers from inadequate public transport links to Manhattan, while the Van Wyck is a nightmare for commuters and travelers alike, largely as a consequence of Moses' obstinacy.

Worse still, in creating his web of urban expressways Moses destroyed long-established neighborhoods with as little thought for the consequences, or compassion for those he dispossessed, as if he were exterminating cockroaches. As the city's slum-clearance czar, he routinely tore down thriving, if untidy and dense, tenement districts and replaced them with clusters of characterless, semi-high-rise apartment blocks—"projects"—that did nothing to beautify the city and rapidly deteriorated into vertical ghettos. Small wonder, then, that he had few if any qualms about dispossessing people in order to construct expressways— yet at times his planning seemed perverse beyond mere callousness. There is a point where the Cross Bronx Expressway takes an inexplicable juke to the north—inexplicable because this deviation cost the homes of thousands of people, whereas an equally viable route, taking advantage of public land, would have required the destruction of only a small number of buildings. Residents of the doomed East Tremont section of the Bronx fought long and hard to save their neighborhood, but all in vain, because public officials one after another backed down from their support of the citizenry when confronted with Moses' ire and scorn. The nearest Moses ever came to explaining why he would not consider the less destructive alternate route was to suggest that it would have entailed destruction of a bus depot—which belonged to a transportation company that possessed a good deal of political clout. It has been suggested, though never proved, that one reason Moses passed over the alternate route was because its implementation would have involved destruction of property belonging to one of his cronies.

Cronyism finally caught up with Moses. He was far too high-minded to accept graft himself, but the power structure he created was dependent upon the support of less scrupulous individuals, some of whom benefited enormously from the roles he assigned them in the realization of his grandiose projects. In the late fifties and sixties this began to draw the attention of the New York press, which had previously treated him as if he were infallible, and unfavorable media stories gradually turned the tide against him until politicians like Nelson Rockefeller were able to call his bluff and strip him of his titles and power.

The story of Robert Moses' passage from idealist to despot has been told in suitably epic terms by Robert A. Caro in *The Power Broker,* which is essential reading for anyone who wishes to understand the impact of the automobile and the highway upon American life, and especially upon the city. The complexity of the story makes it impossible to summarize, except to say that today's New York is still in large part the creation of Moses. He left exquisite parkways, magnificent bridges, beaches and recreation areas that are essential to the region's wellbeing. Yet his urban expressways did enormous damage to the fabric of the city and set up a pattern of transit that at times threatens to bring New York to a standstill. Mercifully he was never permitted to drive his expressways across Manhattan, as he wanted to do.

At least Moses was forced to finance his own follies. His involvement in spending federal money after passage of the 1956 Interstate Act was limited by New York City's location and the fact that the Port Authority controlled the Hudson River approach to Manhattan, hence the link between New York and New Jersey upon which federal funding of Interstate highways depended. By forming a temporary alliance with the Port Authority, Moses was able to participate in and control the building of the Verrazano

Narrows Bridge linking Staten Island and Brooklyn, which is part of the Interstate system and which he considered his finest achievement. There is no telling what he might have attempted had he had greater access to federal funding. As it is, his very prominent example seems to have inspired many colleagues elsewhere who *did* receive financing from Washington.

Two of the most attractive cities on the West Coast, San Francisco and Seattle, have had substantial sections of their picturesque waterfronts ruined by thoughtless placement of especially ugly superhighway structures. Public criticism of such eyesores did not prevent planners elsewhere from proposing schemes that were chilling in their disregard for the existing urban fabric. To give a single example, a section of Interstate 310, the so-called Riverfront–Elysian Fields Expressway, was slated to run as an elevated highway smack through the historic French Quarter of New Orleans, despite the fact that the entire Vieux Carré was designated a national landmark. Not surprisingly this proposal ran into fierce opposition, but the planners adhered stubbornly to their scheme for several years, until the route was eventually vetoed by John Volpe, President Nixon's secretary of transportation.

Such extreme abuses were not the main problem, however. Rather it was that superhighways tend to be out of scale with the preexisting architecture of most older cities. The American landscape can absorb expressways without much difficulty, and in spread-out cities like Los Angeles and Houston, elevated highways can take on a monumental and sculptural character that is positively exhilarating. In San Francisco, on the other hand, the freeways entering the city seem to have been placed there by some childish giant and bear no relationship to the proportions of the architecture that is so crucial to the city's character. Few other cities display the delicacy of architectural balance to be found in San Francisco, but even so they are seldom able to accommodate the urban expressway with any degree of grace; older cities have found that neighborhoods in the shadow of the expressway are subject to accelerated decay. Beyond that the urban expressway contributes to the congestion of the city it supposedly serves and is both directly and indirectly a major source of pollution.

Another by-product of the growing web of Interstates, especially on the fringe of the cities, was the evolution of a new kind of highly concentrated shopping strip located near entrance and exit ramps. These strips did not replace the old ones, which in many places continued to thrive, but they had a character of their own. They did not grow gradually in slow increments of Mom and Pop businesses but rather mushroomed overnight, fueled by the capital available to chain stores such as Sears and Safeway and by the explosion of franchise outlets selling everything from fried chicken to bar stools and dinette sets. Often the focus for a given strip was provided by a cluster of businesses herded together to form a shopping center, a format that would eventually be superseded by the mall. Often, too, lodging was to be found on these exit-ramp strips, usually in one or more of the new franchise-type supermotels such as a Howard Johnson's or Holiday Inn.

The credit for this new kind of supermotel—actually half auto court, half city-style hotel—belongs chiefly to Kemmons Wilson, a Memphis builder who launched the first Holiday Inn in the early fifties, apparently inspired by his difficulties in finding satisfactory accommodations while traveling with his family. Postwar tourists who wanted to see America first and the younger breed of traveling salesman were looking for a degree of comfort provided by relatively few of the prewar "tourist courts." Wilson envisioned a motel with rooms large enough for two double beds, modern toilet facilities, a clean restaurant, Coke machines and free ice, a swimming pool and some of the services offered by city hotels. The prototype he built had 120 rooms, making it huge by the standards of the day. It quickly proved popular. From the outset, Wilson was thinking in terms of franchising Holiday Inns (the name was borrowed from the eponymous Bing Crosby–Fred Astaire movie). Initially he encountered a good deal of resistance to the idea of franchising something as expensive to build as this kind of motel, especially since he would have no truck with lowering the standards he had established. The first investors found themselves doing solid year-round business, however, and momentum began to grow rapidly as people realized that each well-managed Holiday Inn would generate business for every other Holiday Inn.

By the time the Interstate building program began, Holiday Inns were well established in many parts of the country, their presence being made known, day and night, by "the great sign," an extraordinary piece of fifties heraldry, a fragment of Vegas glitz colonizing the hinterland, a free-standing cousin of Hollywood's kidney-shaped swimming pools. The masterpiece of an otherwise unsung artist named Eddie Bluestein, "the great sign" had the virtue of being a conspicuously recognizable piece of public sculpture while at the same time being capable of embodying a degree of intimacy. The emblematic star and arrow were instantly recognizable from the highway, yet the sign also accommodated a movie theater–style marquee that was apt to greet the tired new arrival with such salutations as CONGRATULATIONS BOBBY JEAN! or WELCOME IDAHO ELKS. Even if you were not Bobby Jean or an Idaho Elk, it gave you a warm feeling to know they were there.

The rates at Holiday Inns were modest, but even so some people couldn't afford them. Among this group in the mid-fifties was Colonel Harlan Sanders of Kentucky, who at the age of sixty-six was attempting to franchise his recipe for fried chicken. That recipe (actually the chickens were cooked in pressure cookers) had earned him local fame and the honorary title of Kentucky Colonel, bestowed by Governor Ruby Laffon when he operated Sanders Court, a restaurant on Route 25 in Corbin, Kentucky. The restaurant was a success for close to twenty years, until Interstate 75 was opened in 1955, taking traffic seven miles to the west. Overnight the Colonel's business was destroyed and he was forced to auction off his property. On the day his first social security check arrived, he set out to franchise his secret chicken recipe.

While his own restaurant was still in operation, he had signed licensing agreements with half a dozen other eating places to use his recipe, and this was the shallow foundation on which he hoped to build. Traveling around the South and the Midwest, often sleeping in his car for lack of funds, he would try to persuade restaurant operators at least to try his formula. Confronted by this quaint character with his goatee and white suit—a persona he had perfected at Sanders Court—many managers were convinced they were dealing with a lunatic. The few who listened were persuaded to let him cook for their staff after hours. If the staff was impressed (and in those days the Sanders product was excellent), the Colonel asked to stick around for a few days and cook for regular customers, free of charge. Working this way he managed to sell a few franchises, charging his new business partners four cents for each chicken cooked according to his secret formula. Gradually he built up a reputation and restaurateurs began to seek him out. Still running his operation from the tiny office he had built at the back of his house, by 1960 Sanders had over two hundred outlets that by 1963 had grown to six hundred.

Ray Kroc was a dozen years younger than Harlan Sanders when, at almost exactly the same time, he made his grab for the brass ring. During prohibition Kroc had played piano at the Silent Night, an upscale Florida speakeasy. The thing that he always remembered about this operation was its amazing efficiency, which was based on streamlined service. There were only three items—steak, lobster and roast duckling—on the menu, and all drinks cost one dollar, whether you ordered beer or champagne. He rediscovered that same efficiency three decades later when he first set eyes on Maurice and Richard McDonald's drive-in, located just off Route 66 in San Bernardino, California.

After his stint as a pianist Kroc had worked as a salesman, selling first paper cups, then the Multimixer, a device that could prepare five milkshakes at a time. Both these jobs brought him into contact with large chain-store and franchise operations, such as Walgreen and Dairy Queen, and provided him with a basic education in the science of mass marketing.

In 1954 Kroc's interest was piqued by the fact that a single drive-in in San Bernardino, McDonald's Famous

Hamburgers, would find it necessary to place an order for eight Multimixers. What kind of place required the capacity to produce forty milkshakes at a time? A little research confirmed that the McDonald brothers were doing land-office business, and at the first opportunity Kroc jumped on a plane to check out the drive-in for himself. What he found was a smallish octagonal building in the middle of a sizable parking lot. A little before eleven A.M., Kroc sat in his rented car and watched as employees crisply dressed in white shirts, pants and hats began to arrive and to haul potatoes and ground meat from a shed to the drive-in. At eleven precisely the first customers arrived. They were served with amazing briskness, purchasing their hamburgers at one window, french fries at another. Lines quickly developed, but even so there was no long wait, and the food was extraordinarily cheap, even by mid-fifties standards. A hamburger cost fifteen cents, fries were a dime, and a sixteen-ounce milkshake sold for twenty cents. That was the extent of the menu. Kroc talked to some of the customers and learned that most of them were frequent visitors to the drive-in. Some came daily and almost everyone cited reliable quality and low price as the reasons for the McDonalds' success. Fast service helped too, as did well-maintained rest rooms and a general ambience of cleanliness and efficiency.

According to most published accounts, Kroc was the man who first thought of franchising this operation. In fact the McDonald brothers had already begun to license their business, and by the end of 1954 eight franchises were scattered from Phoenix, Arizona (the first), to Sacramento, California. Unlike the San Bernardino operation, these branches even featured the Golden Arches—they were actually structural elements in the buildings—the brothers having commissioned Stanley Meston, a California architect, to come up with an eye-catching design. The McDonalds' ambitions were limited, however. They saw the restaurants as traditional drive-in operations, with little or no indoor seating. They thought their success was dependent on the year-round mild climate found in California and the Southwest.

Kroc thought otherwise. He believed that the basic idea could be adapted to other situations and climates. The brothers were skeptical, but Kroc persisted and persuaded them to let him use their name and expertise, in return for which they would receive a royalty for every franchise sold. Returning to his Chicago base, Kroc set about building a pilot unit in Des Plaines, Illinois, not far from the site of O'Hare Airport.

Over a period of about a year, Kroc and his staff labored at perfecting both product and procedures. The McDonald brothers' french fries, Kroc realized, were absolutely crucial to the success of the San Bernardino operation. He claimed they were the best he had ever tasted, but try as they might to reproduce the San Berdoo fries, his cooks found something was always missing—the fries were not quite crispy enough. Then one day Kroc discovered that the problem was not in the actual cooking process but in the prestorage of the potatoes. The San Berdoo fries were made from potatoes that had been naturally cured by the dry desert air. Kroc installed an electric fan in the basement of his Des Plaines restaurant and attempted to reproduce the desert environment. After considerable experimentation he succeeded in curing potatoes in just the right way; he finally had discovered the secret of making his ideal french fries.

While perfecting the product, Kroc also worked on streamlining service, as it was his intention to improve upon the already speedy San Bernardino operation. His target was to supply the customer with a burger, fries and a milkshake in fifty seconds flat. Everything would be standardized—somewhat like a Model T Ford. Buns would be exactly 3.5 inches in diameter; the basic hamburger patty would be 3.875 inches in diameter before cooking and weigh 1.6 ounces. It would contain not more than 19 percent fat and no offal or cereal.

Another lesson Kroc learned from the McDonald brothers was that the restaurants should be kept immaculately clean and that they should appeal primarily to the family trade. Teenagers were not discouraged from the San Bernardino drive-in, but the McDonalds made a point of providing no jukeboxes, pay phones or cigarette machines, so that the restaurant remained an efficient food-serving machine rather than becoming a hangout for hot-rodders. Kroc enthusiastically embraced the same policy.

In 1955 he began to sell franchises, and by 1957 thirty-seven units were operating. Two years later the magic one hundred figure was passed, and as new branches opened people were driving miles just to see this remarkable place where hamburgers still sold for fifteen cents. Each unit was built according to Kroc's exacting specifications and was fronted with the Golden Arches, which like "the great sign" and Kentucky Fried Chicken's revolving tub became ubiquitous at exactly the moment in time that the new Interstate exit ramp strips were proliferating.

Financial success for the growing McDonald's chain came in several different ways. Individual franchisers purchased instant recognition—along with national advertising—and an easily set-up and efficient operation that required only minimal management skills to be profitable. Kroc and his associates made money from providing the meat patties and other comestibles served on the deliberately circumscribed menu, and from licensing revenue. They also made an even greater fortune in real estate, the province of a Kroc associate named Harry Sonneborn. Once the company was financially healthy, Sonneborn advocated that McDonald's should purchase suitable properties and lease them to the franchises. At first relatively inexpensive sites were selected, in the middle of a block rather than close to the prime and hence more expensive corner sites, but positioned nevertheless to take advantage of traffic flow. (In the new strips as in the old, the corner sites tended to attract the gas stations belonging to the big oil companies.) Such center-block locations served Mc-Donald's very well and soon rival franchises came to cluster near them; hoping to catch spill-over business, they incidentally greatly enhanced the value of McDonald's own property. When, starting in the sixties, McDonald's began to move into city centers, they found themselves in control of many enormously valuable properties and a real estate empire that stretched from New York to San Diego.

Still the old and new commercial strips provided franchises like Kentucky Fried Chicken and McDonald's with their natural habitat. Drivers could roll off I-95 or I-10 wherever they saw the Golden Arches and be sure of exactly what they would find, in terms of both menu and quality. To say that a revolution in eating habits had been achieved is no exaggeration. When Colonel Sanders ran his Sanders Court restaurant, from the thirties to the early fifties, customers stopped there because he could offer them a unique gastronomic experience, the best chicken dinner on Route 25. A few years later they were exiting from I-75 to eat at a Kentucky Fried Chicken franchise—any Kentucky Fried Chicken franchise—because it promised a homogenized approximation of those once legendary chicken dinners. Security and sameness were what the franchises offered, and whether one likes it or not, it was what the American public wanted. When a McDonald's franchise was opened opposite the McDonald brothers' original San Bernardino drive-in, the drive-in was forced out of business.

If Kentucky Fried Chicken and McDonald's were among the leaders, they soon had plenty of company: Burger King, Wendy's, Arby's, Dunkin' Donuts, Taco Bell, Pizza Hut, Popeye's and the rest. Nor was the company just fast-food outlets. Very quickly the franchising craze spread to everything from specialized auto repairs to health care, fueling the growth of companies like AAMCO Transmissions and United Dental Networks, not to mention beauty-shop chains such as Edie Adams's Cut & Curl, real estate offices like Century-21, and tax specialists owing allegiance to H & R Block.

One of the most surprising successes was that of Midas Muffler, which took one of the humblest and most easily replaceable items in the automobile's bag of tricks and repackaged it so that it seemed almost glamorous. It's easy enough to understand why someone would bring their transmission problems to AAMCO or Mr. Transmission, since gearboxes are notably arcane items not to be entrusted to gas station mechanics, or to specialists with dollar signs in their eyes. The transmission franchises offered reliable service and reasonable fixed prices. But a muffler replacement can be entrusted to just about anyone in oil-stained dungarees, even if he has a watchful friend called George and answers to the name Lennie. Midas painted its mufflers gold and launched a massive advertising campaign aimed at women drivers and other presumed auto-illiterates. "You probably don't give much thought to your muffler," was the tenor of the campaign, "but it might interest you to know that it serves a very important purpose, and the chances are you could use a new one." Enough people listened to this seemingly innocent message, with its blatantly scornful subtext ("What do you know about cars, anyway?"), to enable Midas Muffler to thrive and eventually to offer more demanding specializations.

The lesson was that anything suitably packaged could be sold, and anything that could be sold could be franchised. So it was that the great franchise chains grew up alongside the widening network of Interstates. Now it was possible to buy the same hamburger in Spokane that you purchased last week in Savannah, or sleep in the same bed in Bakersfield that you slept in in Bowling Green. There was no states' rights problem as far as the franchises were concerned, and regional or ethnic accents were just something to use in television commercials to push ribs or pizza. Southern Fried Chicken was the same whether you found it in the Deep South or in Alaska. This was the melting pot in action. Chicanos in Texas served Arthur Treacher's Fish and Chips while blacks in Ohio learned to build tacos. And that melting pot worked more efficiently in the franchise world than in America as a whole, so that soon its consequences were manifested in identical signs, identical color combinations, identical mansard roofs, proclaiming the presence of identical products from coast to coast. If the old commercial strips had been anarchic in character, the new ones (not to mention colonized sections of the old) were an expression of pandemic conformism.

In his book *Open Road*, Phil Patton has written at length about the utility and symbolism of the mansard roof. For the franchisers of the fifties and sixties, this distant derivative of the roofs of Paris served three key purposes.

At a purely functional level, it was an easy way of dressing up a simple glass-and-concrete box and turning it into something sculptural and eye-catching. At a symbolic level, it spelled instant respectability, recalling, for instance, the architectural language of the tasteful restaurants, usually built from local stone, that had been approved by local authorities for lay-bys on parkways and early turnpikes. It was also a valuable advertising tool, since there were innumerable ways in which it could be personalized. If a chain was selling fried chicken and wished to signify its down-home roots, the mansard might be covered with carefully rusticated shingles. A chain selling quasi-Mexican food might clad its mansard with Spanish pantiles, either real or molded onto plastic panels. Or the mansard could simply be painted in bold stripes. Sometimes it was topped with a vaguely *moderne* pagodalike spire.

Under those hard-working roofs the structures were usually very basic, but even so they were carefully thought out. Some businesses, especially fast-food outlets, retained the drive-up windows of the classic drive-ins, if not the curb service. Almost all franchise operations made a feature of huge, panoramic windows. Few of these windows overlooked scenic views—rather, they tended to provide vistas of the parking lot and the highway, but that was the whole point. Fast and inexpensive service—whether food or a transistor radio was being purchased—was the purpose of the exercise, and this was integral with the notion of mobility associated with the automobilized shopping strip. Franchised businesses were designed to be noticed from the highway. Once they had captured a consumer, however, they permitted him to retain visual contact with the highway so that his secondary mission—to be on his way as quickly as possible—might not be forgotten. McDonald's was not alone in not wanting its restaurants to turn into hangouts. Inner and outer space flowed together in a way that made consuming a sundae at Dairy Queen part of the highway experience.

The shopping centers that also sprang up near exit ramps had some things in common with the new commercial strips, but in other respects they operated on a different philosophy. Certainly they displayed their share of mansard roofs, but they did not pretend to interact with the highway in quite the same way as Bun N Burger or Mister Donut, because they sought to encourage the motorist to stay and browse awhile, or at least to provide him with that option.

Although the car-oriented shopping center had its roots in the era of the Model T, in the fifties the concept really came into its own. The idea of a number of structurally related businesses sharing a single parking lot was an almost inevitable offshoot of the commercial strip. Such proto–shopping centers were transformed, however, by the arrival in the suburbs of department stores looking for new customers, as well as by the growth of large drugstore and supermarket chains. The participation of such big-time operations in the development of shopping centers led to the replacement of random growth with careful planning. A typical complex of the fifties would have a branch of a department store chain at one end and a discount store or large drugstore at the other, joined by a row of smaller businesses. Some of the latter were franchise operations but many were locally owned stores of the sort that might previously have established themselves along the highway on some commercial strip. A supermarket was sometimes integrated with this complex, or located adjacent to the other stores while still sharing the parking lot. Often one or more free-standing restaurants, either franchise outlets or old-style diners, would be located at the perimeter of the lot with their own parking facilities and direct access from the highway.

The complex was conceived in such a way as to give customers an option. Someone needing a can of paint, for example, could park a few yards from the hardware store, run in, make his purchase, hurry back to his car and be on his way in minutes. On the other hand, a couple with a greater number of purchases to make might be tempted to linger and even impersonate old-time pedestrians. The department stores in particular encouraged a very leisurely shopping pace. Understaffed, by city store standards, they operated almost like supermarkets, permitting the customers to wander among the racks and take all the time they needed. The grouping of department stores with smaller operations also offered the possibility of comparison shopping on a limited scale, so that the price of a pair of shoes at Penney's could be weighed against the price of a similar pair at the Shoe Inn. Businesses in shopping centers tended to downplay show windows. Unlike their cousins along the nearby strip, they had no interest in promoting the continuum with the highway. They understood very well that they were dependent upon the automobile, but they were intent on holding on to customers as long as possible. They saw themselves as surrogates for the Main Streets of yesterday, frequently adopting names such as Delaware Village, or Greenwood Acres, that suggested a link with the past.

Such shopping centers and their flashier descendants still exist by the thousands, but they were soon superseded by a new concept that was to have more far-reaching consequences. In the mid-fifties a few developers were beginning to experiment with more elaborate shopping complexes: some were built around attractive patios, others were double-decker centers such as the one the Rouse Company built in Baltimore. Meanwhile, Dayton's, the Macy's of Minneapolis, and Hudson's, the Gimbel's of Detroit, joined forces to develop suburban sites. Their first effort was a complex called Northland in Detroit. Far more than just a shopping center, its 250 acres eventually encompassed a hotel and a hospital along with apartment and office buildings. The architect of Northland, Victor Gruen, was hatching an even more radical scheme, however: an entirely enclosed, multilevel shopping complex that drew inspiration from the pedestrian arcades of such European structures as the Galleria Vittorio Emanuele in Milan. Like the Galleria, it would be a place where people came not only to shop but also to meet and eat and be entertained. In Gruen's mind, such a place would be both a commercial complex and a social center. It would accommodate two competing department stores (a heretical idea at the time) as well as scores of smaller businesses, including cafés and restaurants. Because all these smaller businesses would be within a single basic structure, they would be cheaper to build than in a conventional shopping center, and they would of course occupy less ground space.

This scheme ran into considerable skepticism, but it made a great deal of sense to the directors of Dayton's; they saw that such a plan was ideally suited to their home turf, where bitter winters made the operation of conventional shopping centers marginal for months at a time. An enclosed, climate-controlled shopping center seemed entirely sensible to men who worked in a city where enclosed bridges between buildings and heated sidewalks were already a winter commonplace. They approved Gruen's basic scheme and located a suitable site in Edina, a Minneapolis suburb.

Southdale, as the complex was christened, opened in 1956 and from the first it was a triumphant success. Not only did it provide a comfortable place to shop in subzero weather, it also offered an exhilarating visual experience. To come upon the soaring central garden court was like stepping for the first time into the lobby of Radio City Music Hall or the concourse of Grand Central Station. This was not just an architecture of convenience; it was an architectural event. And the drama of the garden court was matched by the general gracefulness with which the entire enterprise was realized. Even today, Southdale, considerably expanded, is a handsome complex. In 1956 it must have seemed like a wonderland. Moreover it did impressive business, proving that the American consumer could be converted into a pedestrian once again. The catch was that this consumer would still need a car to reach the place where he could practice his rediscovered art. The parking lot around Southdale was the largest in the state, until Metropolitan Stadium was built a few years later in next-door Bloomington to accommodate the Minnesota Twins.

Southdale remains a landmark. In one bold step, Victor Gruen and his astute backers had created the Great American Mall.

Taken during a 1953 Los Angeles smog alert, these photographs show
thickening pollution over Hollywood at one-hour intervals,
starting at 8:00 A.M. *UPI/Bettmann*

Chapter 12

AUTOMOVILLE II

Wednesday, September 8, 1943, was a day that traumatized the city of Los Angeles. It was far more unexpected than an earthquake, as shocking almost as the attack on Pearl Harbor. Quite a few citizens did, in fact, think that this was the prelude to a Japanese invasion. Drivers approaching the city that morning on the new Arroyo Seco Parkway and commuters on Pacific Electric's Big Red Cars saw to their horror that the entire downtown area was smothered in a blanket of sulphurous fumes. City Hall, the tower of the library and other landmarks were almost invisible. And the blanket spread far from downtown, plunging Hollywood into gloom, making eyes smart from Watts to Beverly Hills. LA had been smothered by the first of the great Southern California smogs.

This was not the first time smog had struck an American city. Air pollution was well known in industrial centers back East, and the term "smog" had been used in the thirties to describe the chemical-laden fogs that sometimes enveloped the Pittsburg area. But this was different! This was the land of eternal sunshine! Things like this were not

249

supposed to happen in LA. And how was this smog being generated? It seemed out of all proportion to the density of industrial pollution in such a spread-out city.

The Spaniards who initially colonized the Los Angeles basin called the area the Bay of Smokes, an allusion to the persistence of the Indian campfires so characteristic of the LA littoral that sailors could recognize it from far out at sea. There were plenty of Indian campfires elsewhere, of course, but south and north of the Los Angeles basin the smoke from those fires was dispersed by morning and evening breezes blowing either off the ocean or down from the mountains. Around the Town of Our Lady the Queen of the Angels of Porciuncula, however, campfire smoke generally behaved differently. The breezes there were for the most part too gentle to dispel it. Except when the dreaded Santa Ana winds blew, creating other problems, the air above the Los Angeles littoral and the adjacent inland valleys was remarkably still. Later, after the arrival of the first Yankee migrants, the same phenomenon was noted when citrus ranchers lit smudge pots to protect their crops on frosty nights. The following day the smoke would often hang there for hours. More significant from a pollution point of view were the backyard incinerators that became the normal way of disposing of garbage in many LA neighborhoods, until they were banned in 1957. These too produced plumes of smoke that frequently just hung in the air as if they had nowhere to go.

In retrospect this phenomenon can be seen as a warning, though one that nobody could have recognized at the time. The Los Angeles basin happens to be extremely well suited geographically and meteorologically to the nourishment and containment of smog. The persistent smoke plumes were a symptom of this.

Clearly, though, the LA smog was in some ways different from anything that had been observed back East or in Europe. There the obvious culprits were industrial emissions or, as in the case of London, the burning of soft coal. The smog in Los Angeles had little to do with smoke and nothing to do with fog, and if the saffron blanket itself came as a shock, the discovery of its primary cause was equally sensational. Certainly there was an industrial element to LA smog, but the chief culprit was the automobile, the very thing that had enabled Los Angeles to develop into a modern Arcadia. Motor vehicles pumped tens of thousands of tons of unburned hydrocarbons into the atmosphere above Los Angeles every day in the form of gasoline vapor. In the early sixties, a smog engineer estimated that the unburned fuel escaping into LA's air every day would fill a mile-long line of tanker trucks parked bumper to bumper. Motor vehicles also emitted nitrogen oxides and other chemicals as a by-product of the combustion system. Because of the relative stillness of the air, these chemicals were slow to disperse. Often they were further trapped by high-pressure systems moving in from the Pacific Ocean, systems that created a temperature inversion by placing a "lid" of warm air over the cooler air beneath. This lid caused hydrocarbons and other potential pollutants to be caught between mountain ranges, or between mountains and the ocean. Sunlight "cooked" these trapped substances, which underwent a photochemical process that turned them into smog, the noxious vapor that endangered the health of humans and animals and was capable of killing crops and trees, as eventually happened in the Los Angeles National Forest and elsewhere.

This was trouble in paradise, but it failed to cause total despair among the hardy optimists of Southern California. As it happened, the arrival of the smog coincided with a tremendous spurt of growth for LA and the surrounding communities, the greatest since the twenties. Few other cities benefited as much as LA from World War II. The war sent to the West Coast new industries such as steel production, and created a boom in aircraft manufacture as well as in a variety of high-tech fields. The war also brought tens of thousands of servicemen to California; some were stationed there and some were en route to the Pacific theater, but many of them were sufficiently impressed with what they saw to return after the war seeking jobs.

Among the typical sights of LA in the Depression were abandoned developments where streets had been laid out but only a handful of homes had been built before the economy went into its decade-long slump. As the forties progressed, the mesquite and poppy fields that had overgrown these tracts were mown down, the cracks in the concrete roadways were filled in, and new houses began to spring up, reviving dreams that had crashed with the stock market. From Pacific Palisades to Torrance, many of the open spaces—lyrical wastelands—that had been so characteristic of the city in the thirties began to disappear. And out beyond the existing limits of the metropolitan area, in Orange County and parts of the San Gabriel Valley that had been ignored by the interurbans, brand-new auto suburbs began to appear, just as they did in other parts of the country. Here there was greater urgency, as developers brought in heavy equipment to crop hillsides so that houses could be perched perilously above canyons that had previously been home to coyotes and sidewinders. It was a pattern of development that would continue until the Los Angeles metropolitan area had become the second most populous in the nation.

One area that saw especially rapid development in the postwar years was the San Fernando Valley. The real estate significance of the Valley had been recognized as long ago as 1909, when the Los Angeles Suburban Homes Company, founded by Harry Chandler and Harrison Gray Otis of the *Los Angeles Times,* among others, acquired 47,500 acres of wheatland there. Because of its location near burgeoning Ventura Boulevard, much of this acreage was developed relatively early, aided by William Mulholland's aqueduct, which brought water to the Valley in 1913. The wholesale peopling of the Valley did not begin until the mid-forties, however, when its 150-plus square miles suddenly came to seem like a developer's dream. Here was a vast expanse of flatlands that was relatively inexpensive and easy to build on because no terracing of hillsides was required (except at the foot of the mountains where spectacular views made the erection of luxury homes viable). Only a few sections of the Valley enjoyed public transportation, but the already completed section of the Cahuenga Freeway—soon to be the Hollywood Freeway—

gave quick access to downtown and Hollywood, while good surface roads through Laurel and Coldwater canyons and the Sepulveda Pass provided access to the Sunset Strip area, Beverly Hills, the fashionable residential West Side, and also to the ocean. A freeway through the Sepulveda Pass was promised for the near future.

It was easy for realtors to sell homes in the San Fernando Valley, especially in the late forties and fifties, when there were still ranches and alfalfa fields here and there to give it a semirural character. Its limits clearly defined by mountain ranges, its gardens made green by water from the Owens Valley, 240 miles away, this was Shangri-la for the middle class and even for blue-collar workers such as those who worked at the Lockheed plant in Van Nuys. Humble residents of the Valley were even provided with a touch of glamour by proximity to movie studios like Warner Brothers, Universal and Disney, and to movie star homes in enclaves such as Toluca Lake. In fact, movie and radio stars like Bob Hope played a significant role in the postwar development of the Valley.

All you needed to enjoy this Shangri-la was an automobile. This was especially so when the Pacific Electric began to curtail service. Beginning a couple of years after the war, traffic in the Valley changed dramatically. There had been a time when streets like Sherman Way and Reseda Boulevard were given over largely to farm trucks. Now they became busy thoroughfares traveled by thousands of cars every day, cars that came home at night to the new grids of tract homes that had been fitted into the larger, irregular grid of broad boulevards with which the Valley was already provided. The consequences were not long in appearing. The San Fernando Valley proved to be an almost perfect breeding ground for smog, and by the early sixties health alerts there were more frequent than on the other side of the Santa Monica Mountains. It was discovered that the population brought there by the automobile was actually changing the climate: sprinklers and swimming pools were perceptibly raising the humidity, making summers less pleasant than before. The Shangri-la image became somewhat tarnished, but still people

continued to pour in because the Valley remained an affordable place to live and continued to have more to offer than many other cities and their suburbs. Smog and a paltry increase in humidity notwithstanding, for many people the climate was still preferable to anything found back East, and the Valley still provided easy access to the ocean and to spectacular mountain and desert wildernesses, as well as to the glamour of show business. Jokes about the Valley, common by the sixties, might hurt, but you weren't likely to hear them from your neighbors as you strolled the spacious aisles of a Von's supermarket or cooked T-bone steaks on a gas-fired barbecue under the pepper trees in your backyard.

The Hollywood Freeway in the 1950s, when freeway driving was usually a pleasurable experience. *American Stock Photos*

The San Fernando Valley took on symbolic significance, first for Los Angeles and eventually for the whole country, as the ultimate example of the motorized suburb. The fact that it is a patchwork of communities—Burbank, Encino, Reseda, and so on—with distinct personalities to those who live there was lost in this collective identity, an identity that was strongly reinforced by the arrival of the freeways.

The war had interrupted development of the freeway system, and progress remained slow for several years after the war, but this was for practical, financial reasons and not in any sense because the city or the state had backed off from the belief that a network of superhighways was needed to knit the metropolitan area together. An increase in state taxes in 1953 provided capital to begin freeway building on a substantial basis once more, and the passage of the Interstate Highway Act in 1956 gave the impetus needed for full commitment to a freeway system. In 1959 the California State Legislature adopted a program that called for 12,500 miles of freeways statewide. Of this total, 1,570 miles were to be concentrated in Ventura, Los Angeles and Orange counties. In effect this meant that LA's prewar freeway plan could now be implemented in its entirety. Since seven of the area's freeways would be considered part of the Interstate System, the bulk of the funding would come from the federal government, the remainder from a California gasoline tax and other car-use taxes.

Because there is little high-density housing in the Los Angeles area, situations such as that created by the Cross Bronx Expressway's invasion of the East Tremont section in New York were largely avoidable. Even so, one freeway, the seventeen-mile-long Santa Monica Freeway, required the acquisition of 4,129 parcels of land at a cost of 95 million dollars. Close to 15,000 people lost their homes and numerous businesses were displaced. Despite this there was relatively little protest. The prices paid for properties were considered fair on the whole, and Angelenos displayed a willingness to move that was very different from the mood in long-established New York neighborhoods threatened by expressways.

Among the first freeways to be built after the war were the Santa Ana (an extension of the Hollywood Freeway south into Orange County) and the Harbor Freeway (the southward extension of the Arroyo Seco Parkway). These intersected at downtown Los Angeles where they were later joined by the Santa Monica Freeway, which fed into a beltway system that hooked up with the San Bernardino, Pomona and Golden State freeways. The intersections thus created in and around downtown LA were extraordinarily complex and often confusing to visiting motorists. Much photographed, for a score or more years they were treated as one of the wonders of the modern world. This convergence of superhighways, most of them eight lanes wide, helped restore to the downtown area a focus it had been losing as the city spread outward. The convergence did not prevent downtown's degeneration as a residential area, however. Rather, it encouraged the development of new office buildings and large hotels, a trend that gained momentum when the building code was revised to permit the erection of full-scale skyscrapers. These generated an increasing need for parking lots and garages, until it was estimated that close to two thirds of the ground area downtown was given over to either moving traffic or parked vehicles.

But LA was different from other cities in that downtown was not necessarily the primary hub of the superhighway system. Long before the freeways were built, the metropolitan area had developed other significant centers, for example, Glendale and Pasadena to the north, Pomona and San Bernardino to the east, Long Beach and San Pedro to the south, Beverly Hills and Santa Monica to the west. In addition the freeways helped open up relatively underbuilt areas, such as much of Orange County, and encouraged the growth of new commercial complexes like Century City, a high-density office, retail and residential development built on the site of the Twentieth Century–Fox back lot. Not all freeways led to Rome. Instead, in this system many significant points in a wide-spread metropolitan area were linked by a network of limited-access highways that were deliberately designed to enhance the decentralized character of the area. The majority of the millions using the system once it was in place rarely set foot in downtown Los Angeles.

The first of the postwar freeways were hardly miracles of engineering. Parts of the Santa Ana, for example, were built to prewar standards that barely matched those achieved by the first autobahns twenty years earlier. The consequence was that the Santa Ana quickly became notorious for accidents and rush-hour congestion. Conditions rapidly improved, however, especially following the injection of federal funds into the program. Later freeways were the equal of highways built anywhere until that time, and the finest freeways were examples for the rest of the world. Some details of the system, such as the graceful intersection of the Santa Monica and San Diego freeways, raised civil engineering to the level of art and can be compared with the finest achievements of bridge builders in the nineteenth and twentieth centuries. This intersection and others in the system are dramatically beautiful to look at and exhilarating to use. Given good driving conditions, in fact, the freeway system as a whole is exhilarating to use, and driving its elevated sections is the LA equivalent of viewing Paris from the Eiffel Tower: the city spreads out below, clusters of tall buildings and lines of palm trees stand out against the mountains. The movement of the car through space lends an essential element to the way the city is perceived.

Although imposed upon an existing cityscape, the LA freeway system seldom seems out of scale because it relates less to the man-made elements in the landscape than to the landscape itself—mountains, broad valleys and plains, the ocean. Since LA lacked monuments and monumental architecture, the freeways had nothing to belittle. Instead they became a monument of an entirely new kind, giving LA its final identity, making it seem like a world city at last instead of an overgrown if fascinating frontier town. The freeways did for LA what skyscrapers did for Manhattan. They authenticated its ascendency and provided the city with an instantly recognizable identity. And because the LA metropolitan area is so expansive, so low in population density, it was possible to install the freeway system with relatively little damage to the existing fabric of the city. A few slums were created, but in general the freeways came into being with amazingly little disruption (always allowing, that is, that the interurban mass transit system was already doomed and was in fact being replaced by the freeways). Nor were these freeways roads to nowhere, since they did perform the function they were supposed to perform: they knit the horizontal city together.

In general they avoided almost all the negatives that came to be associated with urban expressways. The one problem they could not avoid was the one that plagues planners everywhere. Any new urban highway—no matter how many lanes it provides—will eventually generate enough traffic to choke itself.

But that did not happen at first, except for a few bottlenecks, and there was a period when driving the freeways could be a pleasurable experience, especially if rush hours were avoided. During that brief golden age when the LA freeways were able to accommodate the needs of the region's drivers, they were an amazing phenomenon, though visitors from other parts of the country were sometimes terrified by them. A stranger's first sight of the system was often from the Century Boulevard access ramp to the San Diego Freeway, near Los Angeles International Airport, where he suddenly found himself dealing with streams of cars and trucks rushing toward unknown destinations as if on invisible rails. All at once, as if released by some unseen agency from its assigned route, a Corvette or a souped-up VW would abruptly veer across five lanes of traffic in a single, smooth maneuver before settling on a new course. Even New Yorkers used to the Long Island Expressway were taken aback. On the LIE there was plenty of jostling for position, but it was a one-on-one kind of combat: a honk of the horn or a flicker of the headlights preceded a dart into the passing lane, fleeting eye contact was possible as Pontiac skipped by Plymouth, both drivers muttering, or yelling, "Asshole!" On the LA freeways things worked by a different set of rules, cars switching lanes at speed as logically as bits of information zipping through the microcircuits of a computer. But this logic could be learned, and those who understood it found that driving the freeways was about as pleasant an experience as you could have in a car (except maybe at a drive-in movie). As long as you understood the rules, people were actually polite. Angelenos might make a big deal out of the kind of car they drove, but the driving itself was another matter—they took it for granted. Driving was a way of getting from place to place and the freeways made it possible to do so with maximum efficiency. Freeway driving, for a decade or two, was a marvelous marriage of private transportation and superbly designed public carriageway.

In his excellent book on Los Angeles, the British critic Reyner Banham suggested that the extreme concentration required while driving the freeways brought on a state of heightened awareness that some Angelenos found positively mystical. This heightened awareness was necessary because of the lane discipline required in driving a system as sophisticated as the LA freeways. Banham contrasts this sophistication with what he calls "the kindergarten rule of the road" employed on Britain's high-speed motorways with their designated slow, fast and passing lanes. "The three, four, or five lanes of an Angeleno freeway," he points out, "are virtually equal, the driver is required to select or change lanes according to speed, surrounding circumstances and future intentions." The freeway driver, he submits, acquiesces to "an incredibly demanding man/machine system"—one that despite some evident flaws works remarkably well. Its efficiency relies upon a combination of "enlightened self-interest and public spirit," which permits a heavy flow of traffic to move with relative ease.

As early as 1939, Norman Bel Geddes had suggested that drivers on the superhighways might be required to give up personal control of the automobile to some automated system that would control distance between vehicles, lane changes, and so on. The dawn of the computer age made such a system more plausible, but Banham suggests that the proven efficiency of the LA freeways probably rendered such futuristic notions redundant before they were even practical. An automated system might improve efficiency to a marginal extent, he surmises, and might prevent some accidents, but the gains would hardly prove cost-efficient. As it was, Angelenos' sophisticated driving habits had made the freeways almost as smooth-running as a machine, yet individual drivers retained the illusion, at least, of freedom of choice.

Banham's experience of the freeway system was accumulated in the late sixties, before the freeways were overtaxed by sheer volume of vehicles. At that time freeway traffic was not only fast, for the most part, but also extremely safe in terms of accidents per passenger mile. One problem with freeway driving, however—as with all expressway driving—was that accidents, when they did occur, were likely to be more serious, so that a single collision could set off a domino effect that would sometimes involve dozens of vehicles. Also, a mishap such as a jackknifed tractor-trailer or a spill of cartons from a produce truck could back traffic up for miles.

Such mishaps were sometimes bizarre. One afternoon in 1963, a ranch hand named Simms Reddin was heading east on the Ventura Freeway with a load of four steers bound for the slaughterhouse. Near the Van Nuys off-ramp, he felt his cargo move and pulled over onto the shoulder. He checked the truck and everything seemed in order, but, as he drove off again, the steers fell against the tailgate and out onto the freeway. One steer, in attempting to avoid a passing car, ended up on that car's hood and was carried a short distance before rolling off. Eventually it was apprehended by a police officer and a passing veterinarian and tied to the center divider. Reddin, meanwhile, took off in pursuit of a second steer, lassoed it and then dragged it through oncoming traffic till the rope broke. Uninjured, he managed to bulldog the steer and soon it, too, was tied up to the center divider.

The third and fourth steers ambled west, against inbound traffic. One left the Ventura by way of the Sepulveda off-ramp before discovering another off-ramp, this one descending from the San Diego Freeway. Inexplicably it decided to head up this ramp, immediately causing a collision between two cars attempting to leave the freeway. Cornered by a policeman and the driver of a flatbed truck, the steer charged, tossing the truck driver into the back of his own vehicle. Finally this steer was caught and tied, while its uncaptured mate continued west of the Ventura Freeway till it was at last boxed in by two trucks.

This reminder of LA's none-too-distant frontier past held up traffic on the Ventura Freeway for four hours, while also causing huge backups on the San Diego Freeway.

To avoid such situations, regular users of the freeway system came to rely increasingly on their car radios. Notice of a major tie-up was broadcast in the form of official "sigalerts." From 1957 onward, drivers could also tune in to KMPC's Airwatch, an ongoing account of rush-hour traffic broadcast from a helicopter or light plane that flew over the busiest parts of the system and reported problems as they cropped up. This service, later imitated all over the country, was the invention of Captain Max Schumacher, a former Marine Corps pilot who when stationed in Orange County had been in the habit of reporting to his control tower any road accidents that he spotted from the air. Once out of the military, he approached KMPC with the idea of instigating airborne traffic reports, and soon his voice became as familiar to Angelenos as that of any newscaster or disk jockey. "There's a three-vehicle accident with injuries on the inbound Hollywood Freeway just before the Vermont off-ramp," he might report. "An emergency vehicle is on the scene and traffic is backed up as far as the Hollywood Bowl, plus it's slow in the outbound lanes because of rubbernecking. If you're inbound through the Cahuenga Pass you might consider taking surface streets." The information was sound and the voice was soothing and good-humored. It was a front-page story and the city mourned when "Captain Max" was killed in a helicopter crash in 1966.

In some instances, freeways were constructed parallel with and close to existing major thoroughfares that had become home to typical commercial strips. This was very much the case with the Ventura Freeway, which was conceived as a replacement for Ventura Boulevard as the chief east-west arterial road through the San Fernando Valley. For considerable stretches the freeway runs within a block or two of the boulevard so that shoppers on the boulevard are always aware of its presence. Merchants along the Ventura strip were fearful that the freeway would cause customers to bypas their businesses, and initially these fears were confirmed. For a brief period sales were off sharply. Quite rapidly, however, the situation began to turn around. Within eighteen months of the freeway's opening, stores and restaurants were reporting that receipts were up by 40 and 50 percent. What happened was that the strip was no longer largely reliant upon transients passing through. Less cluttered now, because free of long-distance and intermediate-range traffic, Ventura Boulevard became far more attractive to local customers, so that gradually it evolved into an attenuated Main Street for the entire southern edge of the Valley. In addition, the boulevard benefited to an extent from off-ramp business since it was adjacent to freeway exits at approximately one-mile intervals.

For a while the Ventura Boulevard strip retained a good deal of its former, anarchic character and the fifties saw the construction of some striking neo-*moderne* stores, car washes and restaurants. In particular, this was the heyday of the Los Angeles coffee shop, when architectural firms like Armet & Davis and Martin Stern, Jr., challenged the motorist's attention with flying roofs, acres of glass and revolving kidney-shaped signs, all picked out in neon. Ventura Boulevard was well supplied with examples of the genre, but gradually the strip came under the sway of the chains and franchisers so that those universally familiar signs and mansards began to pepper its length. Once it became apparent that the freeway had enhanced the boulevard's commercial value, rather than blunted it, developers recognized its value as a potential focus for upscale, white-collar businesses, leading to the construction of anonymous office towers, especially in Sherman Oaks near the intersection of the Ventura and San Diego freeways—the very spot where the steers had run rampant, like a Merrill Lynch commercial come to life. Ventura Boulevard was entering middle age.

Much the same thing happened to several of the established commercial strips, while others, such as Lincoln Boulevard in Santa Monica and Venice, preserved a good deal of their chaotic charm despite the arrival of the franchises. Inevitably there was a flowering of shopping centers all over the area, but in the fifties and early sixties these were mostly of the traditional type, largely because the open-air format was so appropriate to the climate. A little later, however, the success of enclosed malls like Southdale would be appropriated by Southern California entrepreneurs, ushering in the era of the Galleria.

Throughout the great freeway-building period, LA appeared frequently in the national press as the acknowledged center of automobile culture. There were the freeways themselves, of course, but attention was also directed toward such LA products as the sometimes Flash-Gordonesque inventions of car customizers like George Barris and Ed Roth, not to mention the hot rods lovingly tuned to perfection in garages from Chatsworth to Anaheim. Alongside the good manners of freeway driving, the antisocial aspects of car culture continued to attract disciples. Illegal drag racing still thrived in LA, and now there was also organized, professional drag racing with its needle-nosed "fuelers" and souped-up "funny cars." Another coterie of LA enthusiasts prepared off-road vehicles for the annual race down the Baja peninsula or simply for leisure driving in the surrounding desert. A subspecies of the off-road vehicle evolved into dune-buggies, many of which made use of the VW Beetle chassis. Thousands of LA youngsters took old cars and transformed them by chopping them or submitting them to other radical modifications. A "chopped top" described a sedan that had had its roof lowered. Another popular modification involved lowering the chassis to the point where the drive shaft was so near the ground that any encounter with a section of uneven pavement could produce a shower of sparks. The California legislature became so concerned about this practice that a law was passed stipulating, rather inelegantly, that "no modified motor vehicles may be driven on the highway if any portion of their bodies other than the wheels are lower than the low point of any rim of the wheels." An alternative to the wholly lowered body was the lowered front end, which produced a car that was dramatically raked forward. Later, young Chicanos would make a cult of lowering the rear end, raking their cars backward to create a unique species of "low rider," often equipped with hydraulic equipment designed to make the front end bounce vertically to a singular kind of automotive salsa beat.

Hot rods, chopped and raked cars, along with hundreds of more conventional vehicles, made a weekly appearance on Van Nuys Boulevard—a used-car buyers' paradise in the Valley—to cruise up and down slowly all evening long, girls piled in seven and eight to a convertible, appraising the boys, boys appraising girls and cars alike. It was the motorized equivalent of riding in the Bois de Boulogne or strolling the Ramblas in Barcelona. Radios blared while friends and strangers called to one another across the sea of hoods and the rumble of engines slowly turning over. These events had nothing to do with speed—cars crawled from block to block—but they were very much about the automobile, the way it looked, the way it exuded power and sexuality. With so much latent potency on display, sporadic outbreaks of violence were as inevitable as the duels that arose from insults uttered during rides in the Bois.

For more sustained violence, there were the motorcycle clubs. Motorcycle gangs in LA had a history dating back to the thirties at least. (There was even a leather-jacketed movie industry gang, consisting of Clark Gable, Victor Fleming, Keenan Wynn, Andy Devine, Ward Bond and others.) The character of these gangs changed radically after World War II, however, when the Hell's Angels were founded in Fontana, out on Route 66 near San Bernardino. With their Harley-Davidson choppers, their long, unkempt hair and beards, their Nazi helmets and swastikas, their steel-tipped boots, metal-studded vests and motorcycle-chain belts (invaluable weapons during rumbles) the Angels were instantly recognized and feared and created an impression that rapidly led to the formation of chapters all over California and throughout much of the country. LA remained one of the Angels' prime centers, however, and it was not long before these extremely mobile buccaneers of the highway were involved in a wide variety of criminal activities, from drug running to prostitution. To the public, however, they were more to be feared for the random violence they espoused. Arriving at a truck stop or public park, they could spread chaos in moments, then just as quickly be on their choppers and lost in freeway traffic before anyone knew what had really happened.

Just as LA was a city made up of many communities, it was a city made up of many subcultures, and since it was so highly motorized, each subculture had its emblematic vehicles, which were every bit as important as a private slang or way of dressing. Surfers, for example, favored "woodies"—old, wood-sided station wagons— then gradually evolved toward a taste for VW Beetles and Minibuses, both of which took on a peculiarly raffish el-

Los Angeles drivers have long been partial to exotic cars, as is the case with this couple in their British Triumph roadster.
American Stock Photos

HIGHWAYS TO HEAVEN

egance when carrying surfboards on their roofs. More than anywhere else in the country, LA was open to foreign cars. European sports cars had been established there for a long time, but as the fifties turned into the sixties the MGBs, TR2s, XK-140s and Porsches were increasingly joined by smart foreign sedans like the Mercedes 220 S and the Jaguar 3.4 as well as a significant sprinkling of more modest imports such as Volvo and Peugeot. Superluxury cars, Rolls-Royces and Bentleys, had always been highly visible in parts of LA and continued to be so.

In the early sixties, if a visitor drove around the residential sections of upscale communities like Beverly Hills and Brentwood he would already be struck by the amazing number of foreign cars parked on driveways beside the Cadillacs, Lincolns and Imperials. Clearly there was an equation here between the symbolism of the luxury homes—ultimate expression of American success—and the cars that sat beside them. Fewer and fewer of these affluent people (for the most part nouveau riche) were finding Detroit's best an adequate expression of their aspirations. After all, if your house imitated some European style—Norman manor house or a Palladian pavilion—then you might as well complete the picture with a European car or two. This was an ominous sign. It was one thing for European manufacturers to outdo Detroit in producing economy cars. It was quite another for Detroit to be losing the luxury-car war. Soon the American automobile industry would find itself being squeezed from both the top and bottom ends of the market, and it was in LA—ultimate American autopia—that this first became evident.

Unloading European imports at Baltimore, c. 1971. *UPI/Bettmann*

Chapter 13

MINIS AND MUSCLE CARS

*A*mong the foreign cars appearing on LA's freeways in the early sixties was a sprinkling of Japanese vehicles—Toyotas and Datsuns were the first to arrive—launched in the California market because it was known to be more adventurous, and because of the West Coast's relative proximity to Japan. At the time these cars attracted very little attention except as curiosities. Their triumph was still a decade or so away, yet their presence was a highly significant portent of things to come.

The history of the Japanese car industry to that point offered little to suggest that it would one day achieve a dominant position in the world. Datsun's roots dated back to 1912, but it did not really become a manufacturer of consequence until 1934, when the corporation was reorganized as the Nissan Motor Company Ltd. In the thirties it was best known for small cars based on the British Austin Seven. Founded in 1935, Toyota rather imaginatively took the Chrysler Airflow as the starting point for its first model and until World War II built American-style automobiles in small quantities. The war brought private-car production to a complete halt, and it did not resume until 1947, when 300 were built. For several years after the war, as Japan rebuilt, truck production took precedence over car production; 50,000 trucks had been built by 1955 as opposed to just 20,000 cars. A mere 46 cars were exported in 1956, and just 410 the following year. The majority of Toyota cars sold domestically were derivative of European models.

Nissan was building the British Austin A50 under license; Isuzu, founded in 1937, was manufacturing another British car, the Hillman Minx; while Hino, a subsidiary of Toyota, had an arrangement with Renault to build rear-engined 4CVs. Wholly Japanese-designed cars of the period included the Datsun 1000, the Toyota Crown and the Toyota Corona, none of which was very distinguished from either a design or engineering viewpoint. Still, the Japanese car industry continued to expand rapidly, becoming the eighth largest in the world by 1960, at which point farsighted executives began to look more seriously at the potentials of the export market.

Their first efforts to penetrate the United States were not especially successful, for the cars were still poorly engineered, by Detroit standards, but a foothold was established in the early sixties so that Datsun and Toyota engineers—soon to be followed by others—could gain first-hand experience of what would be needed to succeed in America. The Japanese learned their engineering lessons quickly and added an understanding of production techniques that put American manufacturers to shame. For the most part the results were well made, if derivative, cars that offered two things customers wanted: economy and reliability. The latter took a while to establish (a car must be driven for a few years before the driver knows how reliable it is). Economy, on the other hand, was evident from the first, although it didn't really come into play until events in the Middle East caused the American public to alter its entire point of view toward the automobile.

These events wouldn't happen for years, but when they did, the Japanese designers and engineers sought to learn everything they could about both the state of the art in

HIGHWAYS TO HEAVEN

automobile design and the needs of the motorist in a rapidly changing world.

One of the models they turned to was a British car that never sold in America in any significant quantity, yet had an enormous influence on future car design in Japan, Europe and America: the BMC-Mini. To this day American highways are heavily traveled by its legitimate and illegitimate descendants. In the postwar decade, Europe had produced some distinguished and radical small cars—not only the VW Beetle but also the Citroën 2CV, the Renault 4CV and the Fiat 600. In 1956, after the Suez crisis had caused Europeans to consider the realities of gasoline shortages, Alec Issigonis set out to design the ultimate small car for the British Motor Corporation. Significantly, the commission came at the very time when Detroit designers were vying with one another to put larger and larger Wurlitzer organs on wheels.

Issigonis had already designed the classic Morris Minor, and now the only limitation placed on him was that he should design his supercompact vehicle around a modified version of an existing BMC engine, which meant that he could not employ an air-cooled motor (like the VW) but had to rely on a water-cooled, four cylinder unit. Actual fuel economy was largely determined by this power plant (later a number of different engines were used). The task Issigonis set himself was to create a car that in addition to providing good mileage was extremely small overall yet roomy inside, with adequate power and optimum roadholding qualities. It was his belief that even the best of the existing small cars sacrificed space for styling. For this exercise in miniaturization—the ADO 15 project—Issigonis sought to combine engineering compactness with the ultimate in minimalistic yet efficient design.

To achieve maximum passenger space it was essential to eliminate the driveshaft required in any conventional front-engine–rear-wheel-drive car. This meant either a rear-engine–rear-wheel-drive vehicle, like the Renault 4CV, or a front-engine–front-wheel-drive vehicle, like the Citroën 2CV. He chose the latter, because it would provide better weight distribution and road handling, but he went the 2CV one better, revolutionizing car layouts by mounting the engine transversely, with the transmission in the block, thus saving an enormous amount of room. He also fitted the car with ten-inch wheels, thus cutting down on wasteful fender-well space, and designed a spatially efficient suspension system, with trailing arms at the rear. As a consequence of all this, the Mini (as the ADO 15 project eventually came to be known) was only ten feet long, and Issigonis was able to boast that eight of those feet were devoted to passenger space.

Despite Issigonis's disdain for styling, the Mini was a handsomely functional-looking little car and its performance was remarkable. Even with their standard 848 cc engine, producing 34 hp, the original 1959 versions, designated Morris Mini Minor and Austin Seven, could achieve a speed of 75 mph, largely because the car weighed just 1,340 pounds, and later versions such as the 100 hp Mini Coopers were much faster. But the real glory of the Mini was its road handling and stability. If ever a car turned on a dime (or a sixpence) this was it. It was a car in which you could nip in and out of traffic as nimbly as if you were driving an MG. So good was its performance that it soon became a favorite among European rally drivers: one of the great sights of the Monte Carlo Rally in the sixties was to watch a Mini Cooper in full trim—headlights taped, covered in decals—slipstreaming behind a Lancia on the open road or zipping past a Porsche on the twisting curves of the Corniche. The Mini Cooper was so well adapted to this kind of event that it won the Monte Carlo Rally outright in 1964, 1965 and 1967, beating scores of larger and more powerful rivals.

Like the VW Beetle, the Mini had real character and enjoyed great success in Britain as well as a number of export markets (five million were built). It was not a perfect car—although it carried four adults with reasonable comfort it barely provided trunk space for one—but its layout inspired other designers from Turin to Osaka. Perhaps the Mini was a little too small for most purposes, but it had demonstrated brilliantly how the transverse, front-mounted, front-wheel-drive motor could permit a compact car to be built with a spacious interior and superior performance and handling abilities. Issigonis himself came out with the similar but larger 1100 series in 1962, while European manufacturers were right behind, like Peugeot with the 204.

Meanwhile, in Japan, Honda was on the move, producing automobiles for the first time in 1962 after achieving international recognition with its motorcycles. The first successful Honda car was the 1966 N360, the inspiration for which was so obvious that it was immediately dubbed the Mini Honda. What makes the N360 (and hence the Mini) significant for American drivers is the fact that it was the immediate precursor of the Honda Civic, another transverse engine, front-wheel-drive small car that in layout and other particulars acknowledges the British Mini as its honorable ancestor. With the Civic, Honda would make its first impact in America, and even today's Honda Accord can trace its roots to the Mini, as can a whole rash of compact cars produced in Europe, Japan and America. The Mini started a revolution that has been felt every bit as much in the USA as in the rest of the world.

Back in the early sixties, however, American car manufacturers were still struggling to come to terms with the notion of the compact car. Of those launched in answer to the VW challenge, by far the most interesting was the Chevrolet Corvair, a car that might have helped prepare Detroit for the Japanese challenge but that instead set the industry back, for reasons that were not totally the fault of GM.

Few cars have received as much criticism as the Corvair. It was a near miss fraught with problems that could have been solved, given time. Certainly it was a better car than the first Japanese imports, but there was a big difference. Datsun and Toyota, with nothing to lose, could afford to take their time perfecting the product. Chevy needed immediate and continuing success in order to justify persisting with the Corvair. The immediate success was forthcoming—here was an interesting-looking car that sold in an extremely low price range—but the car's shortcomings were quickly apparent.

Ed Cole, Chevy's chief engineer, never quite acknowledged that he had taken a page out of VW's book when he designed the Corvair. Nonetheless, the car that emerged had an air-cooled engine in the tail driving the rear wheels. It did not look like a VW, however, its unit-construction body–cum–chassis design being conventionally American in appearance, though it sported a distinctive "bathtub" ridge at fender-top level and was remarkably clean and free of excessive chrome by the standards of the day. Empty it weighed 2,400 pounds, almost twice the weight of a Mini but still light compared with standard American cars. The problem was that too much of this weight was at the rear end, and as unwary drivers quickly discovered, this adversely affected the car's handling.

The front-engine, rear-wheel-drive cars Americans were used to tended to understeer, making them feel very secure to drive, if sometimes a little sluggish in response to the wheel. The Corvair was extremely prone to oversteering, so that drivers found it supersensitive to any movement of the wheel. This tendency could be kept under control to some extent by keeping front tire pressures lower than rear tire pressures, but nothing could eliminate the oversteering completely, and on slick roads even skilled drivers sometimes found that the Corvair was a terrifying vehicle to drive. When cornering at even modest speeds, on wet or icy surfaces, the heavy rear end tried to overtake the lighter front end, throwing the car out of control.

Many accidents were attributed to this handling characteristic, and critics suggested that they often had more serious consequences for the car's occupants than was necessary because of flaws in the Corvair's construction. Although unit-body construction is generally considered relatively crash-proof, the notorious X-frames employed by GM made the Corvair especially vulnerable to serious damage when hit from the side, and its particular handling problems made such side hits all too likely.

Most prominent of the car's critics was Ralph Nader, who made the Corvair a prime target of his 1965 book, *Unsafe at Any Speed.* By the time the book appeared, the

Corvair was already scheduled to be phased out (it survived till 1969), sales having dropped off significantly because of the public's perception of its inadequacies. The irony is that by 1964 Chevrolet had solved most of the Corvair's handling problems, so that it was no longer the same car that Nadar demolished on paper.

Unsafe at Any Speed was not simply an assault on the Corvair. It was an indictment of GM's policies as a whole, and of the entire American automobile industry. As such it made many valid points, though these were blunted somewhat by the fact that Nader wrote as a man who seemed to have no feeling for the pleasures of driving. In his polemic, he is particularly biting about the conservatism of Detroit engineering and, paradoxically, acknowledges the innovations represented by the Corvair even as he points out its failings. Unfortunately, the consequence of all this was that he appears to have helped reinforce Detroit, and GM in particular, in its conservatism. *Unsafe at Any Speed* may have been unintentionally instrumental in killing off adventurous compact designs for a number of years and so perhaps contributed indirectly to Detroit's failure to be prepared for the battles of the seventies.

Nader's book also had a dramatic impact upon a sizable section of the American public. The growth of import sales showed that a considerable number of Americans were prepared to doubt the wisdom of Detroit's policies; now here was a book that set out the American car industry's failings in great detail. Ever since Henry Ford revolutionized automobile production, most Americans had regarded their car builders—especially the Big Three—with something like awe. It was American enterprise at its most scintillating, weaving vast fortunes for a few while satisfying the needs and dreams of the great American public. The bosses of Ford, GM and Chrysler had been accepted as demigods—and now there was hard evidence that these men might not always have the well-being of their customers at heart. It was shocking news, and if not everyone believed all of Nader's charges, he certainly managed to sow many seeds of doubt. Were American cars the safest and best built in the world? If not, what could the consumer do about it? Nader also helped make the American car buyer self-conscious in a way that was quite novel. Perhaps it was absurd to be driving a dreamboat as big as the Ritz. Perhaps there was an alternative.

This is not to say that every consumer paid attention to Nader's arguments, or to suggest that Detroit lacked successes in the sixties. At Ford, for example, Lee Iacocca oversaw the development of the phenomenally successful Mustang. Originally a two-seat semi-sports-car with a relatively modest price tag, it appealed to the youthful wing of the market and sold a million between 1964, when it was introduced, and 1966. Later Mustangs, such as the Mach I, were larger four-seaters and came equipped with a variety of powerful V-8's generating up to 375 hp. The biggest of these engines gave the Mach I the capability of reaching 140 mph, making it a true muscle car.

The muscle car was an expression of everything that Ralph Nader deplored about Detroit engineering. It involved mounting a gas-hungry, high-output power plant in a conventional, standard-size chassis and wrapping it in a sedan or hard-top shell that hinted at capabilities appropriate to an Indy car. Certainly Indy cars, with their big Offenhauser and Ford V-8 engines, were one inspiration for the sixties muscle cars, but more important than Indianapolis-style racing was stock-car racing, which had become an enormous attraction after the war, first in the South and then throughout the country. It was appropriate that the archetypal family of muscle cars, the big Pontiacs, should establish its reputation with successes on the stock-car circuit.

The story of the Pontiac muscle cars began with the introduction, in 1955, of the powerful, overhead-valve, Strato-Streak V-8 engine. A few months later, Semon "Bunkie" Knudson was named head of the Pontiac Division, and he set about reversing the marque's staid image, seeking instead to capture the adventurous, youthful (or young-at-heart) driver. To do so he ordered a new approach to styling and also made an all-out assault on the stock-car

The Ford Mustang is unveiled to the media in 1964. *UPI/Bettmann*

HIGHWAYS TO HEAVEN

circuit. Almost at once Pontiac began winning major NAS-CAR races, which it continued to do until 1963, when GM forbade its divisions from entering such events. Meanwhile, Royal Pontiac, a dealership based in Royal Oak, Michigan, built and raced modified Pontiacs, with great success, in the Super Stock category at national drag meets. By 1959, the marque's styling had changed dramatically (the split grille made its first appearance that year), and suddenly the Bonneville, Star Chief and even the low-end Catalina were cars to be seen in.

The Bonneville was a big car, but it was very clean compared with other Detroit products of the period. There was relative restraint in the use of chrome and a total absence of baroque excess. There were fins, but they emphasized the overall lines of the car rather than interrupting them. A certain amount of fifties *moderne* detail persisted, but basically this was a car of the sixties, and Pontiac was able to stay with the package—modifying it from year to year rather than introducing wholesale change—for two decades. By 1961, a year in which the division won thirty out of fifty-two Grand National stock-car races, Pontiac became the third-best-selling car in the country—helped, admittedly, by its newly introduced Tempest compact. In 1962 came the Grand Prix—built on the shorter Catalina wheelbase but with all the appointments of a Bonneville—then, in 1964, the GTO, a smaller yet decidedly muscular car evolved from the basic Tempest and its sportier Le Mans derivative.

This family of muscle and minimuscle cars lived on into the seventies with new arrivals like the Trans Am and the Grand Am, but it was at its peak in the sixties and in a transitional period when the industry was not at all certain where the future lay, it was a demonstration of what Detroit did best. In many ways, cars like the Bonneville and the Grand Prix were the ultimate driving machines for the newly built system of Interstates. They were not as nippy as sports cars (though they handled well), but they had the power and smoothness to take advantage of those broad, sweeping highways with their near perfect surfaces and carefully planned sightlines. And they were handsome machines whose styling stands up well in retrospect. There was nothing ridiculous about their lines, and if they borrowed from the aviation aesthetic, they did so in a less gimmicky way than their forebears had. From a sexual point of view, they were far less ambiguous than the cars of the fifties, being as straightforwardly masculine as any cars produced since the war.

With the Pontiac muscle cars the lines were drawn. If you espoused the Detroit viewpoint and understood its virtues, you drove a Bonneville or a GTO. If you were convinced by Ralph Nader's arguments, you threw up your hands in despair and wrote a letter to your congressman.

The real muscle on the new Interstates, however, belonged not to Pontiac or any of its direct rivals but rather to the trucks that now plied from coast to coast in increasing numbers and at increasing speeds. The trucks in use by the sixties bore little relation to those of the prewar period and one respect in which they had changed drastically was the replacement of the diesel for the gasoline engine, which had once been almost universal. The diesel offered the advantages of lower fuel consumption and longer engine life, a fact that was demonstrated by Cummins and GM—as well as by several European and Japanese companies—in the 1930's, when diesel trucks and buses first began to appear in significant numbers. In the fifties, however, diesel development took off in a big way. Mack Truck introduced its heavy-duty Thermodyne power plant in 1953, while GM became competitive with its own distinctive two-stroke diesels. The Perkins company of England began to supply many medium-size diesel motors to the Chrysler Corporation, while in 1954 Volvo came out with a turbo-charged diesel truck, a development that would prove influential on both sides of the Atlantic.

As the superhighways spread, engines became more powerful. Simultaneously, many other technical improvements—air brakes, engine retarders, air suspension systems, two-speed back axles, etc.—permitted trucks to become larger and larger and to carry heavier and heavier loads. Multiaxle rigid trucks such as the Reo Tri-Drive were designed and built to carry huge payloads, but more and more the emphasis switched to articulated rigs, especially where big loads and long distances were concerned. Tens of thousands of these big rigs crisscrossed the country, and by the late sixties their drivers were evolving a new and distinctive Interstate subculture.

Since the Interstates, including the urban freeways, were designed to accommodate both trucks and regular passenger traffic, increased truck activity inevitably brought car drivers into conflict with the pilots of the big rigs, especially in and near cities. All too often truck drivers behaved as if they owned the highway, showing little courtesy to commuters or leisure drivers. At bottlenecks it was the trucks that because of their sheer bulk seemed to be causing the traffic jams (though their operators could hardly be blamed for this, since they were simply trying to move goods in the cheapest possible way and use the Interstate System as it had been intended). Most frequently, car drivers complained about trucks emitting fumes, and this was the unkindest cut of all.

The exhausts from diesel engines may be ugly and smelly, but they are far less dangerous than the invisible emissions from gasoline engines, contributing very little to the photochemical process that creates smog. For the most part diesel exhaust fumes simply sink to the ground and are quickly dispersed.

By the 1960s, the phenomenon of photochemical smog had visited itself on many cities other than Los Angeles and was beginning to be taken seriously as a national problem. Starting in the early sixties, a variety of partial solutions was explored, with California leading the way in legislation that required automobiles to be fitted with antipollutant devices. From 1962 on, special crankcase devices were fitted to new cars that reduced hydrocarbon output by 30 percent. Exhaust controls, introduced in 1966 models, reduced hydrocarbon emissions still further, and in 1970 the State of California brought in stiff new laws, including the requirement that cars be fitted with equipment to inhibit fuel evaporation when the car was not in use. As much as 15 percent of smog, it had been calculated, was generated by parked cars, especially in a city like Los

Angeles with many warm days and millions of acres of open-air parking lots.

Another antipollution development of the sixties was the introduction of lead-free gasoline, a move instigated largely by Ford, which pointed out that the lead in gasoline was fouling up the antismog devices they fitted to their cars, thus rendering them useless. Until then the oil companies had assiduously been pushing high-lead gas because it corresponded with high octane, and high octane was a primary selling point. With Ford and then the other major manufacturers demanding unleaded fuel, however, the oil companies had no choice but to fall into line.

Predominantly, then, the sixties was a decade of change. Detroit remained dominant in the world of automobile manufacture, but it faced increasing competition from abroad and serious criticism at home. The majority of cars on American roads were still huge by world standards, but the smaller vehicle was finding its niche. The problem of pollution was growing, but it was also being addressed seriously for the first time. As for highway culture, the old roadside commercial strips survived to some extent, but gradually they were being transformed by the arrival of the franchisers, or being superseded by wholly new franchise-oriented strips. More and more, too, the strip itself was being outmoded by the more compact shopping center, which in turn was evolving more and more into the shopping mall.

The success of the mall came as a surprise to many. As already noted, the mall depended upon the notion of turning motorists back into pedestrians, though without eliminating the need for the automobile for basic access. This was counter to prevailing theory, but doubters might have taken note of the success of Disneyland, whose failure had also been predicted. Disneyland was the archetypal pedestrian environment predicated on the automobile. Walt Disney had selected the site because it was close to the route of the Santa Ana Freeway, which in fact was not completed until after the theme park was opened in 1955. The freeway gave people access to Disneyland from all parts of greater Los Angeles, but once there they left their cars and were taken by tram to the entrance. After they entered the gates they were in a pedestrian world, except to the limited extent that they wished to take advantage of Disneyland's own public transportation system (antique vehicles, narrow-gauge railroad, monorail, etc.). In some respects the theme park resembled a World's Fair, but with the significant difference that there were no major national or industrial pavilions vying with each other for attention. Rather, Disneyland was designed so that everything seemed equally enticing. If the line was long for one ride, there was always another ride in view at the end of the street, or a restaurant or refreshment stand nearby to pause at. Major attractions were distributed equally about the grounds so as to maintain circulation. Families with children, couples, groups of teenagers could each find their own pace, their own priorities, just as might have happened on Saturday afternoon in a small Midwestern town at the turn of the century, except of course that there was more to do. The scheme worked so brilliantly that the science fiction writer Ray Bradbury proposed that Walt Disney be elected mayor of Los Angeles, suggesting that he was the only man who could make the city function efficiently. Disney was not really dealing with city-planning problems, though; rather, he was creating a self-contained, pedestrianized enclave that permitted people to temporarily escape from the perceived failings of the urban environment. On a smaller scale, malls did the same thing.

As they learned their business, malls began to function like theme parks. Their primary function was different, in that they made money chiefly from retailing rather than entertainment—though movie theaters and rides for children became commonplace. Beyond that, though, the principles involved were much the same. People arrived by car but then became pedestrianized. As at Disneyland, they normally stayed for considerable lengths of time, though provision was made for in-and-out shopping for those in a hurry. Once there, people circulated according to their priorities, so that teenagers and parents with younger kids were provided for according to their various wants. The main attractions, the department stores, were spaced to ensure a steady flow, while focal points such as clusters of food outlets were provided to create social centers. Interestingly, these food outlets were seldom operated by major franchises and helped revive some of the grass-roots enterprise of the old strips. The malls provided a perfect opportunity for franchising in another area, the retail store, and soon they were filled with outlets like The Gap, Athlete's Foot and Radio Shack, which produced an homogenizing effect. Still, like Disneyland, the malls did offer an experience that approximated that of the small or medium-size town in the preautomobile era. Malls had some advantages over Disneyland: they tended to attract customers from a relatively small catchment area, so that shoppers were likely to run into friends, making the mall a genuine social arena. Teenagers quickly discovered this and began to hang out at malls, whether they had disposable cash or not.

Another phenomenon of the sixties was the downtown pedestrian mall, an attempt to revive sections of inner cities by closing streets to motor traffic, except, in some instances, public transportation. A typical example of this is the Nicolette Mall in Minneapolis, located in the heart of the business district, which encourages pedestrians to stroll among retail stores, cafés and hotels and even provides access to an enclosed minimall.

Both the enclosed mall and the downtown pedestrian mall were perhaps a sign that Americans were turning against the automobile as the be-all and end-all of progress. At the same time the sixties can be seen as a high point for quality of driving, with the Interstate System largely in place by the end of the decade and still adequate to the volume of traffic, except for occasional trouble spots. Speed limits varied from state to state (some, like Nevada, placed no limit), but in general it was possible to cruise for long distances at around 70 mph safely and without attracting the interest of the highway patrol.

Car interiors were more comfortable than ever and onetime luxuries such as automatic transmission and power steering had now become standard on many cars, so that the driving experience became easier, and at the same time somewhat passive. The passive driver had more freedom to enjoy the incidentals of driving, such as listening to the radio. Radio had enjoyed a renaissance, beginning in the mid-fifties, partly because of the rise of rock 'n' roll and partly because the car radio had become virtually universal, a development that was helped by the advent of the transistor. The morning and evening rush hours—actually two-hour periods in typical urban areas—provided radio advertisers with a captive audience, giving birth to the phrase "drive-time radio." An increase in the importance of FM stations, especially in the post-Beatles era, led to the increasing sophistication of car radios, and by the end of the decade the arrival of the prerecorded eight-track tape casette made it possible to convert your car into a mobile entertainment center.

The songs on the radio had changed. The make-out ballads and happy-go-lucky rockabilly and doo-wop of the fifties had given way to something far more complicated. There were songs of protest now, and convoluted lyrics that attempted to capture the hallucinative experience of the acid trip. There was a British invasion on the radio, too—matching the invasion of the foreign car—and all of this rock world activity was being played out against America's involvement in Vietnam, and the rising tide of opposition it had provoked, especially among the young. The two things existed side by side over the airwaves, casualty statistics and Bob Dylan, massacres of Asian civilians and the Frug. That was the texture of drive-time in the late sixties, and it had its effect. Large numbers of young Americans were in flight from what they perceived as a materialistic society, seeking a new and more spiritual reality. For pundits and gurus of this new generation, the motor industry was one of the ultimate symbols of materialism. To the enlightened young, Detroit was no longer a name that automatically conjured up Ford and Chevrolet. For a few years at least, Detroit would be as famous for the Motown Sound as for cars.

Yet this was still America. The hippiest of the hippies, the druggiest of the dropouts, still needed wheels. He needed wheels to get to Woodstock or Altamont, to ship his crop of marijuana from Marin to Market Street. The solution was to transform the car by treating it as a floating "pad." The most beat-up VW would serve just fine, especially if it was spray-painted with psychedelic designs to create a kind of anticamouflage that paradoxically dematerialized it while making it stand out from the chrome-trim crowd. Better still, given the prevailing devotion to the idea of communal life, was a minibus that could accommodate an entire extended hippie family or minitribe, permitting stoned migrations to nowhere and libidinous bivouacs beneath the stars.

Thomas Pynchon concludes his novel *Gravity's Rainbow* with a nuclear explosion that puts an end to what he presents as the madness of the Southern California freeways. In *Vineland*, by contrast, he offers at one point the ritual crossing of the Golden Gate Bridge by a busload of hippies headed for the redwoods and backroads of Northern California (inevitably calling to mind Ken Kesey and his busload of Merry Pranksters). In reality the two apparently divergent worlds—LA auto-eroticism and Mendocino mind bending—were not as far removed from each other as might at first be thought (which *Vineland* makes very clear). Certainly the Merry Pranksters themselves made many antic incursions into LA, and it wasn't long before marijuana ranchers from the north were trading in their minibuses for BMWs and buying up estates in the foothills of the Santa Monica mountains.

In those foothills, in Benedict Canyon, on August 9, 1969, the two worlds collided head-on. Charles Manson—messianic ex-con who had taken on the mantle of hippiedom—had begun recruiting his "family" in San Francisco but eventually settled it in a movie ranch–cum–ghost town within striking distance of Los Angeles. On that fatal date, Manson sent a small group of his followers into the city to commit "a crime that would shock the world." Driving into LA, they stumbled, by chance, it seems, upon the Bel Air home of director Roman Polanski. They invaded it and, crazed with drugs, did commit a crime that stunned the world, brutally murdering Polanski's pregnant wife, Sharon Tate, and four others.

They picked the Polanski estate because it was so isolated. It was the kind of Southern California luxury home that would never have existed without the automobile. Two days later, another Manson raiding party entered another foothill home, this time killing Leon LaBianca, a supermarket tycoon, and his wife. More than any previous crimes, these senseless attacks sensitized affluent Angelenos to the fact that the benefits of living in an auto-dependent Arcadia came with a built-in element of vulnerability to violence in a world where everyone, even the most psychotic outsiders, had access to wheels. Overnight, from Malibu to Los Feliz sophisticated security systems were perceived as a necessity and guard dogs were called in to patrol the sweeping driveways of Brentwood and Holmby Hills.

The automobile was normally regarded as a friend, but it could quickly turn into an enemy, transforming careers overnight. Just three weeks to the day before Sharon Tate's mutilated body was found, the police in Edgartown, Massachusetts, were called to a tidal channel on Chappaquiddick Island. There Police Chief Dominick J. Arena found a black 1967 Buick partially immersed in the water. Further investigation revealed that the car contained the body of Mary Jo Kopechne, a former secretary of the late Senator Robert Kennedy. The Buick was registered in the name of his brother, Senator Edward Kennedy. The ensuing scandal may have changed the face of American presidential politics.

By an ironic coincidence, the Chappaquiddick incident was driven off the front pages by a story that had been set in motion by President John F. Kennedy. JFK had instigated the program that would place man on the moon, a program that came to fruition the day after the Buick was pulled from the water. Edward Kennedy's presidential aspirations ended in a black 1967 Buick. John Kennedy's life ended in a blue 1961 Lincoln convertible as it moved slowly through Dealey Plaza in Dallas on a Friday in November 1963. This, surely, was one of the key images of the sixties—or sequences of images, as seen in the famous Zapruder film: the President jolting forward, reaching for his neck, his wife cradling his head, Special Agent Hill leaping aboard the Lincoln as it sped off toward the triple underpass.

Once again the automobile had played a critical role in the drama of American history.

PART

3

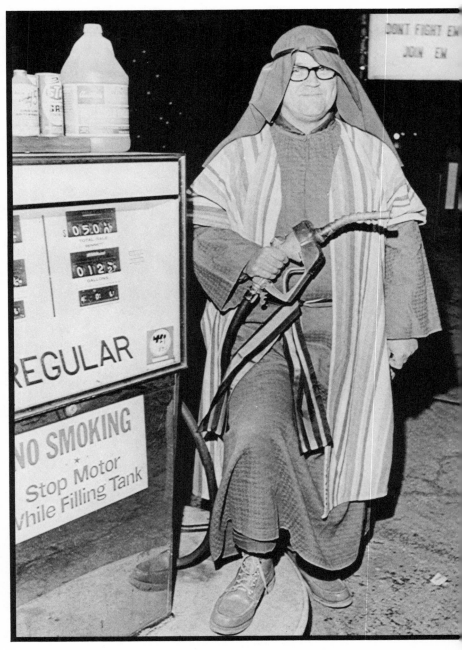

During the 1973–74 gasoline crisis, a Pennsylvania gas station manager attempted to maintain his sense of humor by adopting the native garb of the supposed villains of the piece. *UPI/Bettmann*

Chapter 14

CRISIS

*A*lthough it was over in the blink of an eye, the 1973 Yom Kippur War between Israel and its Arab neighbors had an impact on the American motorist every bit as dramatic as World War II. Yom Kippur, the highest of the Jewish high holy days, fell on October 6, and on that day Syria and Egypt invaded Israel. Taken by surprise, Israel appealed to the United States for aid, and the U.S. government authorized an airlift of arms and ammunition that helped turn the tide of battle, so that the Israelis not only repulsed the invaders but were able to drive Egyptian forces back across the Sinai Peninsula to the Suez Canal. Other Arab states affiliated with the Organization of Petroleum Exporting Countries responded to this intervention by increasing the cost of oil by 70 percent and imposing an oil embargo on the United States. The unthinkable had happened, and with a suddenness that took consumers totally by surprise, petroleum-dependent America was faced with an oil crisis.

There is substantial doubt that an actual oil shortage ever existed, at least as a simple consequence of the OPEC embargo. The lines at the gas pumps were real enough, however, and there had been spot shortages in some areas—Colorado and Kansas, for example—earlier in the year, well in advance of the Yom Kippur War. These were attributable in part to the big oil companies' attempts to force independent, cut-price distributors out of business, creating the appearance of a shortfall in supplies even before OPEC suddenly announced its boycott of the American market.

On the surface, though, the scenario seemed all too straightforward and depressing. Since 1947 America had been importing more oil than it produced, and now, it appeared, the chickens were flocking home to roost. Fossil fuel reserves, it was recognized, were finite, and the bulk of unexploited petroleum fields were to be found in the Middle East in Islamic countries that, though of variegated political persuasions, were united in their opposition to the U.S. government's support of Israel. Some of these countries had already nationalized oil industries founded with American capital and expertise, and now they were ready to hold the world to ransom. America might be the target of the embargo, but other nations were victimized by being forced to pay the new and radically higher prices dictated by the OPEC cartel.

That's the way it appeared to the driver on the street—tuned in to WCBS or KNX at drive-time—as Thanksgiving approached and passed and Christmas lights began to twinkle in the malls. If he lived in certain parts of the country, especially in the Northeast, he was already becoming accustomed to lining up around the block for a tank of gas and to finding that on Sundays there was not a service station open for miles around. And it was all the fault, he was told, of tin-pot dictators like Muammar el-Qaddafi and a bunch of jumped-up desert sheikhs whose fathers had lived in tents! If lack of victory in Vietnam was humiliating, this was downright mortifying.

Not everybody was taking this simplistic view of the "crisis," however. Some politicians, journalists and students of the oil industry were forming the opinion that the facts just did not add up. In the summer of 1973, well before the embargo, representatives of the states of Connecticut, North Carolina, Michigan, Massachusetts, New York and Florida had appeared before the Senate Antitrust Subcommittee to suggest that the major oil companies were creating an artificial shortage. New York State Assistant Attorney General Charles La Torella, Jr., pointed out that as of June 1, U.S. gasoline reserves totaled 202.5 million barrels, substantially more than in 1972, when no "crisis" had developed. When the embargo went into effect, the now geopolitically legitimized shortages showed up in a decidedly erratic way. By year's end, motorists in the Northeast were waiting three hours and more for gas that was still plentiful in Seattle, Dallas and even Denver, which had been heavily hit by the summer shortage. The West Coast as a whole was for the time being largely unaffected by the crisis, except inexplicably, for Oregon. Inexplicably, that is, unless credence was given to the view that Oregon had run afoul of the oil companies by passing some stringent environmental protection laws. Soon Oregon was forced to impose a form of rationing in which motorists could buy a maximum of ten gallons of gas on only odd or even dates, according to the final digit on their license plates.

Similar forms of restriction, official and unofficial, occurred across the country, and violence began to break out in the ever longer lines. Gas station operators were beaten up and even killed, and similar fates befell motorists trying to cut in on lines. Gradually the irregular patchwork of shortages spread to cover the entire nation, finally reaching even California, which by February 1974 was forced to adopt odd/even-day rationing along the lines pioneered in Oregon.

But still the skeptics were not convinced. Stories circulated about fully loaded oil barges backed up for miles on the Ohio River because storage tanks were full to capacity, and tankers waiting for weeks in New York harbor, unable to unload because there was nowhere to put their cargoes. Nor were these just regional aberrations. It was whispered that in many parts of the country storage facilities were at capacity. Even the American Petroleum Institute, an industry mouthpiece, admitted in January that inventories of most refined products were higher than they had been a year earlier; yet the so-called crisis continued. Could it be, informed observers wondered, that the oil industry was stockpiling petroleum products until demand rose to a point that would permit a quantum leap in prices? Could it be that the industry was taking advantage of the OPEC embargo to provide itself with a smoke screen? Could it be that the multinational character of the big oil companies might mean that they were tacitly in league with OPEC? Could it be that the Nixon Administration's deep-seated ties to the oil industry were causing the federal government to turn a blind eye to the entire situation?

The shah of Iran seemed to think so. Interviewed by Mike Wallace for CBS, he asserted that the United States was receiving more oil than ever before and frankly suggested that the major oil companies were creating artificial gasoline shortages as leverage to raise prices and increase profits. When Wallace asked the shah outright if he believed fraud was involved, the shah replied, "Well, something is going on for sure." He might have noted too that the spectre of shortages had been used by oil lobbyists to help steamroll approval of the trans-Alaskan pipeline through the U.S. Senate, despite heavy opposition from environmentalists. That was in July 1973, and by the time the House voted on the issue in November, the OPEC embargo was in full swing so the oil lobbyists could relax, knowing that their work had been done for them. The House approved the pipeline by a resounding 361–14.

Not everyone on Capitol Hill was taken in by the oil companies' scenario, however, and much interesting testimony was elicited in the spring of 1975 during hearings held by the Senate Foreign Relations Subcommittee on Multinational Corporations, chaired by Senator Frank Church of Idaho. The Church hearings did not focus on the immediate causes and circumstances of the 1973–74 "shortages," ranging instead over the preceding decades to provide a background that helped clarify the character of the "crisis" by describing its antecedents. Testimony made it clear that countries like Iraq had been so exploited and

By February 1974, lines at the gas pumps were found from
coast to coast. *UPI/Bettmann*

misled by avaricious U.S. and European oil companies that
they had every reason to feel anti-American, even without
the festering sore of the United States' support of Israel.
These hearings suggested that the OPEC embargo should
have caught no one by surprise, certainly not the multinational oil companies, who through various operating
agreements were actually benefiting financially from
OPEC's action. If nothing else, the Church hearings
brought out the fact that all components of the oil indus-

try—multinationals and members of OPEC alike—were irrevocably locked into a single worldwide system. If an embargo against the United States would benefit OPEC by permitting the establishment of new price levels, it could not help but benefit American-owned oil companies at the same time. And if those American-owned companies manipulated the market to their advantage (and hence ultimately to the advantage of OPEC), the executive branch of government had historically done little to discourage them, to the extent that the oil industry seemed virtually immune to serious antitrust prosecution.

The bottom line of all this was that any rise in oil prices benefited all those affiliated with oil producers and almost nobody else. True-blue, America-right-or-wrong, love-it-or-leave-it holders of Exxon and Mobil stock found themselves in bed with Middle Eastern "bogeymen" like Colonel Qadaffi. As far as the American economy was concerned, the consequences were all negative, since any rise in oil prices inevitably contributes to inflation.

The rises were significant enough, even if pump prices did not reflect the extraordinary price increases that took place in the world market. (A barrel of OPEC oil increased in cost by 400 percent over a twelve-month period.) Before the OPEC blockade American motorists had been paying an average of less than thirty-seven cents a gallon for regular unleaded gasoline. Shortly after the blockade was lifted, on March 18, 1974, that same gallon cost fifty-four cents, an increase of almost a third, and the price would continue to ascend gradually for a half dozen years, until another "crisis" caused an even more dramatic climb.

Suspicion that the oil companies might have helped engineer the price increase was by now rampant among consumers, yet the perception remained that OPEC did genuinely have the whip hand, and the Arabs' anger over U.S. intervention in the Yom Kippur war was clearly real. There was an understanding, too, that many new factors had come into play. With the Suez Canal closed in the aftermath of the war, tankers from the Middle East would have to make their way around Africa, increasing costs. American producers, so their own propaganda argued, might need to turn to more inaccessible and expensive sources, such as oil-bearing shale reserves, to make up the domestic shortfall. This would involve enormous outlays, the argument continued, taxing the liquidity of even the wealthiest companies. Under such circumstances, surely it was forgivable if a company like Occidental Petroleum was showing profits up by 718 percent in the first quarter of 1974!

A period of fervid reassessment followed, during which President Nixon launched his "Project Independence," aimed at freeing America from its thrall to foreign energy producers by the year 1980. The scheme was both convoluted and hazy and involved such notions as the Administration's raising $100 billion to develop a synthetic fuel industry. Some pundits urged the activation of America's vast coal reserves (which, not incidentally, were largely owned by the multinational oil companies). Environmentalists flinched at such an idea, pointing instead to the untapped possibilities of the sun's energy, and before long socially conscious movie stars were heating their swimming pools with the help of solar panels. As for the average motorist, he remembered the long lines and saw the climbing prices on the gas pumps. He thought about the continuing threat of OPEC and, thanks to the television network news, came to learn the names of obscure Gulf emirates where robed figures drove stretch limos across the desert at speeds that would have been considered obscene on the Interstates. Middle Eastern princes even invaded California, buying Beverly Hills mansions and painting pubic hair on the garden statuary. The average motorist marveled at all this and concluded it was time to trade in his gas guzzler for something a shade more practical.

When the "crisis" finally reached LA, early in 1974, the prices for used Volkswagen Bugs soared, so that a 1968 or 1969 model in decent condition often sold for considerably more than it had brand-new. This was due to the simple fact that there was a sudden demand for reliable small cars, a commodity in short supply. As recently as October of 1973, standard size cars had been outselling compacts and subcompacts by 2 to 1. In November the ratio dropped to 5 to 4, and by December smaller cars were selling at the same rate as larger vehicles. In January and February the big V-8's sat on the showroom floor while compacts were driven away as fast as retailers could supply them. Foreign car dealers were experiencing an unprecedented boom. The reason was simple: 1974 standard model American cars averaged less than twelve miles to the gallon (only half the mileage per gallon American cars had offered in the early fifties). A typical import would give seventeen miles per gallon, and a Beetle even more.

Of course, not everybody wanted a Beetle, used or factory-fresh. Many buyers were looking for a car that approximated the style and comfort of a standard American car while offering greater economy. To some extent American compacts fit this bill, but the Big Three were not tooled up to increase compact output significantly. (In the early months of 1974, tens of thousands of workers were laid off at GM, Ford and Chrysler, chiefly because of the sudden fall-off in demand for large cars.) VW was attempting to take up the slack with its relatively new Super Beetle. The real beneficiaries of the postcrisis mentality, however, were the Japanese, especially Datsun and Toyota, with Honda ready to emerge from the wings and Mazda already testing the waters with several models, including the revolutionary rotary-engined RX-2.

Toyota and Datsun/Nissan had paved the way; even before the OPEC "crisis" they had been making impressive gains in the market. In 1956, Toyota had sent to America a three-man survey team, which toured the country and recommended that the company concentrate on Southern California as its export testing ground. Toyota's initial venture into the American marketplace, the Toyopet, was expected to compete with the VW Beetle but failed to capture the imagination of the buying public. A similar fate befell Datsun's ineptly named Cedric sedan, though a small truck introduced at the same time enjoyed some modest success on the West Coast. The Japanese persevered, however, and rather than attempting to go head-to-head with the VW Beetle—which they now perceived as appealing to a finite and already saturated sector of the market—they set about rethinking the small car with the American customer in mind. Newer models such as the jeeplike Toyota Land Cruiser and the sporty Datsun SPL 212-213 kept the Japanese companies alive in America through the early sixties. Then, in 1965, came a major effort to market the Toyota Corona in the United States. The Corona was a conventional-format, 90 hp sedan that was not much larger than a Beetle yet was considerably roomier and more powerful, performing and handling very much like a Detroit compact. Moreover, it had been in production in Japan for several years so that by the time it appeared on American roads all the engineering bugs had been eliminated, which quickly won the Corona a reputation for reliability that soon began to attach itself to Japanese cars in general. Datsun/Nissan's 310 series cars, notably the Bluebird sedan, had similarly established a reputation for solidity and trustworthiness, and by 1966 Toyota and Datsun/Nissan between them were shipping more than 56,000 cars a year to the United States, but they were still behind several European nations, led by Germany, in the import market.

The Japanese motor industry benefited from the low tariffs imposed by the U.S. government, for the American manufacturers felt so secure in their position that they hardly bothered to lobby for trade barriers. By contrast, most European countries protected their car industries with high tariffs, which delayed Japanese penetration of those markets. This meant that Toyota and Datsun could compete with American compacts on pricing, and their advantage increased as some Detroit compacts grew in size to the point where they were not much smaller than standard American cars. With new models like the Toyota Corolla and the Datsun 1200, Japan's Big Two continued to make substantial gains among American customers. By 1970, Datsun had 640 distributors throughout the country, and by 1972 Japan finally overtook West Germany to become the top exporter of cars in the States, selling 697,788 vehicles in America that year. Suggested retail price for the Corolla at the time was $1,953, which meant it undersold Ford Pinto ($1,960), the Chevy Vega ($2,060), the AMC

Gremlin ($2,121) and even the VW Beetle ($1,999). The American auto industry did not yet perceive a serious threat, but the OPEC "crisis"—or, more accurately, its aftermath—would soon change all that.

Before the eventual pattern emerged, however, there was a glitch in the marketplace that caused temporary confusion, especially in the executive offices of Detroit. As noted, during the "crisis" and immediately thereafter, there was a run on small cars—VW's, Datsuns, Toyotas, Pintos, anything that was available. Then, with the return of gasoline—even at inflated price levels—suddenly the American public had a renewed yen for big cars. The thousands who had been laid off at Cadillac and Lincoln and other full-size car plants were now working overtime. For a few months sales of compacts and imports sagged. Perhaps the abdication of Nixon, after the nightmare of Watergate, signaled a return to normalcy. (After all, his successor, Gerald Ford, was a Michigan man.) In any case, Datsun and Toyota dealers found that product was moving slowly, though upstart rival Honda was enjoying a boom, thanks to the success of the Civic. More important in the long run, the American compacts were in the doldrums. By the summer of 1974, Ford found itself with a 96-day backlog of Pintos waiting to be shipped, and the story at GM and Chrysler was as bad or worse. Detroit was caught in a bind. The public seemed once more to want big American cars, but the government was telling manufacturers that it must produce more economical vehicles and demanded an industrywide corporate automobile fuel efficiency of 20 mpg by 1980. This meant that a given company could continue to produce gas guzzlers, but these behemoths would have to be offset by economical cars that would bring down the corporate average. The American giants knew that they had to adjust, but they didn't know how. The Japanese invaders sensed that they had already discovered the correct formula and, despite temporary setbacks, continued with their game plan. By 1975 the wisdom of this was clearly apparent. Many American drivers were finding out firsthand how reliable the Japanese cars were, and doubters were being converted by the excellent road test results being reported in magazines from *Road & Track* to *Consumer Reports.* Japanese cars were already establishing good resale values. Perhaps most important of all, American consumers were beginning to believe in the superiority of the Japanese work ethic to the labor practices of Detroit, with its highly publicized record of layoffs and union disputes.

The Japanese were aided, too, by the failure of European manufacturers to take advantage of the changed American scene. Certain companies, such as Mercedes, BMW and Volvo, cornered sectors of the marketplace, but these sectors as yet had no significant impact on the Japanese manufacturers' plans. The company that might have been expected to challenge Datsun and Toyota was Volkswagen, but Volkswagen found itself temporarily in eclipse. The popularity of the Beetle had declined sharply, and even the Super Beetle failed to reverse that trend. As an interim answer, VW introduced the 411, a conventional European-style small sedan with an 85 hp engine, but it was more expensive than its Japanese competition and less attractive, so that even the company's fine reputation could not guarantee significant sales. VW was pinning its hopes on its next generation of cars, spearheaded by the Rabbit, a moderately priced, Issigonis-format car with a front-mounted, water-cooled, four-cylinder engine and front-wheel drive. Unfortunately for VW, the first Rabbits developed a reputation for mechanical failures, especially oil leaks, and although the model eventually established itself, along with the higher-priced Dasher and Scirocco, VW did not regain full momentum till 1977 or '78, by which time the Japanese had established their dominance in the small-car field.

One thing that helped VW out of the doldrums was the introduction, in 1977, of a variation on the Rabbit powered by a revolutionary small diesel engine. Even more revolutionary, however, was the Wankel rotary engine that helped establish Mazda's name in America. The Wankel engine depended on internal combustion to drive a rotor instead of the conventional pistons. It had fewer moving parts than a piston engine and was highly efficient in terms of horsepower produced per pound of engine weight. It was relatively inexpensive to produce, provided the driver with access to spectacular bursts of acceleration, and was amazingly quiet. On the minus side, it required a good deal of maintenance because of wear and tear on the rotor seals, and it consumed more gas and oil than piston engines of comparable size. Introduced to America a couple of years before the OPEC "crisis," the Mazda RX cars were an immediate success with adventurous motorists, and even Detroit sat up and took note, many experts there declaring the Wankel the engine of the future. But the rise in oil prices and its concomitant emphasis on economy reduced the RX market both in America and in Japan, where gasoline prices had risen astronomically. Almost bankrupt, Mazda was forced to start over virtually from scratch, reentering the U.S. market with inexpensive piston-engined cars such as the Mizer and the GLC (Great Little Car) hatchback, which appeared in 1976 and 1977 respectively.

Another early entry from Japan was Subaru, which made its American debut in 1969 with a minicar that was woefully underpowered and found few buyers. The following year Subaru introduced conventional-looking sedans and coupes that compared with current Datsuns and Toyotas in appearance and price while offering front-wheel drive and some interesting mechanical features. If these cars failed to achieve the popularity enjoyed by Datsun, Toyota and Honda, it was largely due to the fact the Fuji Heavy Industries, Subaru's parent company, was half-hearted in establishing a dealership network in the United States. By the late seventies, however, Subaru began to gain a reputation for reliability and performance, based largely on word of mouth, and enjoyed a particular success with its four-wheel drive vehicles that were especially popular in rural areas. From that point on, Subaru's fortunes began to rise and Fuji responded appropriately.

Of Toyota and Datsun/Nissan's smaller Japanese rivals, the most fascinating and ambitious was Honda. Anything but typical of Japan's business establishment, the company had come from nowhere, being founded by Soichuro Honda, a blacksmith's son who had been apprenticed as an auto mechanic. Honda graduated from producing piston rings to designing a small two-stroke engine that could be used to motorize bicycles. In 1949 Honda built his first motorcycle, and by 1960, with backing and management guidance from the Mitsubishi Bank, had become head of the largest motorcycle company in the world. Fond of women, hard liquor and American-style sports clothes, Soichuro Honda liked to race cars and his own motorcycles and gained a reputation as a playboy eccentric. Americans who found the atmosphere of Japanese boardrooms disquieting in their formality had no difficulty in understanding Honda, whose style was that of a good ol' boy with a Japanese accent. For his part, he felt an affinity for Americans, and when he decided to go into the automobile business he made America his main target, preferring not to go head-to-head with the Big Two in the domestic marketplace—at least not until he was established. His first venture into the auto market, in 1962, was a curious though charming chain-driven sports car, the 500. Soon, however, he was manufacturing knockoffs of the British Mini that evolved quite rapidly into the Civic, which was established in the American market just in time to take full advantage of the aftermath of the OPEC "crisis."

The Civic was bigger than the British Mini, but still smaller than a Beetle; like the Mini, whose front-wheel-drive transverse engine format it borrowed, it offered good road handling, surprising power and great fuel economy, up to 40 mpg on the highway. Moreover, the remarkable CVCC engine could meet EPA emission requirements, yet still run on cheap leaded gasoline. Like the Beetle and the Mini, the Civic had real character, appealing not only to the thrifty but also to motorists who liked the feel of a sporty car. Many drivers thought it was the perfect car for the time, and it established Honda's reputation in America so that by the time the larger and more luxurious Accord appeared, in 1976, the brand was already well established.

Nineteen seventy-six was a pivotal year. For the first time Japanese imports to America passed the million mark (1,129,999), but in many ways it was the arrival of the Accord that did most to convince the American carmakers that a full-scale revolution was under way. The Civic had proved that the Japanese could build a great minicar; the Toyota Celica proved that they could offer a sporty sedan; while the Mazda RX series demonstrated that they were technological innovators. The Accord carried the challenge to a new level. Here was a car that took the logic of the Issigonis Mini to its conclusion, underpinned that logic with sound and innovative engineering, and added exterior and interior styling and finish of a quality that until then had been primarily associated with German luxury cars. The motor purred, the doors closed with a satisfying "thunk," and all this had been put together as an affordable package. Those who had not taken Japanese cars seriously up to that point could hardly fail to be impressed.

Actually, all three of the leading American manufacturers had entered into limited relationships with Japanese companies as far back as 1970. (American Motors, the number four manufacturer, came under virtual control of Renault, the leading French car builder in 1979.) Chrysler had struck a deal with Mitsubishi Motors to develop a small car, eventually known in America as the Colt, that would be sold through Dodge outlets (a variant, the Arrow, was offered by Plymouth dealerships). The Colt was a better-than-decent product but it suffered because Dodge salesmen made higher commissions by selling American-built compacts so didn't push the Colt. The gasoline crunch, however, gave the Colt a second lease on life. Shortly after, Ford bought into Toyo Kogyo, parent company of Mazda, with the hope of gaining access to Wankel technology, while GM purchased partial ownership of Isuzu, which led to a partnership in the production of automatic transmissions and gas turbine engines.

American manufacturers also worked with their European subsidiaries to produce small cars for the American market; nevertheless, when the Accord appeared it was years ahead of anything American automakers could offer. For that matter they had nothing at the low end of the price scale that could compete with the Toyota Corolla, hardly an eye-catching number but a car that provided excellent value for money because it was so soundly conservative from an engineering point of view. America's challenge to the Corolla came from cars like the Ford Pinto and the Chevy Vega, both of which sold well for a while but quickly developed poor reputations. In the case of the Vega, driver complaints amounted to a picture of all-around mediocrity. The Pinto suffered from everything from inadequate driver visibility to a poor maintenance record, and eventually it came to be looked on as a deathtrap, for its gas tank was apt to be ruptured during rear-end collisions, causing fire and explosions.

As for the Accord, there was no American competition for it at all, but by the late seventies domestic manufacturers were desperately struggling to bridge the gap. The most strenuous effort was made by GM, which launched a massive effort to develop a new family of "world cars"—automobiles that it was hoped would have as much appeal in Europe as in the United States. During development these were designated as J-cars—GM executives solemnly swearing that the letter "J" had nothing to do with Japan. Optimism ran high and was encouraged further by a second fuel crisis in 1979, this one occasioned by revolution in Iran. Again there were long lines at the gas pumps and the cost of unleaded fuel, which had stood at around 70 cents a gallon at the beginning of the year, shot up to $1.10 by the fall. Once more foreign manufacturers, led by the Japanese, upped their share of the U.S. market, but this time GM, at least, was ready—or so the GM hierarchy fondly hoped.

When the J-cars—the Chevrolet Cavalier, the Pontiac 1200, and the Cadillac Cimarron—were unveiled, they proved to bear a suspicious resemblance to the Honda Accord. To nobody's surprise they were Issigonis-format front-wheel-drive, transverse-engine vehicles, small but roomy. But they were heavier than the Accord, performed sluggishly by comparison with the Accord, and delivered disappointing mileage. In styling and detail they did not match the Accord, and even the paint job—despite the strenuous efforts of Fisher Body Division—lacked the crystalline finish of the Accord. Automobile journalists were not impressed, and neither was the public. Sales were flat, to say the least.

Ironically, once this second oil crisis was in the past, gasoline prices began to fall and sales of larger Detroit cars rose once more. This did not mean that small-car sales fell, because by now the American car-buying public had split into two major sectors: there were people who would buy full-size cars, presumably out of habit, as long as they could afford to run them. On the other side were people who had discovered that smaller and more economical cars suited their lifestyle and budget, and would buy them whether there was an oil crisis or not. Detroit still owned the full-size car market, but with the failure of the J-cars Detroit had virtually conceded the economy-car market to the imports, primarily the Japanese. Not only did the J-cars not match up to the Accord (which had been significantly improved by 1981), they also failed to match up to other Japanese cars that were now challenging the Accord. GM had not been alone in attempting to meet the Honda challenge, and the Japanese entries in the class included such formidable competitors as Nissan Stanza, the Toyota Tercel and the Mazda 626, all capable of giving the Accord a run for its money. If the Japanese had serious competition it was from European imports such as the Volkswagen Scirocco.

While the Japanese had been winning the numbers game among the imports, European manufacturers had also been strengthening their position in certain areas of the market. There were still American drivers who favored Lincolns and Cadillacs, Corvettes and GTOs, but throughout the seventies Mercedes and BMW had continued to build on their quality image to become, along with Jaguar and a handful of other European imports, the ultimate status symbol cars. Meanwhile, Porsche—not to mention Nissan—challenged in the performance-car area, while Saab and Volvo solidified their grip on small but significant groups of consumers.

Detroit was far from dead in 1981, but to a large extent it dominated the least interesting areas of the marketplace; its constituency had become the conservatives of the motoring world. To be fair, this covered plenty of territory, from the Eldorado drivers living in Boca Raton condos to the Firebird pilots cruising for action in the burbs of Queens and South Boston. Nevertheless, unless the Big Three could turn themselves around, the future belonged to Europe and, especially, Japan.

After **World War II**, BMW fought its **way back** to financial health by manufacturing motorcycles and "Isetta" minicars such as those seen here in New York in 1957. *UPI/Bettmann*

Chapter 15

INVASIONS OF PRIMACY

*T*he radical changes in automobile engineering and styling that came to fruition in the seventies had roots in such economic and historical factors as the rise in gasoline prices, but they also reflected societal shifts in ways both subtle and obvious. Cars changed as functional objects, but also as symbols, fashion accessories and owner surrogates—the sense in which the car parked on the driveway functions as a stand-in for its owner. In the past, prestige had been expressed primarily by size, perceived as an analogue of power, or overt sportiness, perceived as youthful power seasoned with a dash of recklessness. Big cars were sexy. Sports cars were sexy. Small sedans were decidedly unsexy, as exemplified by the failure of the Crosley and the disappointing sales performance of cars like the Nash Metropolitan. Even the VW Beetle was not sexy, its success deriving more from user-friendliness than anything else.

By the seventies, however, small sedans had become sexy, a phenomenon that had its origins in the success of Issigonis's Mini. The Mini was quite unlike any small car that had preceded it in that it did not present itself as a cheap car for the masses. Rather, it was so tiny that it was possible to perceive it as a rich man's toy, like the electric-powered miniature Rolls-Royces that could be purchased for children at Harrod's or Selfridge's. It is difficult to imagine a rich man owning a full-size Rolls and choosing, say, a Vauxhall Velox, as his second car. Yet plenty of British millionaires, from landed gentry to rock stars, supplemented a garageful of high-toned machinery with a Mini to zip around town in. I clearly remember Mick Jagger cruising Mayfair in a Mini with custom-tinted glass, circa 1965. The Mini not only looked like an expensive toy, it actually handled like a real sports car. It was cute and cocky and delivered the performance to make its presumptions palatable. Beyond that it had the good fortune to lend its name to one of the most dramatic fashion statements of the century, a statement that would be taken as a key symbol of a worldwide revolution in morals and sexual attitudes.

It was the French couturier Courrèges who in 1964 gave official notice to the world that hemlines were creeping up above the knee. But in London and provincial centers such as Liverpool and Leeds, British street fashion was way ahead of Paris. Britain, as Americans soon learned, was entering its golden age of rock 'n' roll and the fashion wars between sects like the Mods and the Rockers were thriving, especially at London clubs such as the Marquee (where you might have heard a fledgling group called The Who) and the Flamingo (home to local bands like Manfred Mann and many visiting American R&B stars). Many of the kids who hung out at these clubs made up the dancing audience on television shows such as *Six-Five Special* and *Ready Steady Go*, which helped spread big-city street fashion to the country at large. At some point in 1963, English shopgirls and secretaries began to turn up the hems of cheap skirts and dresses from Marks & Spencer's, and by the time Courrèges's 1964 spring collection was catching the attention of editors at *Vogue* and *Bazaar*, English teenyboppers were wearing skirts up to six inches above the knee. Mary Quant, reigning British fashion queen, was already featuring hemlines that just showed the knee and easily adapted to the street styles, as did younger designers like Sally Tuffin and Marian Foale. Within a couple of years, hems had risen to the point where garterbelts were forced into obsolescence. By then the style had crossed the Atlantic and the colloquial description "mini" was firmly established. Few Americans realized, however, that British journalists had derived the word "miniskirt" from the (for them) ubiquitous BMC Mini. Soon everything "mini" was chic—from minibikes to the minicams used by TV news crews—and the popularity of the word derived from the cheeky but practical Mini.

Although the BMC Mini never made it across the Atlantic, it is perhaps not farfetched to suggest that its namesake, the miniskirt, helped prepare the way for the Mini's Japanese and European derivatives. The miniskirt helped redefine sexiness, replacing the curvaceous look of Marilyn Monroe and Mamie Van Doren with the leggy coltishness of Jean Shrimpton and Twiggy. It would be difficult to imagine Jayne Mansfield emerging from a Honda Civic without seeming grotesque. Her amplitude demanded the scale of a Cadillac, whereas the miniskirted, presumably liberated, model-star of the Aquarian age could make a subcompact seem sexy simply by sliding behind the wheel. More to the point, the miniskirt was a very visible reminder of and advocate for the less-is-more philosophy that took hold in the late sixties and early seventies. As far as clothing was concerned, this philosophy transcended and survived the miniskirt. It was basically an expression of the notion that a young, healthy body, male or female, was apt to be at least as attractive in a cheap T-shirt and well-fitting jeans as in a tailored suit. Such a notion was at the basis of the health and exercise movement (jogging rose in popularity along with the Japanese car) and it affected the way people thought about other purchases, including automobiles. In a sense a Honda Civic was like a T-shirt or an off-the-peg miniskirt. It was something you threw on and looked good in. The Civic, despite its respectable name, was a car that did not wear a necktie. At the same time, like that hard body in jeans and a tank top, it was known to perform, and much the same could be said of other imports that descended from the BMC Mini.

But that was not the whole story. Other fashion changes were arriving from the opposite end of the market, especially the luxury cars imported from Germany. Mercedes-Benz can reasonably be thought of as the oldest car builder in the world (though the two marques Mercedes and Benz did not merge until 1926), and in some respects it is, along with Rolls-Royce, the most traditional. There is a logical progression from the Mercedes Simplex of 1902 to the Mercedes sedans of today, a family resemblance that can be traced through such masterpieces as the SSKs and 540Ks of the thirties and the 300Ss of the fifties. At the same time Mercedes has always managed to keep up with the times, even to anticipate trends, especially in engineering. The secret of the company's continuing success can best be understood as the building of cars that are expressions of a proud engineering tradition. This is what gives Mercedes cars a sense of continuity from decade to decade, let alone from model year to model year. (Nothing could be further from the Detroit philosophy of planned obsolescence.) At the same time the constant progression in Mercedes-Benz technology has ensured that the evolution of the car's gestalt would not merely keep pace with its competition but in fact would make Mercedes the international standard of the industry, and one of the civilized world's most recognizable status symbols. Certainly the innovative character of Mercedes engineering is crucial to the car's personality; but it is the precision of the engineering—perceived as essentially German—that has given the marque a reputation for quality and reliability matched only by Rolls-Royce.

Mercedes has always had admirers in the United States, and in the postwar era the German economic miracle once again drew the attention of affluent Americans to the high standards to be expected from German cars. Grand Prix and sports car championships in the fifties guaranteed the marque's continued legitimacy as a performance car, but this was only one aspect of Mercedes' all-around appeal. Equally significant was the attention paid to safety factors. In the mid-fifties the 180 helped pioneer the notion of a "safety shell" passenger compartment and, starting in 1959, the company launched a systematic attack on both active and passive safety problems, a program intended to make the Mercedes less prone to accidents while at the same time providing better protection, should accidents occur. Over a period of several years this led to innovations such as door locks that would automatically be released in the event of a crash, thus preventing the driver and passengers from being trapped, and antilock brakes.

Volvo, which also placed great emphasis on engineering for safety, developed a reputation for conservatism that suited its market placing. Mercedes, on the other hand, was able to have the best of both worlds, its long sporting history and the performance of its current models enabling it to be perceived as a producer of rather dashing cars even as its position in the market became more establishmentarian by the year. Thus the image Mercedes has projected since the late fifties has been somewhat ambiguous.

A German tailor who had spent some time working in London's Savile Row once commented on the difference between a British custom-tailored suit and its German equivalent: a British tailor would take pains to disguise a customer's incipient paunch; a German tailor would subtly emphasize that same paunch because in Germany's postwar meritocracy a paunch was perceived as a symbol of success. It would be an exaggeration to say that Mercedes in the sixties and seventies became a paunchy car, but it did cultivate a well-fed look that was acceptable because it was expressed in such tasteful and luxurious terms. If one can find fault with Mercedes cars of the modern era, it is certainly not in their performance or all-around engineering excellence, but rather in a hint of smugness in the styling that is probably a consequence of living so long in close proximity to one's own definition of perfection.

Such a successful definition of perfection was not lost on other manufacturers, and certainly not on Mercedes' domestic rival, BMW. Bayerische Motoren-Werke AG had entered the field of automobile construction in 1928 by building the Austin Seven (the same British car that had inspired Datsun in the thirties) under license. By the late thirties BMW had progressed to building splendid sporting cars like the 328, a winner of the prestigious Mille Miglia. After the war the company went through hard times but restored its fortunes by building the economical Italian Isotta "bubble car" under license and by the success of its motorcycle division. Its sights were set on higher things, however, and in 1962 came the 1500 series, a move in the direction of high-quality, compact-sized cars that was to pay off in both the home market and the export trade. For BMW, the seventies was a decade of consolidation in which they developed clearly defined product lines, ranging from sporty, compact four- and six-cylinder cars to sumptuous sedans like the 731. It would be the eighties before BMW established itself as the ultimate yuppie-mobile, but throughout the seventies the marque built its reputation in America as a luxurious but leaner alternative to Mercedes—perfect for the young executives who were beginning to prefer blazers and slacks to tailored business suits. A great car to deposit in your personalized parking slot outside the administration building but also a neat car to be seen in at the beach when you were wearing an Izod-Lacoste polo shirt and your favorite designer jeans. A Mercedes was sexy because it reeked of success. A BMW was sexy for the same reason, but in addition because it shared in some of the less-is-more aesthetic espoused by the Honda Civic. It was a car that acknowledged the more casual lifestyles of the seventies and eighties, yet at the same time could function as a more than acceptable prop for a black-tie evening.

A significant if largely oblique influence on the cars that crowded the Interstates in the seventies came from the great Italian independent designers clustered primarily in the city of Turin. From the earliest days of the automobile, Italian cars had been distinguished by rakish coachwork and stylistic flair, but their modern international influence can be traced back to Sergio Pininfarina's exquisite Cisitalia design on a Fiat chassis, which appeared in 1946. (This is the car that shares a place of honor with paintings by Picasso, Matisse and Mondrian at the Museum of Modern Art in New York.) The Cisitalia Fiat must be considered the fountainhead of all postwar sportscar styling, the automobile that made an ideal of low, sleek, aerodynamic elegance. Soon Pininfarina handcrafted bodies were appearing on high-performance dream cars like the Maserati A6 and the Ferrari 250 GTE. Nor was Pininfarina an isolated phenomenon. Other significant Italian design studios included Bertone (from which emerged bodies for the ultraluxurious Lamborghini GTs), Ghia, Touring, Michelotti and Ital Design, the latter founded by Giorgio Giugiaro, a Bertone protégé.

By the sixties, this elite group of Italian stylists had become the real couturiers of the automobile world. They made their reputations with luxury cars, but because they were independents they were free to take advantage of their up-market success by doing free-lance work for massmarket manufacturers. In 1956, Ghia had collaborated with Volkswagen to produce the striking Karman Ghia. By the sixties, automobile companies in Europe, Japan and the United States were scrambling for the services of the Italian master designers, as consumers turned from elaborate jet plane fantasies to simpler, road-hugging, truly aerodynamic shapes. The 1966 Mazda Luce, for example, had bodywork by Bertone, who three years earlier had been commissioned to design the experimental Chevrolet Testudo, built on a Corvair Monza chassis.

Most prolific of these designers, perhaps, has been Giugiaro, a former portrait painter whose Ital Design studio provides manufacturers with not only prototypes but also detailed cost analyses, plans for machine-tool production, etc. Set up in 1968, Ital Design styled the Scirocco and the Golf for VW as well as economy cars for Fiat, Hyundai and Isuzu, while still finding time to produce upscale designs for companies like BMW, Lotus and Alfa Romeo.

By the seventies, then, there were plenty of Italian-designed cars on American roads, and for every one actually designed by Bertone or Giugiaro, fifty showed the influence of the wizards of Turin.

The genius of the Japanese approach was to attempt to fuse the best of these three worlds—British stylish practicality, German engineering, and Italian brio—into packages that still provided American customers with the basic amenities to which Detroit had made them accustomed. There were compromises, of course. An Accord could not really offer everything you would expect from a BMW 350 CSi, but it came remarkably close, and dollar for dollar it was an extraordinary value. Like the finest European lux-

Part of a rising tide of Japanese imports, these Toyotas are shown on the dock in Boston. *UPI/Bettmann Newsphotos*

ury cars, it had the look and feel of being engineered from the inside out. The typical Detroit car, on the other hand, had the feel of being made up of two distinct components. There was the engineers' contribution and then there was a carefully styled shell encasing it. To a large extent this was a consequence of different divisions at a given manufacturer sharing engineering with one another but packaging their vehicles in varied styles of bodywork, so that a Plymouth, for example, would look different from its Dodge cousin, even though it was basically the same car.

This was a tradition that had thrived in the fifties but made little sense in the seventies, since it virtually prohibited the possibility of achieving that all-of-a-piece look that was so much prized in the European luxury cars.

If you looked at a Mercedes, you had the sense that everything from the camshafts to the chrome trim was the product of a single design process in which it was impossible to tell where engineering left off and styling began. If you looked at an American luxury car of the seventies— a Cadillac, for example—you had the feeling that it was put together in a piecemeal way, like something cannibalized from a half dozen stylistic and engineering sources.

Honda and other Japanese manufacturers realized that the all-of-a-piece approach could be made to work for cars in the midprice range. In an Accord or a Mazda 626, everything seemed to fit together as if it could be no other way, and this gave the cars a tremendously solid feel, very much at odds with what was increasingly perceived as the tinniness of Detroit automobiles. The styling and finish of Japanese midrange cars was excellent, and here, too, the Japanese learned many lessons from the European luxury market. But it was the homogeneity of styling and engineering, with its accompanying sense of logic and solidity, that made it possible to park an Accord between a Mercedes and a BMW without any sense of embarrassment. The Japanese had cracked the secret of creating that special automotive *gestalt* which in the case of European cars had often been attributed to tradition. Tradition, the Japanese showed, could be supplanted by thoroughness.

Thoroughness would not have worked, however, were it not for a fundamental love of the automobile that makes the best Japanese cars not only rational and reliable but also fun to drive and fun to be seen in. One thing the Japanese had on their side was the fact that in their postwar world the car has taken on a special social significance. Young Japanese males (and Japan remains very much a male-dominated society) are faced with a situation in which space and privacy are beyond the reach of those who in America would take the sanctity of apartments or condos for granted. An up-and-coming executive in Japan is apt to be living at home, under crowded conditions, with his parents and siblings. At a certain point he may bring a young woman into this environment, but before that stage is reached other strategies are needed, and for many in that position a hot car becomes an indispensable accessory. The Japanese automobile engineer or stylist grew up with this reality and understands, with even greater urgency than his American counterpart, that a car can be both a status symbol and a haven of privacy. The social stresses may be less formidable in America, the options greater, but the equation of car with sexual display and freedom does not change from one culture to another.

One consequence of post-1973 oil prices is that cars in general do not vary greatly from one culture to another. Gone is the day when the British sports car reflected the realities of one set of driving conditions while an American sports car mirrored the requirements of an entirely different driving environment. There are still twisting country lanes left in Britain, but anyone who drives them at anything like highway speed is taking his life in his hands. There is simply too much traffic to permit the kind of swashbuckling attitude that was once available to the drivers of Morgans and Invictas. For the most part the British motorist drives on well-engineered main roads not dissimilar to their American counterparts, and on high-speed motorways that are the decendants of American Interstates and German autobahns. The basic driving experience in Britain is not far removed from the driving experience in France or Germany or Italy or Sweden or Korea or Japan. Vestigial idiosyncrasies remain, especially where older roads are concerned, but in general it can be said that a homogeneity of motoring environment has resulted in similar driver requirements from country to country and even continent to continent, so that cars have become increasingly alike.

Until 1973, the one thing that insulated the American car industry from this tendency was cheap gasoline, which permitted every man a grandiosity of expression that was forbidden to all but the rich elsewhere in the world. After

1973 many Americans began to play by the same rules as Asians and Europeans, and with this came the sameness of product that afflicts the automobile marketplace today. As fins and grinning chrome radiator grilles slipped into the past, they quickly became objects of nostalgia and veneration. To encounter a '57 Malibu coupe on the street was to be transported back to an America that was simpler, at least in recollection, and that had the blustering self-confidence to support all manner of absurdity.

There were plenty of people who were willing to provide artificial respiration to keep that increasingly mythologized America alive. Significantly, George Lucas's *American Graffiti* was released in 1973, the year of the oil crunch. It was the first of a series of fifties nostalgia movies and TV shows—all of them starring finned Chevys and shark-nosed Fords—that displays no sign of abating. Meanwhile, tens of thousands of ordinary Americans held on to early-model T-Birds, gaudy Coupe de Villes and even Edsels, restoring them lovingly to their original condition and driving them on weekends, refusing to let the dream die even though for everyday commuting purposes they had succumbed to a Toyota.

In the end, those baroque gas guzzlers do not submit to logical criticism. It is all too easy to point out their excesses and inefficiencies, but finally they survive intact in the mind, reminders of a time when dreams were something tangible that you could park in the driveway.

With fuel conservation a national priority, speed limits fell in 1974.
UPI/Bettmann

Chapter 16

INTROVERSIONS

*A*cceptance of the small car, whether American, European or Japanese, was a victory for reason, accompanied, in 1974, by the adoption of a nationwide 55-mile-per-hour speed limit dictated by the perceived need for fuel conservation. As predicted by many experts, this speed limit had the effect of substantially reducing the number of deaths and serious injuries sustained in highway accidents. For the first time in history, Americans were driving modest-sized, fuel-efficient cars, fitted with seat belts (the use of which became compulsory in some places), at speeds that verged on the sedate, on a well-engineered Interstate system that was now virtually complete. For most of the wrong reasons, the forces of responsibility had prevailed.

The shift in spirit since the fifties could not have been more marked. It was far more difficult now for the driver to express his persona by means of his choice of car, except at the luxury-car level, where understated elegance had become the accepted norm. If franchise-oriented strips and malls had started to homogenize suburban landscapes in the sixties, by the late seventies that process of homogenization had spread to their ramps and parking lots. Cars bearing forty different nameplates broke down into perhaps half a dozen basic stylistic types, so that a subcompact hatchback assembled in Japan for an American manufacturer was hardly distinguishable from a subcompact hatchback imported from Europe, or a competing model built in Detroit.

In this look-alike world, manufacturers and car owners both searched for ways to personalize their vehicles. NASCAR, Indy and Formula One racers had for some time carried sponsor ads—for Penzoil, National Van Lines, Budweiser—and now automakers issued whole editions of road cars annoucing their identity in the form of large-scale logos stenciled or decaled onto their side panels. At a stoplight, you might find yourself alongside an otherwise anonymous automobile that bore the legend LE CAR. Stylistically there was little to differentiate the small Renault sold in the United States from several other subcompacts, but by becoming a mobile billboard and advertising itself as LE CAR it acquired a personality of sorts. Other vehicles

Renault's Le Car: the automobile as billboard. *Author's collection*

used the same written-word method to emphasize some unseen characteristic that presumably made that car superior in terms of performance. A car with a turbo-charged engine, for example, might make a prominent feature of the word TURBO as part of its showroom trim.

The power of the printed word on automobiles should not be undervalued. On Election Day, 1964, a truck plastered with Barry Goldwater posters was abandoned, during morning rush hour, in the middle of the Queens-Midtown Tunnel, which connects Long Island with Manhattan. Tens of thousands of drivers were inconvenienced and may even have been influenced to change their presidential vote, not considering the possibility that the truck had been planted there by supporters of Lyndon Johnson.

Every election promotes the personalization of automobiles in the form of political bumper stickers, a means of expression that derives from the venerable campaign button. Bumper stickers are less easily discarded than campaign buttons, however, so there is a tendency for them to remain in place for months and even years after the voters have made their choice, and there is a special poignancy to spotting a fading Dukakis sticker faithfully adhering to a shabby-genteel Volvo wagon as a new round of primaries approaches. The politicization of cars by means of bumper stickers is not limited to support for individual candidates. Many examples are frank statements of basic positions that serve warning of the driver's philosophy, which can be worth knowing when involved in a fender bender. The owner of a Sentra bearing the sticker SAVE THE REDWOODS may hold firm opinions but is likely to be amenable to reason. The owner of a Silverado pickup adorned with MAKE MY DAY and PROTECTED BY 45 MAGNUM should be approached with caution.

In general, bumper stickers fall into three categories. There are those that deliver purely factual messages (THIS CAR CLIMBED MOUNT WASHINGTON) or factual messages distorted by sentimentality (PRECIOUS CARGO ABOARD). More significant is the category of car owner who tries to tell the world something more personal about himself (HONK IF YOU LOVE JESUS or I'D RATHER BE HANG-GLIDING). Most common is the would-be humorous statement (BEAM ME UP SCOTTY, THERE'S NO INTELLIGENT LIFE DOWN HERE) which includes the subcategory of humor intended to demonstrate the driver's superior intellect (AUTHORS DO IT FOR POSTERITY).

A more expensive way of personalizing a car is the vanity license plate, an opportunity for ingenuity that all too often inspires the cute (MY TOY) or the obnoxious (I SUE 4U—spotted on a white Rolls-Royce Corniche parked outside a New York courthouse). The best that can be said for vanity plates is that they do provide a modicum of intellectual exercise for weary commuters, since the whims indulged in are often arcane and occasionally witty (COCO VAN). Less inspired examples with professional overtones (I DOC) can at least serve the purpose of identifying the level of banter that might be expected while undergoing, say, a glaucoma test.

A far more radical form of personalization was sometimes applied to vans, minibuses and recreational vehicles, each of which enjoyed increased popularity during the seventies (though gas prices and shortages set back RV sales at the end of the decade). Hippies in the late sixties had decorated VW buses and converted delivery vans with psychedelic paint jobs. In the early seventies, starting in Southern California, these evolved into custom vans decorated with exotic scenery: desert landscapes and palm-fringed beaches were favorite subjects. Inevitably these vehicles conjured up the notion of a sybaritic lifestyle on wheels, an impression carried through into the interiors, which in some cases were spectacularly plush in a K Mart kind of way. Such vans featured cocktail bars and television sets, radio phones and even chandeliers. And since this was the age of the sexual revolution, they were invariably furnished with comfortable sleeping quarters, sometimes of the waterbed variety. Exterior murals were the least of it. The custom van was the ultimate personal environment rolling down the Interstate on Goodyear Suburbanite Polyglas tires.

While these custom vans were essentially recreational vehicles, an emphasis on the everyday car as a personal environment has become one of the key characteristics of motoring in the past two decades. This notion has to some extent replaced the idea, at its height in the fifties, of the automobile as a form of self-expression. The extroversion of fins and chrome has been replaced by the introversion of reclining bucket seats and CD players.

Luxurious interiors date back to the early days of motoring—excluding the horseless-carriage period—but they were limited to a handful of expensive, hand-build vehicles, and then only to town cars rather than tourers. Such town cars as those constructed on chassis by Locomobile and Isotta-Fraschini sometimes featured hardwood paneling, quilted seats and many of the accoutrements of the Edwardian drawing room. But the real standard of the day was that set by the Ford Model T, which afforded comfort only by comparison with the horse-drawn buggy it replaced. Throughout the twenties and well into the thirties, the great majority of cars on the road were purely functional. Heating systems were primitive and options such as radios were rarities. As the industry entered the streamline era, standards of comfort increased significantly. At the most basic level, seat design improved, making long journeys easier on the spine. At the same time, options such as improved heating and ventilation systems became available in more and more vehicles, especially as customers moved up into the midprice range.

This emphasis on interior comfort accelerated at the end of World War II. The luxuries of the thirties, like radios, became the standard equipment of the fifties. But the greatest luxury of fifties interiors was their sheer spaciousness. The amazing thing about the cars of the seventies and eighties is the fact that they have lost relatively little of this roominess, despite a tremendous reduction in overall size (this is another part of the Issigonis legacy). Some of today's compacts actually offer as much passenger space as did a prewar Rolls-Royce Phantom II, along with creature comforts that were unavailable to the wealthiest car owner not too long ago.

Even the most modest car today is likely to feature a heating and air-conditioning system that provides enough flexibility to satisfy any but the most fastidious motorist.

Similarly, automobile seats designed according to ergonomic principles provide a degree of comfort that is seldom met with in the home. Dashboard metering systems, both digital and analogue, permit the driver to monitor his vehicle's inner workings with unprecedented accuracy. Power-operated windows are now available on moderately priced cars, while wing mirrors are commonly adjustable from within the cockpit. Many automobiles have even been furnished with cup holders that permit the driver to keep his morning coffee handy in rush-hour traffic without danger of its spilling. More than anything else though, electronic gadgets have permitted the motorist to customize the interior of his car till it fits him like a well-cut suit—or a preshrunk pair of jeans. Some of these devices—radar trap detectors, for example—perform a purely utilitarian function. Others elevate the experience of driving to a quasi-spiritual plane.

High-quality radios, if somewhat bulky, were available in the thirties and commonplace by the fifties, but a spectacular development of the seventies was the availability of miniaturized record-playing systems in the form of cassette tape players. Now the motorist was not confined to the radio programs available to him in a given geographical area. This innovation arrived at a fortuitous time, just as radio programming was becoming more and more stereotyped. Instead of being locked into subcretinous Top 40 shows, repetitive news broadcasts and mind-numbing call-in chat fests, the motorist could control his own listening destiny. He could, if he chose to, listen to Erik Satie, Theolonious Monk, Frank Zappa or a novel on tape. He could even learn to conjugate irregular French verbs in preparation for his upcoming vacation. Moreover, the interior of the automobile proved to be an acoustically satisfying environment so that with carefully placed speakers and the appropriate controls the motorist could wrap himself in sound about as efficiently as was possible anywhere outside a recording studio.

A sophisticated automobile sound system can be made to serve many purposes, both social and antisocial. In the hands of an audio-vandal it can destroy the tranquillity of a summer evening. (The notion of transforming cars into boom boxes is an unfortunate example of what can happen when cars begin to lose their glamour as mere cars.) On romantic occasions the sound system can be used to establish mood. But by far the most important use of the "vehicular entertainment center" is to cushion the driver from the outside world when he is traveling alone in his solipsistic capsule, whether sailing across the prairies or crawling toward the city at drive-time. Although he is still connected with the outside world (he can still tune into that traffic helicopter report), the cushioning effect is more significant, since it provides him with the illusion that he is able to invent his own existence, separate from the contingent reality of bottlenecks and traffic jams. By putting Brahms or Chuck Berry on the stereo, the motorist takes on the identity of the music which swells to fill the car as it swells to fill his mind. The car becomes like a miniature cathedral on wheels. As the aisles and apses, the vaults and full majestic volume of a gothic cathedral come wholly to life when it is filled with music, the more modest and very ungothic volume of a BMW or Honda takes on an added dimension when filled with music. However, the motorist is trying to make peace not with God but with himself. The soaring spires of a cathedral seem capable of transmitting Bach or Palestrina to the Heavens. The car is designed to hold everything inside, like a skull. In a sense, the shell of the automobile is a steel cranium, a protective enclosure for self-directed musical prayers that are projected through the speaker system.

The car of the fifties (or of the thirties, for that matter) was personalized as a body, its character expressed as an externalization of its function. The car of the seventies and eighties takes its essential function, transportation, for granted and instead internalizes and intellectualizes its personality. Despite the fact that modern cars are often very powerful in relation to weight (this too has come to be taken for granted), they are prized as much for their intelligence as for their brawn. This is not to say that sleek lines are not appreciated (a lean sleekness that would appeal to a health-club denizen) but they are perceived in a new way, as a computer is perceived as being different from a typewriter. From their electronically controlled ignition systems to their variable-speed windshield wipers they are thinking machines, or at least machines that readily respond to the motorist's thought processes. In reality, the basis of the car is still an internal combustion engine transmitting its power to a set of wheels, a fundamental concept that can be realized as a crude buggy open to the weather as well as a stretch limousine. For the modern motorist, what is most interesting is what separates today's car from the Model T rather than what links the two. What makes today's car different consists largely of elements that have little or nothing to do with the raw idea of "car-ness." Rather the secondary features, such as the quality of the stereo, help define its identity.

The degree to which these secondary features have helped shape personal environments can be measured by motorist behavior. Studs of the fifties combed their ducktails in the rearview mirror, and front-seat passengers have long enjoyed the benefit of flip-down vanity mirrors. But the notion of the automobile as an extension of the bathroom did not really take off until the seventies, when it became commonplace to see men taming their stubble with cordless electric razors as they negotiated stop-and-go traffic. People have become so at home in their cars that they behave as if they are in private, attacking blackheads or applying mascara as if there were no one else present to observe them.

If a car can be a bathroom (it had long had the possibility of serving as a bedroom) or an entertainment center, then it also had the capability of functioning as a mobile office, and here again electronic gadgetry has made this possible. Certainly commercial travelers crisscrossed the country years ago with their samples and order books, and the radio telephone is not a complete novelty, but the development of the cellular phone made the car-as-office concept a reality for tens of thousands of executives and entrepreneurs who did not enjoy the luxury of a chauffeured limo.

The use of the cellular phone while negotiating traffic is a measure not only of the extent to which the car has become a customized environment, but also of the degree to which the act of driving has changed over the years. The technical key to this is the automatic transmission, no longer a novelty, but the real change is psychological rather than mechanical. In the early days of the car and well into the automobile age, the act of driving was very physical and demanded considerable concentration. The constant gear changes called for when piloting a Model T required agility and coordination, and even more conventional shift systems were cumbersome and forced the driver to pay careful attention to gradients and highway conditions. The older highways themselves, with their poor sightlines, blind corners and questionable surfaces, ensured driver alertness.

Interstates, freeways, and automatic transmission changed all that. True, there are still drivers who prefer manual transmission and who remain sensitized to the actual act of driving, but increasingly it has become possible to drive without being fully engaged in the act. The mind doesn't exactly switch off, but rather, like the transmission, operates in automatic mode. Especially on a familiar route, as when commuting, it is possible to turn

The Mercury Lynx. *Bettmann Archive*

driving into an almost passive activity, in which essential maneuvers, such as lane changes, are performed from habit as much as from calculated response to changing conditions. In rush-hour traffic, such an attitude is almost essential. The driver must remain alert to the unforeseen errors of other motorists, but this engages only a relatively small portion of the brain. Plenty is left over for talking to a client or firing a subordinate over the phone.

The mobile office can also be equipped with a fax machine and a laptop computer. The latter can hardly be used by the driver while the car is in progress, but there is nothing to prevent him from completing a spreadsheet while enjoying an Egg MacMuffin in a parking lot, then sending that spreadsheet to his office by modem so that it is printed as hard copy by the time he arrives at work.

When it comes to the motorized personal environment, however, nobody can compete with the long-distance trucker. Accustomed to driving for days at a stretch and covering thousands of miles in a single run, the trucker inevitably looks on his rig as his home away from home. With his sleeper cab—roomy as any RV— and his citizen's band radio, the trucker spends his day in a virtually self-contained world, stopping from time to time only to take on diesel fuel or coffee at a friendly truck stop, which is to all intents and purposes part of a dedicated support system for his mobile universe.

The trucker does not need vanity plates. A multicolored collage of commercial plates from a score of states makes a far more dramatic display. The owner-driver does like to personalize his truck, however, and he often does so by having the names of loved ones—Cheryl, Joe Jr., Bobbie-Jean, Lana, Darryl, Ol' Red—lovingly painted on the exterior of the cab in flowing italic or copperplate script with many attendant scrolls and curlicues. Inside the cab there is likely to be a shrine of snapshots corresponding in large part to the names inscribed without. You may even find Ol' Red along for the ride, providing his master with company by day, guarding the truck by night. If this is a tractor-trailer rig, the trailer unit—and often the cab too—is likely to bear the insignia of some business, local or national, transformed into a supergraphic display. Big as billboards, the sides of these long-distance rigs are emblazoned with the heraldry of commerce, sometimes, like Mayflower Van Lines, advertising themselves, but more often advertising some highway-linked business such as Safeway or Sears.

In reality, all businesses today are highway-related, since the eclipse of the railways as a freight-carrying system has placed the responsibility for the crucial transportation dimension of the economy squarely on the shoulders of the trucker. Without the trucker, fruit does not make it from California to the Connecticut breakfast table, timber for building does not make it from Washington or Montana to the tree-poor Southwest. You could ban the private car from the Interstate System and the country would probably continue to function, but do away with the big rigs and the nation would grind to a standstill. The plain fact is that the trucker has a unique and irreplaceable position in the highway ecosystem. He really is the King of the Road and he is frustrated by the fact that the whole world does not recognize that basic truth (which explains his occasional abuse of power). Truckers are obliged to act like royalty in exile in their own country—Bonny Prince Charlies of the Interstate—and this has led to a long history of self-mythologizing, boosted by powerful shots in the arm from Hollywood and the Nashville wing of Tin Pan Alley.

Long-distance trucking began to gain momentum during the Depression, and during this same period truckers began to come together as a brotherhood, sharing not only trade secrets and favorite eating spots but also a common patois—as arcane as the patois of the railroadmen they were beginning to displace—and a mystique. This was celebrated in 1940 in the Warner Brothers feature *They Drive by Night*, starring George Raft, Humphrey Bogart, Ann Sheridan and Ida Lupino. The early sequences of the film, leading up to the accident in which Paul Fabrini, played by Bogart, loses an arm, constitutes a brief history of trucking in the thirties, from the days of the wood-sided boneshakers to the era of the heavy-duty all-steel truck. More significantly, the movie portrayed truckers as tough, two-fisted, freedom-loving individualists—cowboys on wheels—fighting corruption and injustice as well as the elements, and finding love and companionship wherever they could. If truckers as a group hadn't already hatched an image for themselves, then Warner Brothers did it for them. Not only were these jocks portrayed as hard as nails, they were also shown to be Galahads of the free enterprise system.

After the war, the truck driver's legend was taken up by country and western songwriters and performers. There were some prewar antecedents such as "Truck Drivers Blues" and "Truckers' Ball," but in the fifties a specific market was isolated and catered to with honky-tonk numbers such as Hylo Brown's "Truck Driving Man," Frankie Miller's "Truck Driving Buddy," and the Willis Brothers classic "Give Me Forty Acres (to Turn This Rig Around)." Charlie Moore and Bill Napier recorded western swing-style songs such as "Lonesome Truck Driver," while Jimmy Logsdon with "Gear Jammer" came close to perfecting a kind of half-sung, half-spoken, down-home delivery that would typify many future trucker hits.

These early C&W songs, with their steel guitar and country fiddle obligatos, spawned a whole new genre of radio show, usually coming on at midnight and running to six A.M. and aimed primarily at the all-night trucker. *Truckers' Club* from KLAC in Los Angeles and *The Night Rider Show* from Shreveport, Louisiana, are just two of dozens of such shows that have thrived over the years. Another Louisiana station, WWL, gained an audience when Charlie Daniels established himself as the diesel jocks' top nighttime disc jockey before going on to record such hits as "Uneasy Rider" and "The Devil Went Down to Georgia." The success of these shows in turn gave rise to a new generation of truck songs performed by singers like Dave Dudley ("Six Days on the Road"), Dick Curless ("Tombstone Every Mile"), Red Sovine ("Freightliner Fever"), Johnny Dollar ("Big Rig Rollin' Man") and Del Reeves ("Looking at the World Through a Windshield"). By the seventies, mainstream rockers looking for a country crossover were getting in on the act with numbers like the

Byrds' version of Lowell George's "Truck Stop Girl" and Commander Cody's "Mama Hated Diesels."

The trucker song reached its zenith in January 1976, when C. W. McCall's "Convoy" hit the top of the American pop charts. "Convoy" was different. The traditional trucker song was a plaintive ballad that tended to portray the diesel jockey as a kind of Odysseus in cowboy boots, buffeted by fate as he made his way home, proving his manhood when confronted with assorted challenges, feebly resisting the advances of truck-stop sirens, deriding Smokey the highway patrolman and longing for his girl back in Tulsa. They were like fragments of some lost epic. "Convoy," on the other hand—although it too deals in heroics and derides Smokey—is more like contemporary history, resembling the *Anabasis* of Xenophon more than the *Odyssey*. In "Convoy," McCall describes the cross-country expedition of an army of truckers who band together to protect themselves against the perfidy of the law, expressed in terms of an iniquitous speed limit. What makes it possible for this band of truckers to function so well, despite the forces arrayed against it, is its use of citizens band radio, a device that McCall employs effectively in his song, calling on its jargon to lend the narrative an exotic air.

Certainly, "Convoy" leaned toward exaggeration—it would take a nuclear strike force to stop these jocks—but it rang true because for a while such convoys were a very real part of the truckers' subculture. The 1973–74 oil "crisis" affected truck operators, especially the independents, more than anyone else. Oil prices had a very direct impact on the trucker's livelihood, and this negative was compounded by the federally imposed 55 mph speed limit, which if observed not only increased the duration of a trucker's journey but also caused his rig to perform at below maximum fuel efficiency—most American trucks were designed to cruise at around 62 mph. An immediate consequence was a series of strikes and protests; the Independent Truckers' Association organized a shutdown that led to considerable violence, with road blockades and scab truckers being "bombed" with concrete blocks dropped from overpasses. The shutdown eventually collapsed, but not before the truckers had discovered that they had an effective tactical tool in their CB radios.

CB radios had been legal in America since the fifties and began to be popular with truckers in the late sixties, as transistorization made them more practical. In the wake of the 1973–74 shutdown, thousands more truckers purchased CB's and that was when the possibility of organizing convoys to beat the system became a reality. Talking to one another on their radios, a group of truckers headed in the same general directon would form themselves into a kind of loose chain all traveling at the same speed, significantly above the limit, with a couple of the bolder drivers guarding "the front door" and "the back door." In such a situation, Smokey might pick off one or two speeders but could hardly ticket the entire convoy.

CB radio had many other uses, too, from signaling for help in the case of an accident to reporting road conditions to members of the brotherhood who might be following. Often it was employed simply to allay the loneliness of the long-distance driver by providing conversation, but it also offered an opportunity for the growth of service industries, such as the truckstop hookers who could snare Johns from the comfort of their trailers.

The 1987 version of Chevrolet's rugged S-10 Blazer.
Bettmann Archive

Soon, too, the CB became yet another piece of electronic equipment in more and more civilian cars. Owners justified installing them because of their utility in case of emergencies, but mostly people used them to listen in on truckers' conversations, and, not incidentally, pick up useful information about speed traps. By the late seventies there were enough CB's in regular four-wheel vehicles to call all kinds of new subcultures into being.

In one case, in West LA a six-year-old boy was found listening intently to the portable CB receiver his father had given him for his birthday. There was a puzzled look on his face and he clearly had no idea of the meaning of what he was hearing, though he sensed its urgency. What he had picked up was the voice of someone—these were the days before phone sex—who was masturbating while driving along the Pacific Coast Highway in rush-hour traffic and talking with animation to a female motorist who was all too willing to sponsor his fantasy.

It was perhaps the ultimate way to personalize the driving environment.

A modern Ford assembly line in Atlanta, said to be among the most efficient in the world. *UPI/Bettmann Newsphotos*

Chapter 17

RETRENCHMENT

*I*n a psychological sense, the completion of the Interstate System was equivalent to the closing of the frontier. It is difficult to put a precise date on the completion of the system, but in 1976 the Federal Highway Administration admitted that its role was changing from one in which the emphasis was on expansion to one in which improvement and maintenance were paramount. Though some minor expansion still took place, inflation alone dictated that few new major projects could be undertaken, and it was becoming clear that state and other local authorities would be hard-pressed to find the revenues for upkeep on their own. To adapt to these new circumstances, the Federal Aid Highway Act of 1976 authorized federal participation in the upgrading and rehabilitation of the existing Interstate System.

The heroic age was over. Just as gas guzzlers were giving way to commonsense compacts and Detroit was yielding to Japan, the road-building boom came to an end. The American driving environment had become finite and circumscribed in every imaginable way. In some regards it was actually shrinking, since many of the old highways were literally disappearing, traffic having moved to the Interstates. Parts of Route 66, for example, were totally abandoned and eventually the designation itself was discontinued. Stretches of it are still in active use, and other sections can be sought out by the highway archaeologist, but as a living concept Route 66 belongs to the past every bit as much as the Lincoln Highway or the Natchez Trace.

Of those older highways that remained in active use, many were already in an advanced state of decrepitude. In the early seventies, cars began to fall through holes that appeared without warning in elevated sections of Robert Moses' West Side Highway where it bordered the Hudson River in downtown Manhattan. Barely four decades old, the entire elevated highway below Midtown was first abandoned to joggers and roller skaters and then eventually pulled down while legislators and concerned citizens battled over Westway, a grandiose scheme to bring a new highway, disguised as a park, to the Manhattan shores of the Hudson. Although the park notion was invoked as a justification for Westway, Westway was not planned as a parkway , since the landscaping wasn't designed to be appreciated from a car. Rather, the park was a sop to Manhattan residents, many of whom protested that what they really needed was improved mass transit. The proposed parkland also left plenty of room for real estate development by the kind of entrepreneurs who are much in evidence at $5,000-a-plate political benefits.

The battle over Westway was fought between "progessive capitalists" and environmentalists. Ultimately, the issue that put an end to the scheme was protection of the striped bass, which spawns in the Hudson, a court agreeing that landfill for Westway would destroy the fish's habitat. The political background was far more complex, however: Congress was irritated that federal funds (theoretically Westway would have been part of Interstate 478) were being requested for a scheme that ultimately would have lined the pockets of a few local businessmen without much benefiting the general public in New York City or elsewhere.

The defeat of Westway was a sign that even though old roadways like the West Side Highway were crumbling, people had had enough of highway megalomania for the time being. It was no longer possible to present the construction of superhighways as visionary projects. Road users and those who lived and worked near the highways took the achievements of the Interstate System for granted but were also increasingly aware of its limitations and shortcomings. After a quarter century of carte-blanche expansion, highway authorities were being called to task by a well-organized coalition of public interest groups.

The 1987 Toyota Corolla FX 16 GT-S: a good example of a small car with pretensions that have to be taken seriously. *Bettmann Archive*

Interestingly, traffic has continued to move quite well up and down the western edge of Manhattan without the benefit of any limited-access highway below Midtown. The older sections of the highway system are most vulnerable at points where they span rivers or confront other obstacles, especially where they are carried by a bridge. Bridges tend to create bottleneck situations and they are vulnerable structures. In older cities they were often built before the automobile age and then adapted to motor traffic. This is especially the case in New York City, where elderly structures like the Manhattan and the Williamsburg bridges, key access points to Manhattan from the outer boroughs, have been closed or partially closed for significant periods of time because rotting girders or deteriorating suspension cables have threatened public safety. City engineers report that many New York metropolitan area bridges are in urgent need of major repair. Meanwhile, in upstate New York, in 1988, an important highway bridge was swept away in a flood, causing the loss of several lives. Again, engineers suggested that scores, if not hundreds, of New York state bridges are in need of structural attention.

Clearly this problem is not limited to the Big Apple or New York State. It is to be found in every part of the country and demonstrates that, while America's Interstates are generally well surfaced and maintained, there are thousands of weak spots inviting disaster. During the 1989 Bay Area earthquake, a double-decked section of the Nimitz Freeway in Oakland, California, supposedly built to resist seismic shocks, collapsed like a house of cards, killing a number of motorists. Here, as in the case of the New York bridge swept away by floodwaters, an act of God precipitated the tragedy, but many of the other tragedies waiting to happen require nothing but the passage of time to come to fruition. Attacked by weather and pollution, girders decay and the constant pounding of traffic puts a tremendous stress on the best-designed structure.

The Interstate System has been deteriorating since the moment it was finished—before it was finished, actually, since old parts of the system, like the collapsed section of the Nimitz Freeway, were already antiquated by the time the newer parts were built.

Like the closing of the frontier this decay signals an end to a certain kind of momentum that had been taken for granted. Instead of anticipating a new link in I-95, the driver now begins to count fresh potholes, or to anticipate traffic tie-ups where inadequate earlier planning has necessitated road widening or the strengthening of an overpass. Instead of being a system in a flux of adventurous expansion, the Interstate network has become a system in need of repair. It is beginning to suffer from some of the same problems that beset the railroads a few decades earlier, when improvements in rolling stock were negated by deteriorating roadbeds. A locomotive designed to pull a train at 100 miles an hour must slow to a crawl if the ties are loose and the road ballast crumbling. So it is with the highways. It is difficult to be as excited about the performance of a new car if the highways are deteriorating and overcrowded. Until the early seventies, the American automobile and the American highway system had grown together. From the mid-seventies onward they found themselves out of sync.

Major differences remain between highways and railroads, however. The highway system does still provide the advantage of permitting the driver to go where he wants, when he wants, without being subject to schedules and the whims of management. Despite growing frustrations with an increasingly inadequate system, this apparent freedom of choice continues to massage the motorist's ego, so that he remains willingly dependent on the highways he often curses. Also, the complex interplay between public ownership (of the roads) and private ownership (of vehicles) is a peculiarly democratic arrangement that helps ensure the survival of the system, even if the public sector can no longer keep pace with the private in this symbiotic process.

The truth is that Americans are more firmly wedded to their automobiles than ever. Partly this is because of the way they have come to rely on cars as personalized environments that afford privacy—like treehouses on wheels—rarely encountered at work or at home. Partly it is because of the way Americans are hooked into the roadside culture that has grown up with the highways and that continues to expand even though the highways themselves have ceased to.

When wigwam auto courts and zoomorphic food outlets first appeared along the highways, they relied upon the novelty of their appearance to arrest the progress of the motorist whose chief purpose was to make his way from Bismarck, say, to Rapid City. By the time drive-in restaurants and suburban supermarkets had become common-place, that was already beginning to change. The roadside business was now the final destination of many journeys, and that tendency accelerated rapidly in the era of the fast-food chain and the shopping mall. It is probably safe to say that the majority of car journeys undertaken in America today involve either a commute between home and job or an expedition to a highway-dependent commercial enterprise such as a supermarket or fast-food franchise. A substantial amount of the money earned as a consequence of the daily commute is in fact spent at roadside businesses, so that these two functions of the car are intimately related. The car has become, for most Americans, the intermediary between earning and spending. In this consumer economy, it is as crucial as credit.

The importance to the economy of the automobile industry, including such satellite industries as oil and rubber, is obvious enough. More to the point is the way the retail economy as a whole is tailored to the car and vice versa. This is apparent in changes in automobile design over the years. The car trunk received its name because in the early days of motoring it was literally a trunk strapped to the back of a touring car. It was a conventional piece of luggage, adapted to new circumstances but intended primarily to carry the clothes and personal belongings that would be needed on an extended journey. Soon the trunk became a built-in feature, but it was still intended for the same basic purpose, hence the continuation of the name. For some time these built-in trunks remained relatively small on most cars, but a significant conceptual change arrived with the station wagon, or estate car. Such vehicles first appeared in the twenties and were actually used on estates and ranches as hybrid car-trucks, available for family outings but chiefly looked on as working vehicles capable of carrying cargoes of hay or baling wire. In the thirties they began to be attractive to suburbanites, who liked the rural image they supplied but who also appreciated their cargo-carrying possibilities. The back of a wagon was a great place to carry a picnic basket or stash the family dog. It was also very useful when shopping at the local supermarket, providing room for a week's supply of groceries, far more than could be crammed into a conventional trunk. After the war, wagons became even more popular, while conventional sedans began to offer more and more trunk space. Such space was still useful on long journeys, but it found regular employment in trips to the market, the hardware store and the shopping center. When cars became smaller, manufacturers made certain that they continued to offer plenty of storage space, knowing that this had become an everyday requirement. Even the smallest of the subcompacts was offered in a station-wagon format, and a novel solution to increasing carrying volume was found in the three-door or hatchback formula, which combined the looks of a sedan with some of the features of a wagon. All these developments were designed largely to enhance the automobile as a shopping tool.

In this way, the shopping environment has shaped the car, and reciprocally the car has shaped the retail environment. The original strips evolved into mercantile ecosystems in which the space allocated to parking dictated low-density development. The mall concept permitted the return to a city-style high-density shopping experience, but it too was predicated on the automobile and hence demanded either huge lots or elaborate parking structures. Such parking structures are often handsome, in a functional way, and some are successfully integrated with the architecture of the actual shopping precinct. Often, though, the mall is sited to take advantage of low land values and hence surrounds itself with an apron of raw parking space.

Architecturally, malls vary from the banal to the Byzantine. A few, such as architect Frank Geary's Santa Monica Place Mall, are distinguished statements by any standard. More common in recent years are eclectic postmodern exercises that combine elements as varied as the Crystal Palace and marine architecture of the ocean liner *Normandie* vintage. Few of these very practical fantasies will find their way into the orthodox history books, but often they are enjoyable to contemplate and certainly they enliven the highway landscape. Like the wigwam motor courts, they are attention grabbers, though in a very different way. If the wigwam courts were mercantile folk art, the more inventive malls are the knowing expression of *haut* consumerism, monuments to a world in which names like Ralph Lauren and Donna Karan are as familiar in the hinterlands as they are in New York or LA. This is not to say that everyone is going to the mall to buy Armani suits or Geoffrey Beene skirts, but it's more fun to buy a denim jacket when the luxury goods are on sale next door. The mall is democratic in an upwardly mobile sort of way. In some respects it performs the function once performed by movie palaces, where liveried ushers conducted patrons through ornate lobbies into auditoriums garnished with twinkling stars and trompe l'oeil evocations of Guadalajara or Capri. The movie palace was designed to make the man in the street feel like a somebody, at least for a couple of hours, and this is equally true of the best malls.

The aesthetics of the mall are actually quite traditional, certainly as far as the interiors are concerned. Superior examples are well built from high-grade—even luxurious—materials. They echo the Galleria in Milan, or the Burlington Arcade in London, by emulation rather than the purloining of symbols. Certainly they use modern structural devices, and their layouts are often novel, but Sir Christopher Wren could time-travel to any of the better malls and not be thrown into a state of shock. Recently, malls have come to thrive on good taste (almost to choke on it in some instances) and this separates them from the original aesthetic of the strip which for years reveled in frank plebian glitz.

For decades, the call of the open road was the primary motive for leisure driving. Lately it has been replaced by the call of the open mall. Since the open road is increasingly hard to find, destination becomes all-important, and for tens of millions of motorists every day, destination means the local Galleria or the attendant strip: Burger King, Dunkin' Donuts, AAMCO, K Mart, Egg Head Software or the Route 30 Cineplex. These enterprises, and thousands others like them—both franchised and independent—make up an exurban fabric we have come to take for granted. For many, it is also something to deplore as crass and vulgar and ugly, yet clearly there is something about it that is attractive to millions of people.

The point to keep in mind is that the typical commercial strip should not be compared to Venice or Paris any more than the typical comic strip should be compared to a Titian or a Dégas. In order to enjoy the comic strip, you must accept its conventions and devices. It is unlikely ever to produce practitioners capable of scaling the heights of sublimity reached by Titian or Dégas, but in the hands of artists like George Herriman (*Krazy Kat*), Cliff Sterrett (*Polly & Her Pals*) or Milton Caniff (*Terry and the Pirates*), its own complex aesthetic can provide the basis for a popular art form that is rich and occasionally surprisingly subtle.

The commercial strip is to the highway what the comic strip is to the newspaper. Both had humble beginnings (the comic strip in its modern form is the elder by a couple of decades) and both caught on very quickly. Both unfold in time, and both depend upon bold graphic devices, whether urgent neon signs or panel-bursting talk balloons. Both borrow devices from more traditional forms. Milton Caniff's utilization of chiaroscuro, for example, is equivalent to the food-franchise architect's use of the mansard roof. Each was once current in high-art circles and hence brings a cachet of respectability, or at least recognizability. At the same time each can be made to serve a novel and dramatic purpose, the chiaroscuro being turned to narrative ends, the mansard being transformed into an advertising idiom.

A typical commercial strip may draw on dozens of architectural vernaculars, from Mediterranean to Cape Cod. Similarly, a comic strip may purloin plastic or narrative techniques from the novel, the movies or the advertising industry. But borrowing is far from the whole picture, since both kinds of strip evolved so rapidly that they quickly became self-referential, comics cross-fertilizing one another, and the structural trusses of one fast-food outlet soon being echoed in the architecture of a rival outlet across the way.

Fast-food architecture is characterized by an evolution of style and technical devices every bit as well defined as that of mainstream architecture. The most salient example of this is the architectural truss. Trusses are cantilever elements that can be used to span wide spaces without the need for columns or other intermediate supports. This means that the walls of a building can be all glass so that the play between interior and exterior space is very free. The buildings can therefore be extremely sculptural, a major plus when trying to attract the attention of passing motorists. The structural truss aesthetic, in which style and technical device are as one, is characteristic of the penultimate phase of strip architecture, in which demotic exhibitionism was wed to high-tech engineering (as in a Harley-Davidson or a '55 Chevy) and space age quasi-modernism. The use of structural trusses is by no means unique to commercial strip architecture, but at a certain period trusses were perfectly adapted to the kind of building intended to interact with the highway.

The truss concept in highway architecture was first popularized by coffee shops like Ships and Norm's that began to appear in Southern California in the early fifties. Some of these depended so heavily on theatrical cantilevers that their roofs seemed to be floating in midair, as if suspended in an antigravity field—making for a highly dramatic appearance when viewed from the highway. The style was quickly picked up in modified form by chains like Denny's, which spread it coast to coast. The early McDonald's buildings, designed by Stanley C. Meston, were clever minimalist variants on this theme in which wedge-shaped roofs were suspended from twin structural parabolas that doubled as the Golden Arches. The ensemble was eye-catching and easily recognizable from the highway by day or night; consequently it was much imitated, though seldom equaled.

Back in the fifties and sixties, when they were current, such "sculptural" buildings were commonly despised by critics and high-minded citizens. Today—now that they are disappearing—it is easy enough to recognize their virtues. An early Meston-designed McDonald's in Downey, California, has been entered into the National Register of Historic Places. By the era of the oil "crisis" and the Japanese invasion, however, the texture of the exurban strip was already changing, a change that can be symbolized by McDonald's shift to the mansard roof, inaugurated in 1968. Changing taste had something to do with this, but equally important was the fact that more and more customers wanted to eat their Big Macs indoors, at a table, and so it was necessary to come up with a new concept that allowed for a much larger dining area. (Some older McDonald's had no indoor seating, just benches outside.) In thinking about a new design, McDonald's executives could afford to take into account that their buildings no longer had to double as billboards. Television carried the weight of the advertising now. A relatively modest sign would be enough to identify a given location. The restaurant itself could afford to be tasteful, within the parameters of the fast-food industry. McDonald's had not merely arrived, it had become an institution.

As McDonald's went into transition from space age modern to mansard revival, others followed. Not all of them imitated McDonald's closely (though many did), but by the early seventies there was an inexorable movement toward better taste as defined by the lowest common denominator of tastemakers. If the previous, flying-roof phase of strip architecture might be described as the Jetson era, its replacement can be called the Mary Tyler Moore period, which has been with us for two decades now. In part this has been brought about by the challenge of the malls, especially of the minimalls, which are often integrated into an established strip. In part it is a response to a change in the self-image of the American shopper. Retail stores must now be sensitive to the needs of customers who eat croissants and sushi and watch shows such as *Masterpiece Theater*.

Unfortunately, good taste in this context has little to do with creativity or invention of any kind. Rather, as in network televison programming, it is often a question of offending as few customers as possible. It's fair to say that the commercial strip has gradually come to have more in common with network television than with the comic strip. Not only does it now depend on television advertising, it also subscribes to the kind of values which guarantee that TV programming is a kind of aesthetic mush. As recently as the sixties, the commercial strip was home to a good deal of exuberant invention, however vulgar, which even the franchises subscribed to for a while. Now it tends ever more toward the bland and the homogeneous.

Contributing to this trend has been the entrance into the picture of big developers. In its earlier phases, the strip typically evolved in a somewhat piecemeal way. A given block might feature a gas station, a car wash, an independent coffee shop, a franchised restaurant, a supermarket, a drugstore and half a dozen other retail outlets, each architecturally independent and standing on its own lot. Here and there would be shopping centers, but in most strips the planned complex was the exception rather than the rule. To some extent older strips have managed to hold on to this pattern, but increasingly, newer strips, and those where real estate values have risen dramatically, have fallen into the hands of developers who will purchase an entire block—or perhaps one side of a block—and develop it as an architectural entity, most generally as a continuous ribbon of conjoined stores to be leased to individual retailers, who will have little or no say in the appearance of the complex beyond the right to display modestly scaled advertising signs. From an investment point of view such a form of development makes a great deal of sense, and in the eighteenth and nineteenth centuries a very similar commercial impulse led to the great terraced streets of London, Boston, New York and Philadelphia. The new commercial enclaves, however, have nothing of the substantiality of those terraces. Rather they seem to be built in recognition of the tradition of ephemerality that has marked strip architecture from the outset. It is almost the only thing they have in common with the earlier incarnations of the motorized shopping zone. Although these developments come in many idioms, those idioms are generally so watered down as to seem wholly synthetic, and this synthetic quality is what contributes so much to their insipid sameness.

Curiously enough, relief is coming from an unexpected quarter. Aside from some significant contributions from firms like Armet and Davis, strip architecture developed largely without the input of mainstream architects. When such architects did become involved, especially in the age of the developer, they tended to attempt to impose the prevailing establishment taste of the day—notably the International Style—on the strip. Thus, sub-Miesian glass-and-steel boxes began to appear a quarter of a century ago along Ventura Boulevard and beside the highways of Florida. For the most part they looked ridiculous and out of place. In the past decade the pendulum has swung, and now it is the mainstream architect who finds value in the old Pop Art styles. In the postmodern era, inspiration is as apt to come from a vintage *Superman* comic—remember those Metropolis skylines?—as from the Bauhaus. Such childish inventions often seem mawkish when realized in a traditional urban setting, but alongside the highway they have a refreshing vitality that harks back to the energy of the wigwam motor court. A multicolored shopping center that looks as if it was built from oversized nursery blocks offers the kind of playfulness that is generally missing from strip architecture today. Board-certified, Corbusier-smitten, mainstream architects—those sad, frustrated, would-be visual poets, lost in the jungle of commerce—may yet manage to salvage some of the fun and adventure that once was the currency of the exurban strip.

The highways have also been enlivened in the recent past by a significant revival of the billboard. Back in the mid-sixties there were well over a million hoardings in the United States. The 1965 Highway Beautification Act and various local zoning ordinances cut into that total, but even more significantly the advertisers themselves turned more and more to television as a way of reaching the maximum number of people. The quantity of billboards fell to 500,000, but even as this happened a new philosophy of outdoor advertising was evolving. This came about largely because the cigarette and hard liquor industries were banned from television in the seventies and had no alternative but to take to the outdoors. They found that the billboard had certain definite advantages. For one thing, the Surgeon General's mandatory warnings are hard to read at 55 mph. For another, the billboard makes it possible to target a very precise potential market—a given economic group, for instance—by careful siting of ads. Depending upon the product, this can be much more cost-effective than television advertising, in which a large percentage of the viewers reached by a given commercial may not be interested in the product.

Such a discovery was not lost on other advertisers. According to Bernice Kanner, writing in *New York* magazine in 1989, the billboard costs approximately two dollars per thousand viewers as opposed to seventeen dollars per thousand for a typical television commercial. Throughout the eighties, companies that had abandoned outdoor advertising twenty years earlier began to drift back and find that they were getting excellent value for their money. Tobacco companies remain the biggest presence in the billboard universe, but increasingly they find themselves sharing space with Xerox, Colgate, Hanes, Bell Atlantic, Coors and hundreds of other companies and services. Billboard companies like Patrick and Gannett are thriving.

Success in contemporary billboard advertising depends on a combination of slickness and succinctness. Modern billboards are often huge and use all kinds of picture-plane-breaking graphic devices, but still tend to be less busy than boards once were. The visual point is made as economically as possible and written messages are positively laconic. It is estimated that a driver traveling at 55 mph has seven seconds to absorb the slogan on a given hoarding, so that ideally the message should be confined to seven words or fewer. Once again, the tobacco companies established a precedent for this kind of advertising. Marlboro needs to show nothing more than the rugged face of a wrangler and the words MARLBORO COUNTRY in order to reinforce its image. Similar campaigns have been used to promote very different products, such as Nike athletic shoes, which have been advertised effectively by simply pairing the name with an image of a star athlete such as Dwight Gooden or Michael Jordan in action. Some of these Nike images are even personalized for a specific site, the side of a building, for example. For such a campaign to work, the image must be striking, making for lively highway art.

The future of outdoor advertising promises such novelties as holographic displays and arena-scale high-resolution television screens. For the present, the billboard itself continues to draw the ire of such organizations as Scenic America, and doubtless there are many places where the billboard should not be. Often enough, though, it has a good deal more to offer than the segment of suburban or industrial landscape it obscures.

A crowded Los Angeles freeway in the late 1980s.
UPI/Bettmann Newsphotos

Chapter 18

AUTOMOVILLE III

Nowhere has there been more furor over outdoor advertising than in Los Angeles. Every few years some eager politician or high-minded civic group launches a media putsch announcing that he or it is going to "clean up" the city in the name of "beautification" by demanding some new ordinance that will rid the roadsides and rooftops of billboards. Such reformers resemble missionaries going among the tribes of New Guinea and attempting to convert them not merely to Christianity but to a specific brand of Christianity. Both groups face a tough uphill battle. In LA, for example, billboard users are part of a well-established, motor-age, tribal society. They listen to the newscasts, read the editorials in the *Los Angeles Times*, gauge the seriousness of the threat from the latest irate special interest group, and look for the compromise that will calm things down without seriously interfering with business as usual. In August 1989, the *Los Angeles Times* reported that the local outdoor advertising industry was making every effort to keep billboards simple and tasteful. Zoning laws, not to mention costs, have rendered such Sunset Strip extravaganzas as the 1953 promotion for the Hotel

Sahara in Las Vegas—with its real swimming pool and live showgirls—a thing of the past. Billboards with moving parts are now banned in LA, the argument being that they are dangerously distracting to motorists. This has not been too major an imposition, however, since the national trend in outdoor advertising is toward simplicity. The compromises made by the industry in Los Angeles amount to saying, "OK, we'll wear loincloths but we're not giving up polygamy."

The reality of the situation is that thinking of LA without billboards is like imagining Amsterdam without canals or Brooklyn without stoops. They are an intergral part of the texture of a city that has grown up with the automobile. This seems obvious enough to outsiders, yet somehow it escapes many people who have lived there all their lives.

Despite LA's indisputable eminence as a national and international business and cultural center, many Angelenos remain confused about the city's identity: confused and at the same time guilt-ridden. This identity crisis seems to be rooted in part in LA's image as the metropolis created by the automobile. This is not even strictly accurate—the railroads and interurbans played a big part in the story—but still, outside critics, especially Easterners, have emphasized the freeways and the smog to the point that even Angelenos believe the propaganda. To be formed by the automobile, according to one school of thought, is to be suburban, and to be suburban—or even to become famous as a collection of suburbs—is to have no real identity as a city.

The arguments are familiar and can be summed up in Woody Allen's quip from *Annie Hall* that LA is a city where the only cultural advantage is being able to make a right turn at a red light. Ultimately, that one-liner tells us more about Woody Allen than it does about LA, and this tends to be true of most of the clichéd criticisms thrown at Los Angeles.

"There's no street life," is perhaps the most common of these. This view presupposes that street life has some intrinsic and irreplaceable value; its adherents conveniently overlook the fact that in many older inner cities street life has become a form of urban warfare rather than a medium of cultural exchange. They also place the blame for the supposed absence of street life in LA firmly on the automobile: people are not fermenting a rich street culture because they are prisoners of their cars.

The fundamental error in this collage of half-truths is the built-in assumption that LA should be judged by the standards of other cities. The automobile can properly be criticized for destroying the quality of street life in most older inner cities, by sucking population and vitality away from the earlier residential and commercial centers. But as a decentralized, motorized city, LA has evolved according to a very different pattern. It can offer plenty of pedestrian pleasures; these are not concentrated in one zone, but are spread out among the city's various commercial centers and ethnic neighborhoods. Because of this each pocket of street culture has tended to assume an independent character, with little interplay between one pocket and the next. Only in a few areas, such as Hollywood, Venice and parts of Santa Monica, do black and Hispanic street cultures interact with white middle-class culture to any significant degree. In this LA differs greatly from some Eastern and Midwestern cities, where ethnic neighborhoods and middle-class enclaves are often jumbled together. Still, LA has more street culture to offer than is commonly acknowledged by its critics. If that street culture is car-dependent (how else do you get to Westwood?), this is not so remote from the reality in other cities: the crowds that on the weekend fill Greenwich Village or Georgetown are made up substantially of people who have arrived there by car from the suburbs.

Discussions of street life generally are predicated upon a definition of street life as pedestrian culture. Proponents of pedestrian street life fall into two very distinct categories. In one group are those who seem to feel that rubbing shoulders with crack dealers heightens one's sense of reality in some existential way. In the other are people who perceive street life as an echo of strolling the *grands boulevards* of Paris during the Belle Epoque. The former group should have no difficulty finding existential reassurance in LA. The latter should recall that the *boulevardier* or *demi-mondaine* of Proust's world was as much at home in a carriage as on foot. A man's phaeton carried as much social significance as the cut of his coat.

In LA, too, street life is not exclusively a pedestrian affair. The ritualized cruising of the Van Nuys Boulevard era may be gone, but cruising in a more casual sense—a bunch of Pali High kids in a Cherokee out looking for girls—is a form of street life just as authentic as window-shopping in SoHo. Checking out the Jags and BMW's along Montana Avenue is not really very different from appraising the chinchillas and sables being promenaded along Madison Avenue. People in automobiles interact in many ways with people in other automobiles, and with people on foot, all of which must be taken into account when attempting to define the street life of LA.

Communication between drivers, and between drivers and pedestrians, is inevitably at its most intense within cities. On a crowded street the motorist is most likely to keep his window rolled down for purposes of verbal intercourse with his neighbors, and his fist ready to articulate warnings, friendly and otherwise, with his horn. Because of LA's well-established driving tradition, relatively little of this aggressive form of automobile interchange occurs there, even though conditions today often invite it. Codes of motoring behavior in Southern California were formed in times when the automobile density was lower, so that a "have a nice day" kind of rote politeness is still a characteristic of LA driving. One place where this politeness is beginning to wear thin, however, is on the increasingly crowded freeways, where long delays inevitably lead to frustration and displays of automobile uncouthness that are typically attributed to "newcomers" and "foreigners."

LA's freeways are well maintained and are not subject to the extremes of temperature or the water and ice damage that destroy highway surfaces in many other parts of the country. They are still a pleasure to drive when traffic flow permits, but unfortunately this has become an increasingly rare situation. LA has long been a twenty-four-hour-a-day city, and has become even more so as it has evolved into an interntional business center. Brokers whose day is tied to Wall Street often begin their morning commute at five A.M. or earlier. Businessmen whose profits depend upon dealings in Southeast Asia may find themselves leaving the office at one A.M. In addition, the truckers who must move goods through Greater Los Angeles have found that this is often better accomplished at night. Then there are the night-shift workers, the party animals, the gang members on the move and the twenty-four-hour grocery store habitués who help ensure that the main through routes, such as the Ventura Freeway (I-101), are never less than busy even if the motorist finds himself setting out at three A.M. From the early hours of the morning rush to the prolonged conclusion of the evening rush, the Ventura always has stretches where traffic is reduced to a crawl. Nor is this a unique case. By six A.M. on any weekday morning, traffic on the inbound San Bernadino is likely to be traveling at 20 mph or less, and that is assuming it has not been raining and there are no major accidents to slow things down. By six-thirty the entire network begins to clog.

LA is the world's clearest argument in support of the thesis that construction of highways leads to an inevitable increase in the automobile population. This increase does not merely keep pace with the increased carrying capacity. Instead, the cars and trucks and vans and RV's multiply like rabbits, until the newly built system is clogged as effectively as its predecessor. It is almost as if the community of car owners takes a perverse pleasure in meeting the challenge of increased capacity, not merely beating it but humiliating it, though the same community of car owners suffers the direst consequences. The LA freeway system was the greatest challenge yet devised for the automobile community in a single urban area. The motorists of Los Angeles rose to the occasion and clogged those arteries in double-quick time, astonishing even the most pessimistic prophets of doom. Those whose job it is to predict such things had taken note of the continuing increase of population in the Greater Los Angeles area, but they sorely underestimated the pace at which one-car families became two-car families, and the rate at which two-car families became three-, four-, and even five-car families. In just over a decade, the automobile population of Los Angeles—already the highest per capita in the world—doubled. Sometimes it seems as if that entire population is attempting to inhabit the freeway system at the same time.

It may be a symptom of this problem that Angelenos have gone from calling the constituent parts of the freeway system by name to defining them by Interstate number. In the seventies it was conventional to say, when giving directions, "Take the San Diego Freeway north to the Ventura, then head east on the Ventura as far as the Laurel Canyon off-ramp." Today, the motorist receiving the same directions is more likely to be told "Take 405 north to 101, then head east as far as the Laurel Canyon off-ramp." In a city that loves exotic names (just look at a street map, with its Buena Vista avenues and its Sonora drives) the citizens have depersonalized the freeways, as if in response to the freeways having depersonalized them. In the eyes of the rest of the world, the freeways continue to give LA its identity; their symbolic value has not diminished. But the everyday user no longer perceives them as he did twenty years ago. Just as the Venetian is apt to judge the canal outside his window by the degree to which it smells in the summer or provides a breeding ground for mosquitoes, so the resident of LA has come to judge the freeways by their evident inadequacies.

Tales of accidents and idiocies witnessed are part of everyday conversation. Plans for increasing freeway capacity are commonplace news items. Some favor double-decking the busiest sections, others are convinced that running a new highway down the bed of the Los Angeles River—already concreted over—would relieve congestion in the San Fernando Valley. Still others are committed to the "radical" notion that public transportation is the answer, and billions of dollars are being invested in light rail systems.

Few Angelenos now have much to say in favor of the freeways as they exist in their present state, though the accidents that occur in the system continue to display a lighter side. One famous story—analogous to the legend of alligators in the New York sewer system, though better documented—involves a cargo of chickens (and presumably at least one rooster) that fell from the back of a truck onto the Hollywood Freeway and promptly nested in the scrub adjacent to the shoulder. For years these chickens surprised unwary drivers by making unexpected dashes for the center strip. Motorists in Del Mar were once taken aback by a fifteen-foot Great White Shark (stuffed) that spilled from an overturned trailer onto the Escondido Freeway. Back on the Hollywood Freeway, a Brinks armored truck like a fruit machine gone mad spewed thousands of dollars in quarters and dimes into the path of oncoming motorists, who promptly abandoned their cars and began to scoop up the loose change.

More sinister was the rash of random shootings that occurred in 1987 when it became fashionable in some delinquent circles to take potshots from moving cars at other freeway users, the victims apparently selected at random. A field of glory for the California Highway Patrol, the freeways have been the scene of innumerable high-speed chases such as one, reported in the *Los Angeles Times* in November 1988, in which a woman defied CHP officers at speeds of up to 110 mph until she was finally stopped by a roadblock near San Diego. When interrogated, she offered the explanation that she "just wanted to get away from San Pedro." Clearly, the freeways facilitate the mobility of criminals, but in some cases they seem to actually provide the medium in which the criminal functions. The many Southern California hitchhiker murders fall into this category, as do the rapes and killings committed in the summer of 1985 by Richard Ramirez, known among other nicknames as the Freeway Killer. Ramirez's habit seems to have been to cruise freeways in the Pasadena–San Gabriel Valley area, then, after selecting an exit ramp at random, to pick the first house he came upon with yellow paintwork. If a window was open, he would break in, frequently raping and/or killing the inhabitants. (Los Angeles aside, the link between the automobile and serial killings is very strong. In many of these cases, the mobility provided by the car has been crucial to the perpetrator's modus operandi. The victimization of hitchhikers has also been a factor in scores of these crimes.)

Under rush-hour conditions, some experienced LA drivers will leave the freeways and take to the surface streets, yet apart from a few trouble spots (often near freeway approaches), those surface streets are seldom overtaxed. Despite the huge increase in the total number of cars, major pre-freeway arteries, such as Sunset Boulevard and Sepulveda Boulevard, are not significantly less drivable than they were twenty years ago. The supergrid provided by the freeways has siphoned off the bulk of the additional traffic so that the old street grid has been able to cope remarkably well, especially when a comparison is made to traffic conditions in some other large cities. The freeway system itself may have turned into a nightmare, but a positive consequence is that the city which nurtured it remains an agreeable driving environment. This is small consolation to a motorist who needs to get from Torrance to Riverside in a hurry, but it means that local and mid-range driving—picking up the kids from school, for instance, or driving to the local mall—remains in general a frustration-free experience.

Despite the clusters of high-rises that have sprung up in locations like Westwood and Century City, despite its astonishingly high per capita car ownership, and despite its having become the center of the most populous area in the country, LA remains essentially a low-density city, offering an ease of automobile mobility that is almost unthinkable in other large cities. Everywhere, urban superhighways are clogged, so LA is at no special disadvantage there, but the grade-level streets of LA still allow for a reasonably free flow of traffic, which cannot be said of Midtown Manhattan, the Chicago Loop, or scores of other, more traditional city centers.

In part this is because Greater Los Angeles remains a city without a single center—yet more than ever, to dismiss it as a collection of suburbs is becoming an absurdity. Rather, it has evolved into something like a confederacy of small and midsize city-states that have banded together to constitute a single, powerful, political and commercial entity. Except that it is not involved in military adventures, the confederacy is a little like the Delian League in the age of Pericles. Imagine that a dozen substantial metropolitan areas had been plucked from their native sod, set down beside the Pacific and promptly replanted with palm trees. If you took Minneapolis, St. Paul, Duluth, Des Moines, Bismarck, Rapid City, Kansas City, St. Louis, Fargo, Omaha, Joliet and Dubuque—along with their industries, cultural institutions and suburbs—then reassembled them as a single entity, you would have something not dissimilar to LA. Since many early California migrants came from precisely those Midwestern territories, that is almost how LA did evolve (though it should be remembered that not only the Dodgers relocated from Brooklyn). LA is like a sun-kissed assemblage of Western and Midwestern cities that have grown together while managing to retain at least a tribal memory of the open spaces from which they sprang.

Many older cities are also made up of once distinct entities. In Europe, the City of London and the City of Westminster were formerly separate and self-contained, and Chelsea and Hampstead were outlying hamlets; on America's eastern seaboard, Greenwich Village was originally a refuge from a typhoid epidemic that was ravaging New York to the south, and Harlem was a distant settlement to the north. Eastern and European cities are made up of neighborhoods because they grew from constellations of smaller communities. Los Angeles differs only in that it grew faster and was able to accommodate greater distances between communities.

Culturally, LA differs from New York and the other cities it aspires to compete with, not because it is a collection of suburbs knit together by the automobile but simply because it is a very young city that has not yet had the time to fully mature, which brings with it advantages as well as disadvantages. One advantage is that the city's youth encourages new points of view. For example, living in a thoroughly motorized society has an impact upon the way that Southern California artists and their local patrons experience the world. This was recognized by the Museum of Contemporary Art when it devoted its 1984 opening show to the automobile. Specific automobile imagery is only part of the story, however, and the influence of the automobile is apt to be found also in an attitude to materials, or in a unique spatial sensitivity formed by constant travel through a city like Los Angeles, not to mention a response to the visual smorgasbord that has grown up alongside the city's streets in conjuction with the automobile.

The LA-based film and television industry's love affair with the car is as ripe now as it was fresh when the Keystone Kops first took to the streets. Although many movies are presently shot on location, plenty are still made on home turf, and this is even more the case with television shows. Action series from *The Rockford Files* to *Hunter* have taken LA as their setting. Not only do these shows provide endless variations on the car chase, they also make LA perhaps the most familiar city the world has ever know. If Paris is lovingly conjured up on film with the help of the Eiffel Tower seen across an ocean of rooftops, LA appears on camera as a taken-for-granted background seen from a cruising car with James Garner or some stunt double at the wheel. The beaches and canyons provide picturesque locations, and big Bel Air houses with their sweeping driveways are essential props. Mostly, though, TV cars cruise through the anonymous commercial and industrial strips, past Taco Huts and Texaco stations, past bodyshops and drive-in banks, past parking lots and prefabricated warehouses—man-made sharks contentedly swimming through an ocean they themselves brought into existence.

Such cruising with a camera gives a strong feeling of the texture of the city, but tends to shortchange it as a geographical entity. One thing the automobile has permitted is an easy interrelationship with a spectacular natural setting. Many would argue that the automobile has destroyed that setting, but this was a landscape laid in with a broad brush, and its essential features—the chains of mountains, the valleys and desert plateaus—continue to assert themselves. How many other major urban areas are so thoroughly penetrated with pockets of near-wilderness? The hills rise out of the grid of streets and dominate the architecture. In few other places has man gone to such efforts to establish himself and created a city where none has a reason to be—yet the assertiveness of the landscape, with its accompanying threats of mudslide, fire and earthquake, contrives to make the city seem like a temporary encampment. And the automobile conspires with nature in this regard, since the automobile glorifies motion, and inevitably the glorification of motion is at odds with the idea of permanence.

Yet, curiously, nowhere is the notion of the "home" worshiped more devoutly than in LA. Elsewhere the idea of the city as a conglomeration of single-family homes died with the Victorian era, if not before, but in LA it still reigns supreme. Apartment houses and other multiple-family dwellings have their place there, but even in poor neighborhoods single-family dwellings predominate. This more than anything else contributes to LA's suburban image. The city grew up during a period when the single-family domicile implied flight to the suburbs.

Whereas a typical city is surrounded by a ring of residential satellites, LA has integrated its dormitory areas into the city's infrastructure in such a way as to subtly change the relationship between suburb and workplace. Instead of concentric circles of inner and outer suburbs around a downtown hub, there is a patchwork quilt of residential and commercial districts, so that city life and suburban life are telescoped. To live in the uplands of Beverly Hills is to live in the ultimate suburb, and yet be at the center of things. The trade-off is that there is no single center, but matched Mercedes sedans in the garage can cancel out this shortcoming to a considerable extent.

The worshiped single-family home is not complete without the right car, or cars, to set it off, and certainly a shabby bungalow in Burbank can take on character with a well-maintained muscle car in the driveway. But the most spectacular combinations of car, home and landscape are to be found in the string of communities—Beverly Hills, Bel Air, Holmby Hills, Brentwood and Pacific Palisades—that cling to the Santa Monica Mountains and feed into Sunset Boulevard as it winds westward from Hollywood to the ocean. If the driveway is the umbilical cord that connects the suburban residence with the world at large, then here the umbilical cord is treated with the reverence it deserves.

These communites have little in common with the suburbs of the East Coast or the Midwest, which are at the mercy of the transformations of the seasons. In the summer, an older suburb back East almost drowns in nature, swoons in the humidity, each house standing alone in a pool of shadow cast by mature trees, each family entity cocooned by the hum of insects and lawn tractors. Privacy reigns, except when children and animals spill from one yard to the next. Then in the winter all that is stripped away and the streets stand bare, the white clapboard homes exposed to scrutiny like teeth beneath the dispassionate gaze of a dentist. Families are chased from the front porch to the sanctuary of kitchen and parlor, where they can continue to practice those singular rituals that drive people to live in private residences.

The suburbs of West Los Angeles are different: they remain the same, summer and winter, constantly swathed in vegetation that guarantees privacy year-round. Not that this vegetation is necessarily native to the environment, as is generally the case elsewhere. Just as the architecture may be Spanish, English or even Japanese in inspiration, so the flora comes from all over the world, trees and shrubs from Europe, Central America, Asia and Australia mixing with indigenous plantings and all nourished with the aid of water pumped in from hundreds of miles away.

The conventional suburb represents a flight from the wholly man-made environment to a natural or at least seminatural setting. The suburbs of West LA are wholly man-made environments that employ plant forms as architectural elements. The use of plantings to screen buildings and provide privacy are common everywhere, but the laurel thickets that shelter homes in Brentwood are like living walls, dense and impenetrable. The obsession with privacy is such that houses are often built with their backs to the road, a windowless facade penetrated by a single, palazzo-size door (sometimes so tall it breaks the roofline) that both beckons with its naive braggadocio and rejects with its studied aloofness. But it is not enough for such a building to turn its back on the street; it is likely to be encased in creepers, guarded by ranks of topiary shrubs, shielded by a screen of laurel and a palisade of palm boles. Maintenance of this horticultural architecture requires an army of Japanese and Mexican gardeners, which itself calls on a service industry typified by the lunch wagons that patrol these prosperous enclaves, dispensing hot dogs and enchiladas to the hedge clippers.

At an extreme, then, these homes become foliated fortresses that reveal just enough of themselves to excite curiosity but display nothing of the amenities—swimming pools or tennis courts—that make them so desirable. Nothing, that is, except the three-car garage and the driveway, as significant here as a drawbridge and portcullis would be to a moated castle. Since many of these homes are built on hillside sites, the driveways are often dramatically steep, providing opportunities for spectacular horticultural embellishment that emphasizes their nonfunctional role as sculptural incisions thoughtfully etched into the man-made landscape.

Nothing sets off a car better than these pseudobucolic amphitheaters. Poised at the top or bottom of a precipitous concrete runway, shaded by dense conifers and framed by fleshy succulents, a Porsche or a Saab 9000 looks infinitely more seductive than it does in the showroom. It becomes an advertisement for the beguiling life that is led (the stranger must presume) beyond the bosky portals. Nowhere else is the conjuction between car and house so charged with meaning and glamour. Many of these properties more than live up to the car parked outside, yet it is their purdahlike concealment behind a woodsy veil— the air of secrecy—that invests the car with so much latent sexiness. The car, in return, contributes to the mystery of the house, adds a narrative element to the already heady mix. ("Who the hell could be visiting Felice in an Acura, for God's sake?")

On these tranquil streets with their fairytale and musical-comedy names—Gretna Green Way, Tigertail Road, Sorrento Drive—cars pass with a purr and a swish, the sound muffled by the arboreal fortifications. Here gentility extends to the driver's world; all those ideals of early motoring—the parkway, the manicured landscape served by the automobile—remain alive. To live in these privileged communities is to understand what life with the car can be at its best. (Yet behind these vine-covered walls, you will hear as many complaints as anywhere else about epic traffic jams and feckless mechanics. Even here it is impossible to remove the pain from driving.)

Los Angeles is as full of paradoxes and problems as any major city. In spite of them, this child of the automobile age works better than most modern cities, offering a rich and distinctive culture along with an enviable environment. In many ways it has evolved as any other great city has evolved, being formed primarily by the aspirations of its citizens. That these aspirations involve a lifestyle dependent on the automobile is not incidental, however. Car culture colors the life of the city to an extent that is not to be found in any other metropolitan area of comparable importance.

Some commentators have seen LA as a harbinger of the future, and many urban areas, in America and around the world, have become Los Angelized, but none has evolved quite as LA has, nor to quite such a spectacular size and complexity. LA will remain unique because it is the sole world city formed primarily during the blindly optimistic decades of the automobile age, the years when it seemed to most people that the automobile was a wholly beneficial tool. Any new rivals will be forced to deal with the realities that everyone now recognizes—pollution and the finite nature of the world's fossil fuel supplies. If those problems are solved—if solar energy is finally harnessed, for example—then perhaps another great automobile metropolis will evolve, but it is likely to be very different in character.

For the moment, LA presents a fascinating dichotomy. In one sense it is already a monument to a past Golden Age of motoring. At the same time it is a city that is still evolving, just coming into its prime. In terms of culture and influence, its greatest years are still ahead. In terms of transportation, it is a laboratory in which the problems of the present can be studied and plans for the future hatched. The leading Japanese car manufacturers maintain design studios in Southern California, and authorities there are facing the problems common to all motorized societies more frankly than is being done in other places. What happens in LA will continue to be of major importance to the future of the automobile around the world.

In the last decade of the twentieth century, automobile-related smog
is seen as a symptom of larger pollution problems,
with global consequences. *Reuters/Bettmann*

Chapter 19

ADMONITIONS AND ALTERNATIVES

*F*or the great majority of Americans who live in or near cities, congestion and pollution are somehow accepted, if acknowledged to be undesirable. Cities have always been crowded and dirty. In many ways the cities of the horse-and-buggy era were more congested and certainly filthier than the urban centers of today. The industrial fumes of the Victorian era were as poisonous as automobile emissions, so that in the older cities exhaust emissions seemed almost to be an extension of an established and accepted evil. If smog became associated with Los Angeles, it was largely because, owing to topography and low population density, it is highly visible there, more so than in a similarly afflicted high-rise city, and because it disfigures what was an almost pristine environment prior to the ascendancy of the automobile.

No one can imagine, however, that smog is an exclusively Southern California problem. Take Interstate 90 into Missoula, Montana, on any day when a temperature inversion is in effect, and you are likely to find that what was until recently an idyllic valley is suffocating beneath a saffron blanket that completely conceals the surrounding mountains. Similar pockets of smog are occurring throughout the Rocky Mountain area, wherever concentrations of automobiles occur in conjunction with the temperature inversions that are naturally contained by the mountains, sometimes for weeks at a time.

The visibility of smog depends on photosynthesis, which itself depends on pollutants' being trapped relatively near the ground for an extended period of time. Even when this is not happening—when the air appears clear—the atmosphere in our cities, and in those Rocky Mountain valleys, is still a clearinghouse for scores of pollutants, many of them discharged by automobiles. There is seldom any visible evidence of smog per se at the intersection of Canal Street and Broadway in Manhattan, yet this has been described as the most polluted spot in America. There is far more to pollution than the eye can see, and that pollution is harmful to humans, animals and vegetation—the entire ecosystem.

The oil needed to power and lubricate our automobiles can cause problems for the environment long before reaching the automobile's combustion system. Much crude oil is transported by ship or barge, and significant oil spills into the oceans and other waterways have become almost daily occurrences around the world. In addition, refining crude oil into usable products such as gasoline involves the release of carcinogens and other toxic substances into the atmosphere.

Moreover, the problem of pollution does not exist at ground level alone. Man-made gases such as carbon dioxide, some of them associated with auto emissions, are said to collect above the earth causing the so-called greenhouse effect, which many scientists believe will lead to global warming and attendant environmental consequences considerably more far-reaching than anything predicated upon mere local pollution.

The automobile is not responsible for all of this, but it is one of the chief culprits. The vehicle that first gained popularity because it offered a means of escaping to the unspoiled countryside has become a primary means of the environment's destruction. Every time a father drives his family to the beach, a national park or a favorite picnic spot, he helps propagate the man-made poisons that threaten these national treasures.

The intricacies of the pollution dilemma defy analysis. Nobody can provide an accurate reading of the damage that has already been done, let alone give a reliable prediction of what is to come if drastic steps are not taken to deal with the cause of the problem. Yet to deny that the problem exists would be foolhardy to the point of self-destructiveness.

The origin of life on our planet is a consequence of a precise and fragile balance of elements that made possible the emergence of animate matter, which has the ability to reproduce itself and the instinct to protect its kind by doing so. Millions of species and subspecies evolved from the first configuration of vital compounds, and the entire system was bound together by what might be called an interfamilial instinct for survival.

When man arrived on the scene in the not-too-distant past, he functioned for a while as just another species that could be accommodated by the rest. Ominous as his discovery of fire was, for centuries he was content to burn live or recently dead vegetation, and on a scale that was insignificant from an ecological point of view. His intelligence and insatiable curiosity, however, led him to the discovery that fossil fuels could be burned. He learned too that heat could be used to drive machines, which might be used to improve his life and also to implement his dominance of the planet. Science has enabled humans to unlock the energy contained in fossil fuels but in doing so they have upset the delicate balance of nature. For millions of years, the earth had been a self-tuning system. Man is the first species to interfere with this system, going so far as to tamper with the earth's symbiotic relationship with the sun. And he does so with all the credentials of your local gas station attendant preparing a Penske-Cosworth Special for the Indy 500.

Tens of millions of Americans are sufficiently aware of this situation to express grave concern, yet few of them curtail their driving to any significant degree, even though this could have a discernible impact on a deteriorating situation. The nation is addicted to gasoline, and this addiction is likely to have far more serious consequences than dependency upon heroin or crack. The word "addiction" is no exaggeration because people simply cannot quit the gasoline habit cold turkey. Celebrities appear at rallies deploring the rape of the environment, then have themselves driven home in limos that burn fuel at a reckless rate. Bumper stickers warn against the dangers of global warming, yet the cars that bear them are still on the road.

At the time of writing, Congress and the federal government are working in tandem to draft new antipollution legislation, the first of its kind since the 1977 updating of the 1970 Clean Air Act. The goal, expressed in that earlier legislation, of cleaning up our cities' air, has been subject to innumerable postponements. Even so, automobiles and the fuels they burn are considerably cleaner than they were twenty years ago; but improvements in emission control have simply not been able to keep pace with the increases in car ownership and usage. The new legislation envisions further reductions of auto emissions and compulsory gasoline economy in the range of 40 miles per gallon at highway speeds (this would be the required fleet average for any given manufacturer). According to the Senate bill, the new emissions standards would apply to all new cars by the year 1995, and the 40-miles-per-gallon goal should be reached by the end of the century.

The one thing that nobody suggests is any restriction on the total number of automobiles on the road, or on their usage. It is tacitly acknowledged that any attempt to impinge on the American citizen's right to use his or her automobile is tantamount to political suicide.

As is exceedingly clear from the history of the automobile in America—its rise to a position of dominance in the transportation field—the average citizen equates the car with personal freedom, which is held to be a self-evident and inalienable right guaranteed by the Constitution. The American Revolution did not merely seek freedom for the new republic but also liberty for the individual within that republic. That individual liberty translated into a significant measure of personal power, whether the power to vote or the power to express oneself freely. The advent of the automobile placed in the hands of the individual an instrument that encouraged the expression of personal power at both practical and symbolic levels. It could be an everyday tool, a passport to leisure, a provider of privacy, and at the same time a status symbol. Its significance in twentieth-century America might be compared to that of firearms in Colonial times or on the frontier. Not only does the automobile have a similar practical importance, it can also be looked on as a lethal weapon, because of both the deaths that can be caused by its misuse and the harm it does to the environment in the course of normal use. The right to bear arms guaranteed by the Second Amendment to the Constitution is still capable of stirring great debates. There is no amendment that specifically guarantees American citizens the right to possess automobiles—unless it is acknowledged that car ownership is a form of self-expression and is therefore protected by the First Amendment—but denial of that right would create an outcry alongside which the efforts of the handgun lobby would seem debonair.

The automobile began its life as a recreational vehicle, then took on a utilitarian aspect, but it has established itself within the ecosystem as an instrument of personal power, or imagined personal power. If it were perceived simply as a recreational or functional tool, it would perhaps be possible to conceive of replacing it, especially in light of the damage it does to the environment. What causes people to perceive the car as indispensable is its nonutilitarian aspects, however: for some motorists it functions as a surrogate mistress or lover and at the same time is perceived to make the owner seem more desirable to the opposite sex.

The housewife driving a Dodge wagon to the supermarket may not rely on her vehicle to make her seem sexy, but she does count on it to designate her position within her chosen stratum of society. The baby seat in the back indicates that she is fulfilling her role as childbearer and nurturer. The ski rack on the roof informs everyone that though married she is still active. The SAVE THE WHALES bumper sticker signals that her heart and conscience are in the right places. She may not seek to impress in the same sense as the young stud at the wheel of a Corvette, or the rising executive in his BMW, but her personal power, such as it is, derives from her respectable position in the community and that position is perfectly expressed by her car.

In ways like this the car is locked into the human ecosystem. This is not an exclusively American phenomenon. The situation in Western Europe and parts of the Far East is almost identical, and the party boss driving his Volga sedan to his dacha outside Moscow is participating in the same game. (Leonid Brezhnev was not untypical of Soviet leaders in owning a whole fleet of luxury imports, including a Cadillac, a Mercedes, a brace of Rolls-Royces, a Maserati and a Matra Bagheera.) The automobile is part of the ecosystem because human beings have become the most volatile ingredient in the ecosystem, and in many areas of the world the automobile has become integral to human aspirations, both economically and emotionally. In countries like the United States, the motor vehicle has in fact created a world—the highway world—on which the national economy depends, a world that cannot function without some kind of personal transportation. Any attempt to find solutions to the automobile-related aspect of the pollution crisis must acknowledge this. The personally owned and driven car cannot be removed from the equation overnight, nor even within a generation, without drastic consequences.

At the same time, the automobile's negative impact upon the ecosystem must be reduced—and soon—to avoid consequences that will be still more drastic.

Mass transit is frequently touted as the cure to transportation ills, especially within sizable urban areas (those with a population of one million or more), and there is no doubt that better mass transportation could improve the driving situation, or at least prevent it from worsening, where circumstances make it viable. Such improvements might involve the more efficient use of existing facilities, the building of new but traditional systems, or the employment of novel technologies such as MAGLEV.

MAGLEV—magnetic levitation—is an extension of fixed-rail technology in that it requires a permanent track to be laid, whether at grade level, along an elevated platform or in a subway tunnel. The MAGLEV train uses electric energy, but instead of running on flanged wheels that are in contact with steel rails it employs electromagnetic attraction or repulsion (there are two alternate operating systems) to levitate a vehicle within a car-wide guideway channel that both directs the vehicle and completes the magnetic field. The virtual absence of friction permits speeds in excess of 300 mph with almost silent operation. Unfortunately, MAGLEV is still unproven on a large scale and, like any new technology, is expensive to install, though there is no reason why it cannot take advantage of existing fixed-rail rights-of-way. In addition, its high-speed potential would be largely negated in commuting situations that inevitably involve numerous stops.

Meanwhile conventional fixed-rail mass transit suffers from a poor image, despite the relative success of new subway systems in cities like Washington, D.C., and Montreal, and in the San Francisco Bay Area. All American subway systems tend to suffer from the bad publicity that regularly attaches itself to the New York system, by far the largest and most visible. New York's system is also the oldest, with all the drawbacks that implies for maintenance and customer comfort. In recent years it has been plagued with everything from graffiti (now almost totally eliminated) to failures of rolling stock and periodic epidemics of crime, both petty and vicious. In other parts of the country, it is often assumed that any new public transportation system is likely to suffer the same fate as the New York subway and is therefore not worth supporting.

Yet in reality the New York subway system is something of a miracle, carrying millions of passengers a year, few of whom suffer anything worse than occasional annoyance and minor inconvenience. Without its subways, New York would be a transportation nightmare.

Whether such a system could be built today is highly questionable, for the cost of excavating tunnels is prohibitively expensive, at least on the scale of the New York subway. This alone makes a subway system impractical for most cities with growing mass transit needs; the alternatives are elevated tracks (conventional or monorail), grade-level rail lines, and the rational use of highways. Elevated tracks could conceivably be built above existing highway rights-of-way, but would be expensive to install and probably highly disruptive to automobile traffic during construction. Grade-level rail lines—the equivalent of the old interurbans, sometimes called light rail—either require new rights-of-way or else must be limited to existing but underused tracks.

The inescapable fact is that any new mass transportation system, if built from scratch, would be exorbitantly

Introduced in 1973, the Bay Area Rapid Transit (BART) system—
centered in San Francisco—is a good example of a modern and
efficient rail system offering a viable alternative to the
automobile for thousands of commuters. *Bettmann Archive*

expensive and would require large outlays of public
money, which car-owning voters are unlikely to support
until gridlock becomes universal. Even in high-density
urban areas such as New York City, existing systems require substantial government subsidies in order to operate
while providing reasonable fares. In low-density cities,
where the automobile always offers an attractive alternative, public transportation systems are inherently less
efficient (in that they offer real advantages to fewer people)
and therefore require even greater subsidies.

This doesn't mean that new public transportation systems should not or will not be built. It is a matter of un-

derstanding that mass transportation offers only limited solutions to the traffic problem, especially in low-density cities, and that even these limited solutions are very costly. Given the American form of government and the way it controls funding of large-scale public projects, we are unlikely to see the approval of radical mass transportation experiments until the highway traffic crisis reaches critical mass. In the meantime, the best that can reasonably be hoped for in most situations is improved commuter service on existing rail lines, and an extension of the rational use of limited-access highways, such as the designation of special bus lanes during rush hours to permit the efficient operation of commuter buses.

If mass transportation does not offer short-range or even medium-range solutions, then governments, administrators, scientists, manufacturers and car owners must look to improved automotive technology to reduce pollution, and to rational highway use to reduce congestion.

The technology involved in increasing the fuel efficiency of motor vehicles is sometimes complicated, sometimes extremely simple. Significant gains can be made merely by fitting a car with radial tires and keeping them inflated at optimum pressure. Tractor-trailer trucks fitted with radial tires, variable on-off fans and inexpensive, retrofitted aerodynamic cab fairings showed dramatic performance improvements over trucks not fitted with these features, traveling 5.34 miles per gallon as against 4.29 mpg for the nonmodified rigs. Similarly modified pickup trucks and delivery vans showed even more striking improvements in fuel economy.

Radial tires have become almost standard on passenger cars, and aerodynamic design has improved greatly in recent years. Another way manufacturers have improved fuel economy over the past two decades is weight reduction, the average car today weighing approximately fifteen hundred pounds less than the average in 1975. This is one reason for the popularity of the Issigonis front-wheel-drive format, which not only provides more space in a small car but reduces weight by eliminating the chassis-length drive shaft. Reduced weight will continue to play a role in improving fuel economy, though clearly there are limits here in terms of both size and safety.

Much attention has been and continues to be paid to improving the efficiency of the standard Otto-cycle engine. Turbo-charging is a well-known example that is already quite common but is likely to find even more widespread use. Turbo-charging provides a system in which more air is forced into the cylinders, permitting the size of the motor to be reduced in proportion to its power output. Like aerodynamic styling, turbo-charging can be used to make a high-performance car go faster or an everyday road car more efficient. Diesel engines, inherently more efficient than gasoline-powered Otto-cycle engines, can also be turbo-charged and may well enjoy increased popularity in the near future.

There is likely to be further experimentation with such relatively little known power systems as the Stirling engine, a continuous-combustion engine characterized by low exhaust emissions. Ford and other manufacturers have explored the potential of this motor, but so far its theoretical advantages have not been fully borne out in practical experiments.

One device that shows more promise of early success is the energy-storage flywheel, which can be employed in conjunction with any kind of power plant, conventional or otherwise. A flywheel is a heavy wheel that regulates the speed and uniformity of motion of the machinery with which it is engaged. A flywheel that is introduced between the engine and the transmission of a motor vehicle can ensure that the engine always works at close to maximum efficiency. Normally the efficiency of an internal combustion engine varies enormously as it is called upon to meet the changing requirements of the drivetrain. The flywheel regulates this and evens it out, absorbing all the energy produced by the engine at its most efficient operating level, even when the systems of the vehicle do not require that energy. At the same time, inertia causes surplus energy to be stored in the rim of the flywheel and this energy can be tapped, for example, to decelerate the vehicle and thus function as a braking system. In this way the flywheel serves a double purpose, increasing engine efficiency and storing energy for designated purposes.

Given these advantages, and the fact that the flywheel is a well-known device in other mechanical contexts, it is perhaps surprising that it has not attracted the attention of automotive engineers until recently. One probable reason is that it requires a rather sophisticated continuously variable transmission system capable of transmitting energy in both directions, for acceleration and deceleration. The flywheel speed is not subject to control so that its energy must continuously be matched, by the transmission, to the propulsion needs of the vehicle. For example, as the vehicle gathers speed the flywheel loses speed and the transmission must ceaselessly adjust to this shifting ratio. Several continuously variable transmission systems are available, but they are expensive compared with ordinary automobile transmissions and, along with the flywheel itself, would add considerably to the base price of any car. Experiments in Europe and America suggest that such initial outlay might well be offset by substantial savings in operating costs. Standard production cars modified at the University of Wisconsin to take advantage of the flywheel storage are reported to have demonstrated fuel-efficiency improvements above 50 percent.

Whenever the energy-efficient, nonpolluting automobile of the future is discussed, attention invariably turns to the electric vehicles that attracted so much interest in the early days of motoring. The electric car—almost silent, free of emissions and capable of excellent performance—is certainly attractive, but it still presents the problem that limited its acceptance earlier in the century: given the present state of the art, storage batteries place a limit on the EV's range. New technologies such as nickel-iron, nickel-zinc and zinc-chlorine batteries may soon increase the range of EVs to 100 miles or so without greatly increasing the weight of the car. This range might well prove satisfactory for the second car in a two-car family, one that is used for short-distance commuting, shopping and such, but it is hardly likely to meet with universal acceptance. Even limited acceptance, though, could have a significant effect on overall gasoline consumption, and hence on pollution.

General acceptance of the electric car seems to rest on two possibilities: the development of radically improved batteries and the development of roadway-powered electric vehicles. Existing environmental pressures have fanned interest in producing the necessary "super batteries," and there is real promise in projects such as the aluminum-air battery which can be recharged immediately by the replacement of aluminum plates instead of requiring overnight recharging. This is still in the early developmental stage, however, and its use in production road vehicles may be decades away.

Meanwhile, experiments are being carried out with roadway-powered electric vehicles. Such vehicles would have conventional battery storage systems for neighborhood driving, but would be supplied with power pickups mounted beneath the car for travel over highways provided with a power source. The source would consist of cables buried just beneath the road surface which would transfer their power inductively across the air gap (about one inch) between the road and the pickup device. No mechanical contact is necessary, so the car can maneuver freely on the highway just as if equipped with a conventional engine—indeed conventional gasoline-powered cars can use the same highway. In addition, the battery used for off-highway driving can be recharged from the same magnetic field that provides the traction power.

A mile-long stretch of powered roadway is currently being built in Southern California, and it is there—and in climatically similar regions—that this system may have its chief application. The small gap between the road surface and the pickup device means that roadway power sources are practical only where you have flat, well-maintained highways free of potholes and warping. It might work extremely well for the Los Angeles freeway network, but would have little application in the Midwest or Northeast, where hot summers and freezing winters cause so much damage to the roads.

There might be other drawbacks. Some recent medical studies indicate that magnetic fields may be a health hazard, and these power-source highways would produce magnetic fields of considerable power. A similar problem may confront MAGLEV transportation systems. In addition, electric vehicles of whatever kind will require a great increase in the nation's ability to produce energy, and generating stations themselves are sources of pollution, except where hydroelectric power is available, so to suggest that electric cars would be totally clean vehicles is not entirely accurate.

Even supposing that clean vehicles could be built, however, this would not solve the problem of traffic congestion. It might even make it worse, since now drivers could take to the highways free of the guilt of polluting the environment. If so, traffic management would become more crucial than ever. Various route-guidance systems have been designed and tested over the past quarter century, all of them aiming to give the driver in-car information that will enable him to reach his destination by the best possible route, which means not necessarily the shortest route but the one that will provide the best driving conditions and the shortest drive time.

This is no small challenge. In the Los Angeles area, for example, the permutations of routing decisions that might be involved in driving, say, from Santa Monica to Pasadena are potentially astronomical. Under optimum conditions the freeway system would provide the best route (or routes), but when freeway congestion is taken into account there might well be times when drivers can make better time by occasionally taking to surface streets. A route-guidance scheme would attempt to present these alternatives to the driver who had punched his destination into his on-board receiver, which is in radio contact with a centralized computer system, which in turn might be responsive to information supplied by an observation satellite suspended in orbit directly above the city. In most systems being tested today, traffic information would be fed into the car by means of a screen displaying a map indicating, perhaps by color, traffic densities at given points along the route. In addition the screen might provide textual information ("Take next exit, then proceed east on Mulholland Drive"). Or a voice synthesizer might offer similar suggestions.

One problem with this is that if all vehicles are fitted with such a guidance system, what happens if they all take the same advice at the same time—exiting en masse onto Ventura Boulevard and leaving the 101 freeway empty? Clearly such possibilities must be taken into account, which adds enormously to the difficulties involved in devising such a system on a useful scale.

It is but one step—though admittedly a huge one—from route-guidance systems that provide advice to motorists to guidance systems that take control of the car from the driver and hand it over to a central command system, one that has charge of not only route choice but also such minutiae of driving as lane changes and merging. The technology required to provide for fully automated driving should be available, according to the Jet Propulsion Lab in Pasadena, by the year 2000. Testing such a system would presumably take a number of years, and installation even on a limited scale years more, so that it is unlikely that cities could be readied for automated driving until well into the next century—and that assumes that the enormous expenditures involved in implementing the system are approved.

By then, perhaps drivers will be ready to give up a degree of control, at least when traveling through busy cities. Outside dense urban areas, except perhaps along heavily traveled intercity corridors, automated driving is likely to be prohibitively expensive. The same would probably be true of neighborhood side-street driving, so that there would be numerous conditions under which the driver would be called upon to control his vehicle in the traditional way. Automation would take over only in situations where the driver is normally placed under stress by conditions beyond his control. We already have a situation in which there is an unwritten contract that weds the private automobile to the public highway. If automation is ever introduced, that contract would have to be modified somewhat so that in certain situations the public sector would take over some of the responsibilities that are now assigned to the individual, while the driver would still enjoy the privacy of his own vehicle. In a sense it would be a novel form of public transportation in which the traveler, not the transit authority, provides the carriage and pays for the motive power while the transit authority provides the carriageway and the guidance system.

Whether such a contract would be acceptable to motorists who are accustomed to complete freedom of choice, with all its potential for both elation and frustration, is a matter for speculation. Clearly, the days have already passed of which Reyner Banham could write that the LA freeways worked so well that they defied the need for automation. There must be millions of Angelenos who would gladly give up control of their vehicle during rush hour on the Harbor Freeway or I-405 and hand it over to an automated system that would carry the rider smoothly to his destination while providing the opportunity to read the *Times*, make business calls or even watch TV. Automated driving is still a long way off, but already it begins to seem more appealing than it did just a few short years ago, when the very idea conjured up the image of a robotic police state.

Few people in the early 1890s, when the first horseless carriages were seen on America's streets, would have imagined that the age of the horse would be virtually over a quarter of a century later. So it may be that today's Americans will be greatly surprised by the advances in transportation that will occur over the next twenty or thirty years. In the meantime, however, it is imperative that everyone—politicians, manufacturers and car owners—concentrate on the small but significant improvements that can be made in the forseeable future. The automobile will not just go away, and everyone involved with it must make sure that its fuel efficiency is improved and that the fuels it burns are made cleaner. In the relatively short time since the 1970 Clean Air Act, considerable strides have been made in improving fuel economy and cutting down on harmful emissions. The automobile industry has been reasonably responsive to government directives, and the momentum that has been achieved should lead to even greater improvements in the years ahead. At the same time, complacency is the last thing the world can afford. There is only a finite amount of time available to clean up the air if environmental disaster is to be avoided.

The ultimate responsibility lies with individual motorists. They vote politicians into power. Through the normal mechanics of the marketplace they can influence the kind of vehicles the auto manufacturers build. They can guarantee that today's generation of cars is used efficiently. If every American motorist simply ensures that his or her car's tires are inflated to the optimum pressure, it will save hundreds of thousands of barrels of oil a year and have a measurable beneficial impact upon pollution.

The Ford Escort. *UPI/Bettmann*

Chapter 20

MULTINATIONAL MATTERS

*I*t is significant that one of the success stories of the American automobile industry over the past decade has been the Ford Escort. This distant descendant of the Model T is a true world car—as at home in Djakarta as Dearborn—and thus has fulfilled the ambitions announced by Detroit manufacturers back in the early seventies, and first essayed with those notorious General Motors J-cars. A global bestseller, the Escort provides comfortable space for five, good mileage and better-than-adequate performance in a pleasing if unremarkable package at a reasonable price. It doesn't turn heads, but it is a sensible car that satisfies the needs of many families and commuters. With an all-new version introduced in 1990, the Escort may well prove to have a longevity comparable with that of the Tin Lizzie.

This new Escort is based on the Mazda 323. Ford and Mazda are in an ongoing business relationship that dates back to Ford's interest in the Wankel rotary engine; so the Escort is now an American car only to the extent that it is styled and built in America. The styling is based on the

Ford Taurus, which was a genuinely innovative car when it was introduced in 1985, yet remained within an international stylistic mainstream, owing something to European sedans like the Lancia Prisma and in turn influencing the look of such Japanese cars as the Lexus and the Infiniti. In its basic format, the new Escort is a typical front-wheel-drive economy car deriving from the Issigonis Minis of the late fifties and sixties. This is a world car in every sense of the phrase.

Much the same could be said of one of the Escort's rivals, the Eagle Summit. At least, that is what the car is called when sold by Jeep/Eagle dealers, who are part of the Chrysler Corporation. At Dodge dealerships it is the Dodge Colt, but the Colts of the nineties are not to be confused with the Colts of the eighties. These nineties Colts, like the Eagle Summit, are virtually identical to the sporty Mitsubishi Mirage. For that matter, the Geo Prizm sold by Chevrolet dealers is actually a California-built version of the current Toyota Corolla.

Dozens of such instances could be cited, and it is not just a matter of American manufacturers utilizing Japanese technology. The two-way relationship between American carmakers and their European subsidiaries is well established, while the Japanese have long employed Italian designers and are now entering into development deals with German manufacturers. The automobile industry today has become as much a multinational business as the oil industry.

Given this climate of internationalism, what has happened to the Americanism of the American car? From the Model T to the Mustang, this Americanism was easily apprehended, and during its heyday, from the thirties to the sixties, it was handily described in terms of size and ornament. Detroit manufacturers still produce a few models that fit the old image—the lugubriously boxy Cadillac Brougham, for example, currently billed as America's longest production car—but they are anachronisms that for the most part emphasize everything that was worst about American design, without recalling any of the qualities that made the best American cars of the past such fun to be seen in.

Recognizably American cars are an endangered species. A Jaguar is still very British; with all that walnut interior trim, to ride in a Jaguar is rather like time traveling in an Edwardian sideboard. Mercedes and BMWs positively reek of German engineering, while Italian sports cars, though much imitated, display a blend of arrogance and insouciance that is unmistakably Italian. Of the top producing nations, only the Japanese have never had their own style (which doesn't mean they will not achieve one). They have succeeded by taking proven elements from other traditions and blending them into clever hybrids. American manufacturers, once responsible for the most influential of all national styles, are now themselves reduced to producing similar hybrids.

In its day American design had a powerful impact upon the European and Japanese companies that have become such forces in the international marketplace. It is still vestigially present in some of their products, but the dominant international style derives primarily from the European cars, especially the sports sedans, that emerged in the wake of World War II. The sports-sedan style in particular has come to typify the look of the cars of the nineties, and this has its roots in the graceful lines pioneered in the fifties by companies like Aston Martin and Porsche and by the great Italian designers of Turin, modified by the more sedate but still elegant style favored by Mercedes-Benz.

Two areas in which the American look still dominates are the pickup truck and the four-wheel-drive utility vehicle. The latter, deriving from the still popular jeep, had many foreign imitators, but the basic style remains essentially American, no matter where the vehicles are built. They call up images not only of World War II GIs jolting toward the Rhine, but also of the American West, modern-day cowboys riding the range on heavy-duty tires.

Much the same applies to the pickup. There are aerodynamic pickups, but somehow they look a shade sissified. A pickup is supposed to be a workhorse, even if you use it primarily to take your boogie board to the beach. Like the jeep it ought to look blunt and functional, and that style was perfected by American manufacturers decades ago. Nobody has found any good reason to change it.

Interestingly, then, the European look has become associated with the idea of leisure driving, even when the realities of the owner's routine dictate that the car is primarily utilitarian. A typical owner may use his Hyundai Sonata chiefly for commuting, but when he steps into the showroom he pictures himself zipping along a winding highway on a sunny weekend. It might be a family car, purchased for reasons of economy, but the Giugiaro styling lets him think of it as a four-door sportscar. On the other hand, the four-by-four and the pickup, wherever they are built, come on with a hardworking, ranch-hand, all-American kind of a look, even though many of them are used primarily as leisure vehicles.

The most dramatically new style of vehicle on American roads is the minivan. Part minibus, part station wagon, the minivan did not exist until 1984. It has proved so versatile, however, especially when equipped with four-wheel drive, that by 1990 close to one million minivans a year were being sold in the U.S. market, despite the fact that some of the earlier exercises in the genre—the Plymouth Voyager, for example—were hardly things of beauty. Newer versions are considerably more elegant. The Chevy Lumina APV features a striking, aerodynamic profile suggestive of performance as well as utility. The highly regarded Mazda MPV is handsomely styled and more carlike than the majority of minivans. Most interesting of all, though, is the Toyota Previa, a vehicle that would not have looked out of place in the Futurama pavilion at the 1939 New York World's Fair.

With the Previa, the teardrop shape so beloved of progressive designers in the thirties has become a reality. With its soft curves, its vestigial hood sweeping up without a break into a huge expanse of windshield, this van is as aerodynamic as any Italian sports car and it brings into focus an important fact. The automobiles of the past twenty years have in many ways picked up the evolutionary logic

The 1990 Chevrolet Lumina APV. *Bettmann Archive*

that was abandoned by American car makers after World War II. Influenced by Detroit, some European manfacturers also abandoned that logic, but a few European cars kept the old spirit of progressivism alive while most American vehicles wallowed in chrome and techno-symbolism. The VW Beetle was in reality a very advanced late 1930's car, while automobiles as varied as the Citroën DS, the Alfa Romeo Giulietta Sprint and the BMC Mini (all introduced in the fifties) were innovative designs that extended the established evolutionary logic.

When the gasoline crunch arrived, in 1973, the success of the Beetle in America prepared the way for more economical vehicles, and the example of the BMC Mini provided the Japanese with a format on which to model their world cars. To this they added the clean, aerodynamic styling that characterized the Giulietta. (The Citroën DS's styling was so far ahead of its time that its influence is being felt only in the nineties with minivans like the Previa.) In many ways, the biggest problem with American manufacturers was their stubborn insistence on producing cars that looked distinctively American. This was due in part to customer pressure (or imagined customer pressure, since many buyers were in fact choosing the Japanese and European imports). In part, though, it was a dogged determination to retain an American persona that no longer made much sense in the face of global realities. Even after the gasoline crunch, it took Detroit the better part of a decade to realize that the best way to survive was to return to the logic of automobile evolution that had been abandoned the day Harley Earl had the notion of adapting the P-38's tail fins to GM cars.

In other ways, however, the Detroit influence is very much alive. Those behemoths of the fifties—like the 1955 Chevys—instilled in the mind of the masses the notion that anyone could afford a car that was roomy, fully accessorized and well appointed. (Whether your notion of good appointments ran to leather or Naugahyde was a matter of taste.) In Europe, only luxury cars provided the kind of comforts that were taken for granted in America and it was one of the master strokes of the Japanese manufacturers to understand that even economy cars can have interiors that will satisfy the fussiest owner. The Issigonis format provided plenty of passenger space, even in small cars, and car builders like Honda, Toyota and Nissan furnished that space up to the highest American expectations, setting a standard that has now become the universal norm.

The Japanese also picked up on the techno-symbolism characteristic of American cars in the fifties and adapted it to the automobile interior. Pontiacs and Plymouths—not to mention the Edsel—had in the fifties sought to create interiors that resembled the cockpits of combat planes, the imagery deriving from the early jet era. The Japanese updated this by introducing digital readouts and a whole range of high-tech gimmicks that evoked the aura of the heat-seeking missile age. (Though lately there has been a return to favor of more traditional analogue instrument panels.)

As employed by the Japanese, however, high-tech symbolism tends to promote the idea of the world car, rather than a national style, simply because high technology is universal. There are no strong national trends in the design of personal computers because they are all required to perform similar functions under similar conditions. (Software is perhaps another matter.) In much the same way, Soviet space shuttle designs are similar to American space shuttle designs because they are intended to fulfill the same task. This is the opposite of the situation that pertained in the early days of the development of the automobile, when driving conditions varied widely from country to country, as did driver psychology, which is the software of the car world.

But if the American car is in danger of disappearing, no such fate threatens the American highway landscape. The world created by the American motorist is still very much in place, and its style (or configuration of styles) has spread to most countries around the world where there is a significant automobile culture.

Partly, highway landscapes in Europe or Southeast Asia resemble American highway landscapes because they are home to familiar American businesses and signs—Holiday Inn or Coca-Cola. But the real resemblance comes from the adoption of American-style devices to create the highway strip. Billboards were certainly known in Europe before the age of the automobile, but in the modern era their profusion and style owes a good deal to American influence—and British, French and Japanese agencies are especially skillful at exploiting this medium. Completely American in inspiration are the fast-food outlets now found around the world, while the shopping malls of Stockholm and Seoul have their origins in the suburbs of Minneapolis. Japan's so-called love motels are often built in fantastic forms—boats, castles or onion-domed palaces—to attract the attention of drivers just as wigwam auto courts beckoned to tourists alongside Midwestern highways fifty years ago.

The automobile itself is an object charged with social resonance, but the highway culture it has created is still more complex, and this has permitted elaborate cultural cross-pollination, so that the texture of a roadside commercial strip in Taiwan may be both clearly Americanized and yet distinctly Oriental. In relatively undeveloped countries, auto strips are often to be found thriving at the grass-roots phase that has almost disappeared in America, ramshackle Mom and Pop businesses jostling for attention.

The contrast between the disappearance of the American car and the Americanization of the world's highways is instructive. It suggests that, for better or worse, the American way of doing retail business—from advertising to franchising to shopping by car—has come to dominate the world marketplace, while certain categories of American consumer goods have lost much of their cachet (automobiles being one, electronic products another).

The American highway landscape continues to define the national culture in much the way that a Cotswold village defines a lost England. This is not to say that roadside commercial strips represent the totality of American culture, any more than the thatched cottage represents the totality of England's cultural heritage. Yet it feels proper enough that William Shakespeare grew up in a Warwickshire cottage, and returned to one at the end of his life. So it feels appropriate that American artists of the twentieth century such as painters James Rosenquist and Roy Lichtenstein, with their billboard-size pop images, grew up dealing daily with the commercial strips. These strips have the same brash vigor that we associate with much that is best and most original in American culture, from jazz to Hollywood movies. Over the decades they have changed, however, and while the fever to make money remains, the flights of imagination that characterized the old strips have been dulled by standardization. The old "bad" taste that was so capable of setting the creative juices working has been replaced by an innocuous form of "good" taste—or a hypocritical genuflection toward the notion of "good" taste—so that many strips have become stultifyingly dull.

The early strips were exciting because they were in a constant state of flux, always growing and changing in an anarchistic way. Now the strips have evolved into shopping zones, no longer linear, where growth and change are manipulated by developers and speculators. In many ways they have become like old-fashioned urban shopping areas, except that they depend on the car for customer access. The businesses that make up these zones no longer gesture wildly to attract attention. They have become part of the establishment, fixed points in the daily or weekly routine of their patrons.

In a telling series of television commercials shown in 1990, McDonald's presented middle-aged customers musing nostalgically about the first time they tasted a Big Mac or those famous fries. Flashback. Fade to a parking lot lined with finmobiles. Inside the restaurant the middle-aged narrator has become a nine-year-old happily munching on a burger with his dad and mom. The point was effectively made. McDonald's has been around a long time.

And McDonald's is not alone. The same applies to Safeway and K Mart and Sav-on and AAMCO and scores of others. Every drive-in neighborhood has its constellation of familiar names, and the same patrons return to these stores and restaurants day after day, week after week. They are part of a routine and routine inevitably becomes somewhat dull. Given the fifties nostalgia craze that has been around since *American Graffiti* at least, it's a wonder that some developer or franchiser has not dressed up his properties in retrofitted fifties drag. The success of refurbished diners like San Francisco's Fog City Diner suggests that such a ploy might make good commercial sense. For that matter, it would be interesting to see what kind of response a car manufacturer would receive if it took a modern compact and dressed it up to look like a scaled-down version of a fifties Detroit product. Imagine a Mitsubishi Galant with fins and "chrome" protuberences simulated in flexible plastic with a vacuum deposit of Mylar. It just might catch on.

The car industry has never experimented with nostalgia on any significant scale. The notion has always been progress within the parameters that the public will accept. This could change, but for the time being we seem to be in the midst of an era when the primary sales strategy is the presentation of the car as an efficient and internally luxurious transit capsule. Certain vehicles—minivans and station wagons, for example—emphasize the communal and familial aspects of driving, but even these are found as often as not with a driver aboard and no passengers. More and more, whether they are commuting or driving for pleasure, people relish those private moments in the car, away from spouse and kids and career concerns.

Roland Barthes suggested that automobiles were the cathedrals of the twentieth century, and there was a time, not too long ago, when this made sense. Now, though, they are more like the monks' cells of our fin de siècle (cars like the Lexus are so smooth-riding and silent they offer a sense of peace rivaling anything found in a medieval monastary). Very luxurious cells, certainly, but essentially compact mobile spaces to which individuals retreat for meditation and private communication with High Test, the holy spirit of power.

Given the onanistic character of such cells, they are naturally flooded with ghostly memories and fantasies that have attached themselves to the automobile during its century of evolution. Inside every Subaru Justy is a Duesenberg struggling to burst out. Every Geo, sitting at night on its driveway, dreams of the day it will sprout fins and turn into a '57 Eldorado convertible. Or so the supplicants behind the wheel choose to believe, because they too are capable of formidable feats of transfiguration. Friar Truck, in the cab of his Dodge Ram, can will himself into becoming a cross between Mario Andretti and John Wayne. Despite the homogenization of the past two decades, automobiles are still magic instruments capable of transforming ordinary mortals into heroes—literally, in the case of race-car drivers like Andretti; quixotically, in the case of most motorists.

If clothes make the man, the car he drives makes him even more. Stephen Bayley has pointed out that people who are prepared to live with discount-store furniture and drugstore prints of wild animals are nonetheless fastidious about their driving environments. But it goes beyond this. Many motorists (I would go so far as to say the great majority) feel that they are judged by their car more than by their home or by their clothing. A rising executive may buy suits off the rack at sale time, and hardly think about style as long as his appearance is suitably neat and conservative, yet he finds it absolutely esential to drive a BMW to impress his boss and fellow workers. For millions, the car is the measure of the man.

This is a conformist period for automobiles. One thing that was exciting about the fifties was that the Chevy became as glamorous in its way as the Cadillac. There was something smart about driving a cheap car that had personality and could provide performance. The owner could express his individuality even if he could not afford top-of-the-line prices. Now automotive image is judged by nameplate and sticker price, with the familiar European names—Mercedes, BMW, Jaguar, Porsche—perched at the top of the ladder, despite the challenge of the new Japanese luxury cars. The yuppie as a phenomenon may be on the wane, but his legacy remains and there is a tendency to judge a person's worth in terms of the most conventional of status symbols.

Vestiges of automotive anarchy remain. There is still drag-racing on Queens Boulevard and the low-riders still rule on the streets of East LA. To a large extent, though, the anarchistic side of driving has been ritualized into ever more spectacular movie stunts, organized racing and stadium events featuring off-road vehicles equipped with tires suitable for Boeing 747s. (The Demolition Derby, surely, must be ready for a big-time revival?) America's youth still uses the automobile as a medium of revolt, but increasingly the public is organized against all forms of reckless driving, especially driving while under the influence of drink or drugs.

The rise in legal drinking age in many states has been tied to the threat of withholding federal highway funds, and the days when your host supplied you with a vodka and tonic in a plastic cup as you left the cocktail party are long gone in most parts of the country. Against that, however, the rise in the use of drugs over the past quarter century means that the roads are far from free of drivers under the influence of foreign substances.

Offsetting this is the fact that cars and highways are safer than ever. In terms of deaths per passenger mile,

American roads were at their worst in the twenties and have steadily improved ever since. Even so, they still account for a horrifying number of deaths and injuries and will probably never be completely safe unless and until a fully automated transit system is introduced.

The anarchic aspect of the car found its most unfortunate expression in the ease with which the reckless could transform it into a lethal weapon. Its happiest expression was found in the way it merged with populism—a trend started by the Model T—and helped transform American society, breaking down social and economic barriers, in large part by creating the highway landscape that we take for granted today. That landscape is an example of American democracy at work.

It is not, however, free of faults. It embraces some of the greatest and most aesthetically satisfying engineering feats of all time as well as some of the ugliest commercial structures known to mankind. It combines public works on the grand scale with the almost random proliferation of emphemeral architecture encouraged by the free enterprise system. It blends splendid strokes of imagination with banalities almost beyond belief. Unfortunately the strokes of imagination have become rarer and rarer as the free enterprise system has bred corporations that value consistency over creativity of any kind, a position that is apparently endorsed by their patrons, though those patrons are of course manipulated by advertising.

"Nobody has ever lost money," P. T. Barnum asserted, "by underestimating the intelligence of the American public." In many ways Barnum was the patron saint of the commercial strip—the first genius of hype and flimflam showmanship—and in as many ways the strip seems to bear out his famous dictum. Fortunes are made there by selling cut-rate patio sets by the thousand and mediocre hamburgers by the million. Each highway shopping strip is an exposed vein of the American economy. Once the strips blended the drive to make money with grass-roots invention, but now they are about money pure and simple, money made by harnessing the dull talents of product planners and inventory managers.

No wonder, then, that the automobiles that service these strips are judged in purely monetary terms. Driving a Mercedes becomes the accepted reward for successfully peddling high-cholesterol fast food or dubious weight-loss products. Demean yourself long enough and hard enough and you might drive home in a Ferrari or a Rolls.

To be fair, the commercial strips sometimes remain home to pleasant surprises. Driving in the San Fernando Valley you may come across a diner frozen in time or a quality second-hand bookstore. The strip economy still finds room for marginal businesses that could not exist in more expensive situations. Meanwhile, the first generation of exurbs created by the car have matured and become smothered in vegetation. And the Interstates still offer the motorist a comfortable ride through some of the continent's most spectacular scenery.

Recently, in New Jersey, I found my tank close to empty and was fortunate to come across a general store that dispensed gasoline from a curbside pump of Depression vintage in a village that might have been memorialized in a Sinclair Lewis novel. Such remnants of the old highway culture are still to be found all over, lurking in the shadows of the superhighways. The archaeology of the road is a discipline available to everyone.

The automobile age is far from over. It has reached a relatively stagnant phase, but only because the pressures of saving the environment have put it in the position where great changes must be expected but cannot be forced.

The automobile has remade America in its own image, and that formidable work will not easily be undone.

Bibliography

Anderson, Scott. *Check the Oil: A Pictorial History of the American Filling Station.* Greensboro, N.C.: Wallace-Homestead Book Co., 1986.

Armi, C. Edson. *The Art of American Car Design.* University Park, Penn.: University of Pennsylvania Press, 1988.

Banham, Reyner. *Los Angeles: The Architecture of Four Ecologies.* Middlesex, England: Allen Lane/Penguin Books, 1971.

Bayley, Stephen. *Sex, Drink and Fast Cars.* New York: Pantheon Books, 1986.

Bel Geddes, Norman. *Magic Motorways.* New York: Random House, 1940.

Bonsall, Thomas E., ed. *Big Pontiacs: A Source Book, 1955 Thru 1970.* Baltimore : Bookman Publishing, 1983.

——. *GTO, Volume II: A Source Book.* Baltimore: Bookman Publishing, 1984.

Bottles, Scott L. *Los Angeles and the Automobile: The Making of the Modern City.* Berkeley, Calif.: University of California Press, 1987.

Brilliant, Ashleigh. *The Great Car Craze: How Southern California Collided with the Automobile in the 1920s.* Santa Barbara, Calif.: Woodbridge Press, 1989.

Caro, Robert A. *The Power Broker: Robert Moses and the Fall of New York.* New York: Alfred A. Knopf, 1974.

Chapman, John L. *Incredible Los Angeles.* New York: Harper & Row, 1967.

Collier, Peter, and David Horowitz. *The Fords: An American Epic.* New York: Summit Books, 1987.

Crump, Spencer. *Henry Huntington and the Pacific Electric.* Corona del Mar, Calif.: Trans-Angelo Books, 1978.

Dash, Norman. *Yesterday's Los Angeles.* Miami: E. A. Seemann, 1976.

Duke, Donald. *Pacific Electric Railway: A Pictorial Album of Electric Railroading.* San Marino, Calif.: Golden West Books, 1958.

Fischler, Stanley I. *Moving Millions: An Inside Look at Mass Transit.* New York: Harper & Row, 1979.

Flower, Raymond, and Michael Wynn Jones. *One Hundred Years of Motoring.* Maidenhead, England: McGraw-Hill (U.K.), 1981.

Gebhard, David, and Hariette Von Breton. *L.A. in the Thirties.* Layton, Utah: Peregrine Smith, 1975.

Gibbons, Eric, and Graeme Ewens. *The Pictorial History of Trucks.* Secaucus, N.J.: Chartwell Books, 1978.

Gutman, Richard, and Elliott Kaufman. *American Diner.* New York, 1979.

Halpern, John. *Los Angeles, Improbable City.* New York: E. P. Dutton, 1979.

Halprin, Lawrence, *Freeways.* New York: Reinhold, 1966.

Hebert, Richard. *Highways to Nowhere: The Politics of City Transportation.* Indianapolis/New York: Bobbs-Merrill Company, 1972.

Hendry, Maurice D. *Cadillac: Standard of the World.* Princeton: Automobile Quarterly Publications, 1973.

Ikuta, Yasutoshi. *Cruise-O-Matic: Automobile Advertising of the 1950s.* San Francisco: Chronicle Books, 1988.

Jerome, John. *The Death of the Automobile.* New York: W. W. Norton, 1972.

Kittel, Gerd. *Diners, People and Places.* London/New York: Thames & Hudson, 1990.

Kowinski, William Severini. *The Malling of America: An Inside Look at the Great Consumer Paradise.* New York: William Morrow, 1985.

Kramer, Paul, and Frederick L. Holborn, eds. *The City in American Life from Colonial Times to the Present.*

New York: Capricorn Books, 1970.

Luxenberg, Stan. *Roadside Empires: How the Chains Franchised America.* New York: Viking/Penguin, 1985.

MacDonald, Donald. *Detroit 1985.* Garden City, N.Y.: Doubleday, 1980.

Marcantonio, Alfredo, et al. *Is the Bug Dead?.* New York: Stewart, Tabori & Chang, 1983.

Money, Lloyd J. *Transportation, Energy and the Future.* Englewood Cliffs, N.J.: Prentice-Hall, 1984.

Mowbray, A. Q. *Road to Ruin.* Philadelphia and New York: J. B. Lippincott, 1968.

Murphy, Bill. *Los Angeles, Wonder City of the West.* San Francisco: Fearon Publishers, 1959.

Owen, Wilfred. *The Accessible City.* Washington, D.C.: Brookings Institution, 1972.

Partridge, Bellamy. *Fill 'Er Up.* New York: McGraw-Hill, 1952.

Patton, Phil, *Open Road: A Celebration of the American Highway.* New York: Simon & Schuster, 1986.

Perazik, Juraj. *Motor Cars 1770–1940.* Chichester, England: Galley Press, 1981.

Pettifer, Julian, and Nigel Turner. *Automania.* Boston: Little, Brown, 1984.

Rae, John B. *The American Automobile: A Brief History.* Chicago: University of Chicago Press, 1965.

Rand, Christopher. *Los Angles: The Ultimate City.* New York: Oxford University Press, 1967.

BIBLIOGRAPHY

Robinson, John. *Highways and Our Environment*. New York: McGraw-Hill, 1971.

Robson, Graham. *Pictorial History of the Automobile*. New York: Gallery Books, 1987.

Schisgall, Oscar, *The Greyhound Story: From Hibbing to Everywhere*. Chicago: J. G. Ferguson Publishing Co., 1985.

Sobel, Robert. *Car Wars*. New York: E. P. Dutton, 1984.

St. Clair, David J. *The Motorization of American Cities*. New York: Praeger, 1986.

United States Federal Highway Administration. *America's Highways 1776–1976: A History of the Federal Aid Program*. Washington, D.C.: U.S. Department of Transportation, 1976.

Waitley, Douglas. *The Roads We Traveled: An Amusing History of the Automobile*. New York: Julian Messner, 1979.

Wright, J. Patrick. *On a Clear Day You Can See General Motors*. Grosse Point, Mich.: Wright Enterprises, 1979.

Yates, Brock. *The Decline and Fall of the American Automobile Industry*. New York: Empire Books, 1983.

Index